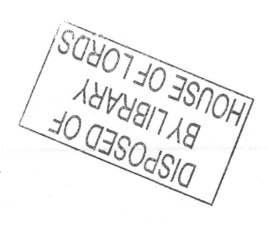

# Workers Versus Pensioners:
# Intergenerational Justice
# in an Ageing World

Centre for Economic Policy Research

# Centre for Economic Policy Research

The Centre for Economic Policy Research is a registered charity with educational purposes. It was established in 1983 to promote independent analysis and public discussion of open economies and the relations among them. Institutional (core) finance for the Centre has been provided through major grants from the Leverhulme Trust, the Esmée Fairbairn Trust, the Baring Foundation and the Bank of England. None of these organisations gives prior review to the Centre's publications nor do they necessarily endorse the views expressed therein.

The Centre is pluralist and non-partisan, bringing economic research to bear on the analysis of medium- and long-run policy questions. The research work that it disseminates may include views on policy, but the Board of Governors of the Centre does not give prior review to such publications, and the Centre itself takes no institutional policy positions. The opinions expressed in this volume are those of the authors and not those of the Centre for Economic Policy Research.

## Board of Governors

*Chairman*　Mr Jeremy Hardie
*Vice-Chairman*　Sir Adam Ridley

Professor Giorgio Basevi
Dr Christopher Bliss
Dr Paul Champsaur
Ms Honor Chapman
Admiral Sir James Eberle
Mr Michael Emerson
Ms Sarah Hogg

Professor Richard Layard
Ms Kate Mortimer
Mr Michael Posner
Ms Sheila Drew Smith
Professor David Stout
Mr Angus Walker
Sir Douglas Wass

## Officers

*Director*　Professor Richard Portes
*Assistant Director*　Mr Stephen Yeo
*Director of Finance and Research Administration*　Mrs Wendy Thompson

3 January 1989

CEPR, 6 Duke of York Street, London SW1Y 6LA, 01 930 2963

# Workers Versus Pensioners: Intergenerational Justice in an Ageing World

edited by
Paul Johnson
Christoph Conrad
and
David Thomson

Manchester University Press
Manchester and New York

in association with the Centre for Economic Policy Research

distributed exclusively in the United States and Canada
by St. Martin's Press, New York

Copyright © Centre for Economic Policy Research 1989

*Published by* Manchester University Press
Oxford Road, Manchester M13 9PL, UK
*and* Room 400, 175 Fifth Avenue,
New York, NY 10010, USA

*Distributed exclusively in the USA and Canada*
*by* St. Martin's Press, Inc.,
175 Fifth Avenue, New York, NY 10010, USA

*British Library cataloguing in publication data*
Workers versus pensioners : intergenerational justice
   in an ageing world.
   1. Great Britain. Old persons. Welfare benefits
   I. Johnson, Paul   II. Conrad, Christoph   III. Thomson, David
   IV. Centre for Economic Policy Research
362.6'3

*Library of Congress cataloging in publication data applied for*

ISBN 0 7190 3038 2 *hardback*

Printed and bound in Great Britain by
Courier International Ltd, Tiptree, Essex

# Table of Contents

# List of Tables

# List of Figures

# Preface

The articles presented in this volume derive from a conference on 'Work, Retirement and Intergenerational Equity, 1850–2050: The Social Economy of the Second Half of Life', organised by the Centre for Economic Policy Research and held at St John's College, Cambridge, in July 1988. We are most grateful to the following organisations for providing financial support for the conference: the Nuffield Foundation, the Centre for Economic Policy Research International Foundation, the Department of Health and Social Security, the Anglo-German Foundation for the Study of Industrial Society, the French Cultural Delegation, and the Rackham Program to Augment International Partnerships at the University of Michigan. We wish to thank both Elizabeth Taylor, the Production Editor, and Paul Compton, Publications Officer at CEPR, for their valuable assistance and guidance in the preparation of this volume. Above all, we would like to express our deep gratitude to Peter Laslett for his encouragement and support for both the Cambridge conference and our research into the study of ageing and intergenerational equity. It was through him that we first met in 1986 and from him that the idea of an international conference arose. We cannot claim that this volume provides comprehensive answers to the issue that Peter has encouraged us to address, but we hope that at least some of the questions have been more clearly defined.

PJ   CC   DT

3 January 1989

# List of Conference Participants

Dr Kerstin Abukhanfusa, University of Stockholm
Professor W. Andrew Achenbaum, University of Michigan
Professor Brian Barry, London School of Economics
Mr Christoph Conrad, Freie Universität, Berlin
Mme Françoise Cribier, Université de Paris VII and Centre National de la Recherche
  Scientifique, Paris
Professor Norman Daniels, Tufts University
Dr Jim Davies, University of Essex
Dr John Ermisch, National Institute for Economic and Social Research and CEPR
Ms Maria Evandrou, London School of Economics
Ms Jane Falkingham, London School of Economics
Mr Ben Gales, University of Eindhoven
Mr Chris Gordon, London School of Economics
Professor Brian Gratton, Arizona State University
Professor Anne-Marie Guillemard, Université de Paris I
Professor Leslie Hannah, London School of Economics and CEPR
Dr Paul Johnson, London School of Economics and CEPR
Professor Franz-Xaver Kaufmann, Universität Bielefeld
Professor Denis Kessler, Université de Nancy II and Centre National de la Recherche Scienti-
  fique, Paris
Dr Jay Kleinberg, West London Institute of Higher Education
Professor Martin Kohli, Freie Universität, Berlin
Dr Hans-Joachim von Kondratowitz, Deutsches Zentrum für Altersfragen (DZA), Berlin
Mr Torsten Krauel, Bundeskanzleramt, Bonn
Dr Peter Laslett, Cambridge Group for the History of Population and Social Structure
Professor Birgitta Odén, University of Lund
Mr Gilles Pollet, Université de Lyon II
Dr Gillis Samuelsson, University of Lund
Dr Steven Sass, Federal Reserve Bank of Boston
Professor Winfried Schmähl, Freie Universität, Berlin
Dr Richard Smith, All Souls College, Oxford
Dr Gerdt Sundström, Institute of Gerontology, Jönköping
Dr Pat Thane, Goldsmiths' College, London and CEPR
Mrs Wendy Thompson, CEPR
Dr David Thomson, Massey University, New Zealand

Dr Richard Wall, Cambridge Group for the History of Population and Social Structure and CEPR

Professor Tony Wrigley, London School of Economics

# 1

# Introduction

## Paul Johnson, Christoph Conrad
## and David Thomson

The rapid ageing of the populations of all industrial countries over the next forty years will be an economic and social transformation of vastly greater magnitude than the 1970s oil price shock or the 1980s recession. Unlike the economic difficulties of the last two decades which arose suddenly and with little warning, the timing and extent of population ageing are fairly predictable, because we know now within narrow boundaries how many people of working age and how many elderly will be alive in twenty or thirty years' time. This process of population ageing is likely to have a profound impact on many established social customs and institutions such as the pattern of work and retirement, the functioning of welfare systems, and the nature of family relationships. The anticipation of this demographic shift and its attendant social and economic problems must lead us to question whether the principles of our social institutions related to work and leisure, income and transfers are well adapted to these future challenges. A growing number of observers think the answer is no.

This volume sets out to analyse one potentially disruptive aspect of the ageing or 'greying' of the welfare state. The design and expansion of public transfer systems since the Second World War have provided the elderly with an increasing, though in some countries still partially insufficient, retirement income. The historical reduction of old-age poverty is one of the great successes of modern welfare society. To continue this redistribution of resources between younger and older adults, however, would put a growing and potentially unsustainable burden on fewer and fewer workers in the productive age groups. Seen from a cohort perspective, not only the ups and downs of fertility in the twentieth century but also the workings of social security have created considerable inequities between different generations. If perceived as such, this injustice between the generations could foster discontent with future social policies and, finally, undermine the 'implicit contract' between generations on which the welfare state is based.

The articles in this volume derive from a conference held at St John's College,

Cambridge in July 1988 which brought together over thirty economists, sociologists, philosophers and historians to develop an interdisciplinary approach to this issue of population ageing and intergenerational transfers. An interdisciplinary approach is necessary because of the nature of the subject which embraces philosophical issues of equity and justice between distinct age groups in the population, economic questions about the efficiency of retirement systems and pension schemes, socio-political concerns about the purpose of public social welfare systems, and historical debates about the origins of social categories such as 'pensioner' which profoundly influence current expectations about economic entitlements in old age. The articles that follow will touch on all these themes and more; they come from France, West Germany, Great Britain, New Zealand and the USA. Because they encompass theoretical considerations as well as specific case studies they can also serve as problem-orientated guides to a wealth of national and comparative research in these countries. The interdisciplinary approach and the variety of national experiences should provide stimulus as well as material for further investigation. We are well aware that the importance of population ageing and intergenerational justice is not limited to income matters. The health system, the provision for long-term care and changing family relationships are all areas of similar concern (see, e.g., Garms-Homolová *et al.*, 1984; Pifer and Bronte, 1986). In focusing on work, retirement and financial transfers, we hope to suggest new ways of analysing their relationships to population ageing and to highlight some of the policy options open to industrial countries if they wish to plan for the inevitable demographic restructuring of the next four or five decades. In this introduction we aim to provide a brief outline of the nature of the social and economic issues that will become most obvious in an increasingly bitter competition for resources between workers and pensioners.

## The demographic background

The essence of the demographic problem is quite simple – the proportion of old people in the population of industrial societies is increasing and the proportion of people of normal working age is falling. However, as John Ermisch makes clear in Chapter 2, the dynamics of this demographic change are quite complex and vary to a surprising degree between countries. All developed countries have seen an increase in average life expectancy over the course of the twentieth century as nutrition and hygiene have improved and medical advances have increased the survival chances of the young. In Britain, for instance, a child aged 10 in 1900 could, on average, expect to live for another 49.6 years. By the early 1980s Britain's 10-year-olds could expect to live for another 62.2 years if male and 68.1 years if female, and this pattern of improvement is found across all industrialised countries. In Japan, which has the highest life expectancy rates in the world, a 10-year-old boy can now expect to live for a further 65.6 years and a girl for 71.2 years. Moreover, life expectancy among the elderly has also increased so that more 70-year-olds now survive to 80 and more 80-year-olds live to 90 than ever before. Yet despite these impressive increases in longevity, the root cause of population ageing lies not in our success in extending the life course, but in our failure to produce more children.

In 1950 the total fertility rate, which measures the expected number of births per woman aged 15–44, was well over 2.1 (the population replacement rate) in all the countries of western Europe and North America. Today only Ireland continues to experience above-replacement fertility, while in West Germany and Denmark total fertility has fallen to the unprecedented level of 1.4. Large and rapid changes have been experienced before, though not of the magnitude of the last twenty years – the 'baby boom' of the 1950s, for example, followed two decades of low fertility during the 1930s Depression and the Second World War. The very low fertility rates evident in some countries today are not expected to continue indefinitely, although few population projections suggest a return to above-replacement fertility rates in the foreseeable future. But even if fertility does return to something approaching the replacement rate by the year 2000 or shortly after, there will nevertheless be an enormous transitional problem by the third decade of the next century as the 'baby boom' generation enter retirement and turn to the small cohorts of working-age adults for economic support (Eversley and Köllman, 1982). The cyclical nature of recent demographic history by itself poses problems for various areas of social policy: processing the baby boom generation through education, into the labour market and, finally, into retirement would challenge social institutions and age relations even without the secular ageing of the population as a background (Waring, 1975).

As Ermisch points out, the ratio of persons aged 65+ per 100 persons aged 15–64 in Europe stood at 15.1 in 1960 and is expected to be 29.1 by 2025; in West Germany the ratio in 1960 was 16.0, but the very low fertility rates of today mean that the expected ratio in 2025 will be 36.5. It should be emphasised that this is an optimistic projection based upon the assumption of a quick return to near-replacement fertility. Taking into account persistent low fertility, late entry into and early exit from the labour force as well as moderate female employment, pessimistic voices in the Federal Republic have recently warned that there may be only one worker for every pensioner by 2030. The French demographer Bourgeois-Pichat has calculated that if all European countries were immediately (and implausibly) to adopt and then maintain the very low West German fertility rate, then the native population of Europe would become extinct within 300 years (Bourgeois-Pichat, 1988).

The fertility decline of the last twenty-five years has been general across all developed countries, and a number of possible explanations have been suggested – religious influences, access to contraception and abortion, the extension since the Second World War of educational and employment opportunities for women, the impact of feminist ideology upon the social and economic expectations of younger women, the rising personal cost to parents of raising children, and more. But whatever the reason for the fertility decline, its effect will be to increase very sharply the proportion of older people in the populations of developed countries in the first three decades of the twenty-first century.

Why does this matter? An increase in the average age of the population need not engender any inevitable economic problems. There is nothing sacrosanct about the age 60 or 65 to make it the dividing line between productive and unproductive phases of life. Indeed, the long-term improvements in nutrition and health care that have worked to increase life expectancy over the course of this century suggest that on average a 65-year-old man or woman today is likely to be physically more capable of sustaining employment than a somewhat younger person at the beginning of this century. However, increased longevity has not been matched by an extension of the working phase of life; the trend has been for the normal age of retirement to fall rather than rise. Furthermore, the typical age for commencement of work in the labour market has risen over the last century as a larger proportion of children have been educated for a greater number of years. These long-term changes in the nature of the employment contract, with work starting later and finishing earlier, have led to a progressive shortening of the productive phase of life despite the overall improvement in health and higher chance of survival which together have worked to increase the productive potential of the individual.

An inevitable corollary of this reduction in the number of years spent in employment is an increase in the length of life spent dependent on the effort and output of that section of the population currently engaged in productive work. ('Productive' is being used here in the conventional but limited sense of remunerated activity, and no comment is being made about the possible wider meanings of the term.) Whether the retired population is supported from its own savings or from state pension and welfare payments does not affect the general proposition that the present consumption of the aged (and children) is provided for by the current output of productive workers. However, the specific pension arrangements that have evolved in each country do determine the nature and degree of exchange or transfer between particular age groups or generations, and in most developed countries it is the state pension and welfare systems that have emerged as the prime agents for transferring resources from productive to non-productive sections of the population.

It has become fashionable among politicians and journalists, as well as among scholars who should know better, to discuss this issue in terms of 'dependency ratios' and 'dependency burdens'. These concepts need to be treated with the greatest caution. Calculations of the numbers of 'active' and 'inactive' appeal to many because of their apparent ready comprehensibility and definite character. But all dependency measures incorporate vague assertions about the meaning of 'productive', 'active' or 'dependent'. Moreover, all carry clear if unspoken connotations of 'good' and 'bad', useful and wasteful, asset and burden. Until demographers and economists proceed a great deal further than they have as yet done in devising ranges of possible weightings and well spelt-out assumptions from which to build dependency measures, all figures on the burdens of the unproductive should be treated with critical circumspection. They are very much less useful than they seem (Crown, 1985; Falkingham, 1989).

In a response to the first round of criticism directed against social security and the elderly in the US, Robert Binstock pointed to one of the dangers of simply accepting this mode of thinking:

Here again we can see the role in framing the discussions which is played by the singular payroll tax financing mechanism of the Social Security system. Few people are discussing how many workers it takes to finance an aircraft carrier, a tobacco subsidy, a renal dialysis unit, or an investment tax credit. By pitting generations against each other, scapegoating the aged ... diverts our attention from other issues of significance to American society. (Binstock, 1983, p. 141)

On a more general level, the particular meaning of 'productive' which is restricted to work in the market and wage-based economy has been questioned. Summarising the arguments which have been put forward by the feminist critique of traditional social policies, Peter Flora writes:

Given the altered demographic parameters, we are thus facing an institutional maladjustment with considerable explosive force, in which the changing relationships between the generations is interwoven with a change in the relationships between the sexes. The nodal point lies in the structural underevaluation of that part of necessary work which is not involved in market exchange and therefore is usually done without independent income and adequate social rights.... Child-raising is an essential part of necessary but undervalued work in our society. (Flora, 1986a, p. xxvii)

The state welfare and pension systems, which are based upon an implicit contract that each generation will honour their obligations to pay taxes while in work in exchange for benefits when retired, evolved during the 1950s and 1960s when economic growth was high and when the immediate cost of increasing benefits or including more beneficiaries was slight. This post-war experience of a cheap and generous state pension system forged a popular perception of the welfare contract as an unbeatable bargain in which the pay-out was much larger than the input. But the ageing of the population, a (possibly temporary) brake to the rate of economic growth, and the changes in the nature of the employment contract that have resulted in a reduction in the length of the average working life, together serve to make expectations of the welfare contract derived from the experience of the recent past no longer viable. To see exactly why these expectations cannot be fulfilled, and why the interests of workers will inevitably clash with those of pensioners, we need to examine more closely the nature, function and evolution of both the welfare contract and the employment contract in modern industrial societies.

## The welfare contract

There is considerable variation in the financial and administrative detail of the different national systems for the transfer of resources from productive workers to non-productive pensioners, but they have tended to follow similar trends since the Second World War (for long-term comparative accounts see Flora, 1986b; Conrad, 1988; and Schulz and Myles, 1989). The case of the United States, considered by Andrew Achenbaum in Chapter 7, serves as an illuminating example. In the immediate post-war period the proportion of the workforce covered by the US contributory state pension scheme – Old Age and Survivors Insurance (OASI) – grew rapidly, and the real value of the pension payment rose sharply. These developments appeared to be costless because expanding the coverage of the scheme brought in new contributors who would not be entitled to draw pensions until the 1980s or later. Revenue rose more rapidly than expenditure, and it therefore seemed appropriate to increase pension payments for retirees to a level far above that which could be justified on an actuarial basis by reference to the contributions those retirees had themselves made. These pension increases may not have been actuarially fair, but they did seem to be morally fair at the time, because they allowed older people who could no longer participate in the productive economy to enjoy a share of the rapid economic advances experienced by workers in the 1950s and 1960s.

In the 1970s, however, as the OASI system matured, the ready sources of additional revenue dried up. By that time the coverage of the scheme had expanded to include nearly all adult workers, so that the scope for finding additional revenue by incorporating new groups of hitherto uninsured workers disappeared. Moreover, larger numbers of workers were beginning to enter retirement and carried with them the expectations of high and rising pension levels such as they had seen their older colleagues enjoy. However, contributions from the current workforce were no longer high enough to sustain these expanded pensions. The social security system faced bankruptcy, and the financial crisis was exacerbated by the reduction in the rate of economic growth and rise in the level of unemployment that accompanied the oil price increases of 1974 and 1979. A unique historical episode, the 'golden age of pensions' as a French economist put it, came to an end (Babeau, 1985).

The way welfare and pension systems reacted to the similar range of problems they faced in the 1970s has led David Thomson to argue, in Chapter 3, that welfare states may be one-generation phenomena. Any tax-funded welfare system operates on the basis of an implicit contract between generations which involves people paying contributions during the productive phases of their life cycle, and drawing benefits during childhood, in periods of sickness, and after retirement. This is analogous, at a societal level, to the implicit contract that exists within families, with working-age adults providing care and support both to their children and to their elderly parents. These implicit contracts work in the long run only if each generation is prepared to honour their moral obligations to both the preceding and succeeding generations. If the contract is broken by one generation that refuse to pay sufficiently or appropriately during their productive phase, there is then a strong incentive for succeeding generations not to invest in the contract at all and to put their faith in self-help rather than expectations of intergenerational transfers.

This is exactly what Thomson believes has happened in the post-war period in most developed countries. Basing his argument on the case of New Zealand, but with examples from a range of other countries, he suggests in Chapter 3 that there has been an unconscious but nevertheless consistent and successful attempt by one broad birth cohort, which reached adulthood during and just after the Second World War, to secure for themselves the main benefits of the post-war welfare state. This 'welfare generation', as Thomson calls them, have gained heavily throughout their lives from welfare and tax systems which provided them with highly subsidised property purchase, large child benefits and an expanding educational system when they were at the stage of family formation and now with greatly increased pension rights as they enter retirement.

Thomson's essential point is both clear and startling – that this 'welfare generation' have consistently refused to honour their obligations towards the younger cohorts upon which future welfare is based. People of the 'welfare generation', he argues, have always been net beneficiaries of the welfare state, and wish to remain so into their very comfortable retirement, despite enjoying a higher income, more assets and greater economic security than many younger households. Crucial to the argument is the reluctance of the 'welfare generation' to curtail their claim on the welfare state at a time when welfare budgets are overburdened, and when many people of working age are themselves dependent on the state because of high rates of unemployment. Despite a clear rise since the mid-1970s in the number of young adults with dependent children living at or below the poverty line, the real value of welfare benefits and tax concessions to this age group has fallen, whereas the increasingly asset-rich elderly have maintained or improved the value of their state pension entitlements. In this economic environment, suggests Thomson, there is a strong incentive for younger voters to break with this implicit welfare contract which seems always to work to their disadvantage, and to support the dismantling of the national welfare system and a return to private provision. Intergenerational competition, therefore, may affect not just the relative welfare of the old and the young, but can also threaten the very existence of state welfare systems.

This interpretation of a selfish 'welfare generation' that have failed to moderate their claims on the welfare state is contentious, but Thomson's point that welfare systems are tending to promote the interests of the increasingly wealthy retired population at the expense of poor children and parents has been advanced by a number of other investigators. In the United States the demographer Samuel Preston has identified clearly divergent trends in the welfare of the young and the old, though he regards this as the unforeseen and short-term consequence of a range of public and private choices about welfare and tax policies, rather than the product of an accumulating history of generational inconsistency and inequity (Preston, 1984). His views have generated a good deal of public discussion, and there is now an active pressure group in the United States called Americans for Generational Equity (AGE) which is campaigning for a reduction in the pension and welfare entitlements of the elderly, and for greater investment in the education and welfare of the children who will make up the next generation of productive workers (Longman, 1987).

This idea of an intergenerational conflict for resources between the young and the old has been rejected by a number of commentators who argue that generation or birth cohort is not an appropriate unit of analysis (Binney and Estes, 1988; Easterlin, 1987). To talk of a 'welfare generation' or of competition for resources between the young and the old implies a degree of homogeneity among the elderly population that may not exist. Class divisions or (because so many of the very old and very poor elderly are women) gender divisions within the aged population may be as significant as any divergence in the age profile of poverty between those over retirement age and those with dependent children. This is to a large extent an empirical issue, but one that cannot easily be resolved because the questions involve issues of long-term influences over the whole of the life cycle whereas most of the available data come from cross-sectional surveys. Even for someone who disagrees with Thomson's results, however, his methodological approach can serve as a model. Following cohorts through time, assessing their collective 'welfare balance sheet', and disregarding the artificial dividing lines between the different welfare programmes and insurance systems are powerful and elegant ways to overcome the segmentation in many expert discussions.

Perhaps not surprisingly, given the newness of the generational approach to social analysis, there exists disagreement amongst those who believe that the intergenerational framework is an appropriate way to think about the dynamic impact of modern welfare states. In particular, there is debate about how an optimal degree of intergenerational exchange might be decided upon. In Chapter 4 Norman Daniels is concerned to point up the confusions that abound in talking about justice between age groups and generations. The two are distinct, and yet individuals are members of both at once. As a result two separate questions are being merged and misconstrued in most discussions of 'generational equity', most especially in the public debate that has developed around this in the United States in the 1980s. On the one hand there is the age group issue – what is due in terms of justice to those who are young or old today. On the other, modern societies face the generation question – what is due to those who may be elderly now, but who perhaps have a peculiar history of contribution to or benefit from society's taxation and benefit programmes. Daniels argues that little is to be gained by searching first for justice between generations: that way lies acrimony, divisiveness and constant tinkering with policies. The long-term interests of all will best be served if primacy is given to determining what a just society wants for the elderly and others, since all now enjoy the near-certain prospect of passing through all ages themselves.

Despite these various reservations about the validity of an intergenerational framework for the analysis of recent trends in welfare state activity, there can be little doubt that the scale and direction of welfare transfers between generations that is projected for the early years of the next century is a cause for concern. In Chapter 3 Thomson argues that welfare states have, since the 1970s, tended to assist the old at the expense of the young; in Chapter 8 Winfried Schmähl shows how this redistribution will become even more pronounced over the next thirty years unless some action is taken to curtail the state pension entitlements of the retired population. If the old-age pension system in West Germany retains its current form, then according to Schmähl's pessimistic scenarios, a payroll tax of nearly 42 per cent will need to be levied on productive workers by the year 2030 to pay for the pension system alone. An increase in the rate of economic growth will not provide any amelioration since the pension payments are effectively indexed to current wage levels. Although the case of West Germany is extreme, because of both the very low fertility rate and the generous nature of the state pension system, Schmähl points out that all western countries will experience similar pressures in the next few decades.

It seems inevitable that the interaction of current demographic trends and current welfare policies will impose a large, growing and possibly unsustainable fiscal burden on the productive populations in developed nations. Since there can be no immediate change in the population age structure, and a rise in fertility would only raise still further the numbers of 'dependants', at least in the short run, it may seem that an obvious way to cope with the rising financial burden of an ageing population is to alter in some fundamental way the welfare contract that operates to transfer resources from the young to the old. Such a re-drawing of the welfare contract is certainly possible, but it is far from clear that this sort of reform is alone sufficient to restrict the economic costs of population ageing.

The impact of policy interventions is further restricted by the 'private-public mix' in the provision of old-age income (Rein and Rainwater, 1986; ISSA, 1987; Schulz, 1988; Schulz and Myles, 1989). Shifting parts of the future burden on to private shoulders seems an attractive way out for many of those concerned with the fiscal crisis. This 'solution' will not, however, change the basic mechanism of redistribution from one age group to the other. Whether retired people receive income from the state via the tax transfer system (or from social insurance) or whether they live off the interest and dividend payments from their past savings, the goods and services they consume are part of the current output of the currently employed population. A doubling in the size of the elderly population will, other things being equal, double the financial burden of support on the working population regardless of how the retired population exercises a claim on output. A sudden curtailment of state support for the elderly would reduce tax burdens at the cost to the retired population of an immediate decrease in welfare, but in the long run, if private income rose to replace the diminished state pension, there would be no net change in the proportion of current output consumed by the non-productive elderly. An immediate reduction in state support for the elderly would not, therefore, solve the long-term economic problems of population ageing. To do this, it is necessary to lower the overall income expectations of the aged, or to change patterns of work, and the scope for action here is determined by the nature of the labour contract in modern societies.

## The labour contract

It has already been noted that the increase in life expectancy at older ages in the twentieth century has been accompanied by a contraction of the productive lifespan because the average age of entry into the workforce has risen as educational opportunities and requirements have increased, and the length of the retirement phase has grown. The long-term trend to lower labour force participation past age 65 has accelerated dramatically since the mid-1970s and has reached those in their later fifties and early sixties. Comparisons with the 1930s indicate that labour market conditions again play a decisive role in this (Conrad, 1988). The discussion in Chapter 9 by Anne-Marie Guillemard of the trend towards early withdrawal from the labour force shows that the average retirement age has fallen in all developed countries over the last twenty years, and that this has occurred independently of any alteration in the age limits for the receipt of state old-age pensions or other welfare benefits. If this trend towards earlier retirement could be reversed the effect on intergenerational transfers between productive and non-productive sections of the population would be immediate and significant, because the additions to the labour force would also be subtractions from the dependent population.

To see what scope exists for reversing the trend towards early retirement, we need to consider why people leave the labour force, and how these decisions are influenced by social security and pension rules, a subject discussed by Denis Kessler in Chapter 5. Individual choices and circumstances play a part; people may opt for early retirement because they no longer need or want to work, or they may be forced into retirement because they lose the mental or physical capacity for employment. Improvements in the fitness and nutrition of the population over the course of the twentieth century indicate that the reduction in the average age of retirement has not occurred because of an absolute decline in the health of older people, although changing popular and medical perceptions of fitness and disability may have worked to counter any objective improvements in health. It seems more likely that the labour force supply of older people has fallen over time because their increasing wealth and pension entitlements have reduced their need for an employment income. However, it can be said with confidence that not all retired people have left employment from choice, even though it is difficult or impossible to determine what proportion of the retired population has consciously opted out of the labour market because of relative affluence. High rates of unemployment among older workers who have not reached retirement age are a sure sign that the declining labour force participation of the elderly is in part a consequence of a fall in the demand for older workers.

A much discussed model developed by Lazear (1979) explains why employers have curtailed their demand for older workers in terms of economics. In large, modern corporations the fixed costs associated with hiring and training a worker are substantial and in order to minimise these costs employers attempt to restrict staff turnover. One effective way to do this is to pay seniority increments to staff with a certain number of years' service. These bonuses are not related to the specific job done by the worker or to his or her productivity – their purpose is to establish an earnings gradient which will provide an incentive for workers to stay with their employer. However, the very nature of seniority payments means that at some point an older worker is likely to be paid a wage or salary greater than his marginal product – in other words, he will be a net cost to the employer. At this point the employer needs to shed this worker, but a straightforward policy of dismissal of older workers would serve to undermine the employee loyalty which it is the purpose of the earnings gradient to promote. The socially acceptable way to shed older workers is, therefore, to offer them early retirement with an advantageous pension arrangement. As long as the cost to the employer of the early retirement settlement is less than the cost of the continued employment of the unproductive worker up to normal retirement age, early retirement is the employer's preferred choice.

As Stephen Sass demonstrates in his investigation of US private and union pension schemes in Chapter 6, it is also the preferred choice of labour organisations. In order to preserve industry-wide wage agreements, particularly when they relate to time-rates rather than piece-rates, unions tend to be as keen as employers to ensure that workers who have an uneconomic level of productivity are removed from their jobs. However, unions have to be seen to be protecting their members, so they are anxious to demonstrate that they can obtain good severance settlements for their older and marginally productive workers. Furthermore, early retirement on favourable terms is frequently the favoured choice of the workers themselves who have come to expect, from their observations of trends in the 1960s and 1970s, a lengthy, healthy and prosperous retirement.

Early retirement seems, therefore, to be in the interest of everyone directly involved in it, if not for the bulk of the working population who have to support the cost of generous pension arrangements either through increased taxes, increased private pension contributions, or increased prices for the products of the companies that promote these expensive early retirement policies. A higher level of labour force participation among older people, which would appear to be in the interest of all western societies now facing the problems of population ageing, seems not to be in the interest of any of the parties involved in the decision – a clear case perhaps of the public good and individual self-interest in conflict. Until recently national governments themselves favoured early exit from the labour force as a means of alleviating the pressure on the labour market. Serious doubts about the cost and the effectiveness of such policies have emerged (Holzmann, 1988) but the aim of shifting jobs from the old to the young is still quite popular. The situation therefore looks like a conflict between two public goods – the short-term labour market concern and the long-term pension cost con-cern. Although one cannot expect to reverse the trend to earlier retirement by political decisions alone, governments will have to make up their mind which way to go on this issue (for international diagnoses and therapies see Casey and Bruche, 1983; and Schmähl, 1989).

There is an alternative, more conspiratorial, interpretation of the process of early retirement, which derives from a marxist view of the labour process. Within this model, the extension of early retirement is viewed not as a consequence of individual choice or the simple working out of microeconomic logic, but instead as the result of a complex process whereby capitalist societies in the twentieth century have deliberately promoted the marginalisation and dependency of elderly people. The state has developed the concepts of retirement and pensionable status in ways which have reinforced the social dependency of the elderly, and which have effectively marginalised older people in the labour market; older workers are seen as a reserve army, called up during times of labour shortage such as war, but cast on to the human scrapheap during periods of high unemployment. This model of structured dependency has had a great influence across a broad range of research in social gerontology, especially in Britain (see Townsend, 1981; Walker, 1980; Phillipson, 1982; and, for an alternative view, Johnson, 1989), and its importance lies in the explicit link it draws between phenomena such as early retirement and the political economy of capitalist society. Whether this explanation of early retirement will generate different policy proposals to the simpler neo-classical model of Lazear when applied to the long-term problems of an ageing population remains to be seen. Where the two views converge is in viewing early retirement as merely one part of a broader problem within political economy.

## Policy options

The effects of earlier exit from the labour force and increased life expectancy at higher ages have joined forces to change radically the nature and meaning of 'old age'. The extension of this life stage which perhaps soon might span from the fiftieth to the hundredth birthday is a challenge to the imagination as well as the problem-solving capacities of all industrial societies (Pifer and Bronte, 1986; Gaullier, 1988; Laslett, 1989). Reforming the policies of public and private transfers figures as only one, albeit essential task in this context. There is growing doubt whether the welfare state can be relied on to deal effectively with its self-created problems (cf. Luhmann, 1981). In view of the still unresolved problems of poverty among older women and the provision of long-term care, it is also questionable whether a claim for 'justice between the generations' can and should simply be added to all the other claims for political intervention. But, as David Thomson points out, much will depend on the 'messages' that policies for transfers in the future send to the younger members of society. Even if the historical uniqueness of the fate of successive cohorts after the Second World

War is probably not prone to political 'compensation', social security reforms must give younger people a good reason for sustaining the common stake that different generations have in the welfare state.

The working of both the welfare contract and the employment contract in modern industrial societies serve to exacerbate the economic and social problems that are a concomitant of population ageing. The problems are manifest and obvious, the solutions less straightforward. If no action is taken to deal with the incipient crisis of population ageing, then it seems certain that western societies will experience major social and economic dislocation, and they may experience this relatively soon. Although demographic ratios and welfare systems may in aggregate change relatively slowly, over two or three decades, the changes experienced by adjacent cohorts in the population are much more obvious. This point is made very clearly by Françoise Cribier in Chapter 10, where she examines the experience of two groups of Parisian workers who retired in the early 1970s and the early 1980s. Although only separated by just over a decade, their income, wealth, attitudes to work and expectations about pension payments and living standards were very different. While many members of the first cohort were the first in their family to experience retirement as a distinct phase of life, and did not trust the generosity of the welfare state, the younger cohort are both more aware of their comfortable situation and have noticed the mounting tensions with younger people over jobs, and they feel concerned for the future of their children and grandchildren.

There is a further reason for action to be taken now, even if the most pressing economic consequences of population ageing do not emerge until the next century. Life insurance and pension companies always stress in their advertising that it is never too early to start thinking about and planning for retirement, and for most individuals retirement income is determined by actions early in adult life. Few people have the opportunity and resources to change their pension plans and pattern of asset accumulation after their mid-forties, so that their social and economic expectations of retirement tend to be set at least twenty years before normal retirement age. If new attitudes to retirement will be needed by the third decade of the next century to cope with the cost of an ageing population, then it is the expectations and actions of today's 20- and 30-year-olds that should be the focus of attention.

Many governments have already enacted certain measures to dampen the expectations of retirees in the twenty-first century, for example by increasing payroll taxes, reducing early retirement incentives and revising the automatic increase of benefits (ILO, 1987; Holzmann, 1988; Schmähl, 1989). These reforms, however, do not touch the principles of existing systems and seem to allow only for cosmetic reactions to the inbuilt inequities. They may even worsen the inequity felt by younger workers.

The most obvious and accessible area for immediate government action is the welfare contract. Changing the nature of this contract will not reverse the long-term problem of a relative decline in the productive capacity of the population, but it can ease some of the transitional issues associated with unfair fiscal burdens. There can be no justification for a pension scheme that takes from poor parents and children and gives to rich pensioners. Of course, many of today's pensioners are poor, and no doubt there will be poor pensioners in fifty years' time, but current trends indicate that pensioners as a whole are getting wealthier. A move from a universal to a needs-related pension system would seem to be both fair and efficient, but politically hardly 'saleable' as yet, before the effects of ageing are more widely considered and discussed. Whether any western government has either the political will or the electoral strength for such a move remains to be seen; recent retrenchment in welfare spending has impinged very little on the retired population, despite the fact that pension expenditure is the most costly element in all western welfare states.

Any action to alter the nature of the employment contract will be more difficult because, as explained above, all parties concerned with the decision seem to prefer early retirement. The legislation enacted in the United States by President Reagan to raise in steps the normal age of receipt of the OASI pension from 65 to 67 between the years 2003 and 2027 is not likely to have any effect on the downward trend in the actual age of retirement from paid work unless the demand for labour increases considerably at the same time. It may be possible to encourage the employment of older workers through various tax concessions, but these would have to be large to overcome the effect of the earnings gradient. Perhaps the shortage of young workers over the next decade will begin to undermine ageist employment policies.

This shortage of young workers, the essence of the demographic problem, could also be affected by government policy. A short-term response to labour shortage would be immigration, but governments are now more aware of the attendant social costs of immigration than they were during the post-war years of labour shortage, and it is unlikely to become a widely adopted policy. An alternative long-term approach is to attempt to raise the domestic fertility rate. Again it is 20- and 30-year-olds who would be at the forefront of any such policy, and until the reasons for the fall in fertility are fully understood, any pro-natalist policy must be somewhat speculative. However, the high rates of married female labour force participation mean that childbirth and childcare involve a substantial and immediate cost in terms of lost earnings for many women. Financial compensation for this loss and free and comprehensive childcare facilities would be two possible ways of raising fertility from the disastrously low levels of today. While the private cost of having children remains so high, there is little likelihood of individuals responding to the public need for a rise in the fertility rate. Substantial incentives will need to be offered to a young adult population to persuade it to sustain the additional cost of more children at a time when it is facing rapidly expanding costs in supporting the aged.

The expected decline in the proportion of the population of working age also makes it imperative that western countries use this human capital in the best ways possible. In less developed countries demographic trends of a different sort mean that the early decades of the next century will see a sharp increase in the proportion of their populations of working age. In less developed countries, unskilled labour will be cheap and plentiful. If western countries are to compete in international markets, they will have to ensure that their small labour force is highly skilled and adaptable. This implies that more effort and resources will need to be devoted to the education, training and retraining of future generations of workers.

The economic and social problems associated with population ageing in industrial societies are not short-term phenomena like balance of payments crises or periods of inflation which can be corrected through monetary or fiscal policy. Even if fertility rates could be brought back towards replacement levels in all countries within a decade, the problems of population ageing would still be apparent in our demographic structure for the next fifty years. It is this long-term aspect which makes population ageing such an unpalatable issue for governments and administrations which are interested in solutions rather than problems, and which like to parade the effectiveness of their solutions at appropriate points in the electoral cycle. Yet it is the long-term nature of the problem that makes it imperative that action is taken now to cope with the costs of population ageing that will become most apparent in thirty years' time. If no action is taken, the competition for resources between workers and pensioners will break the fiscal basis of modern welfare systems, and quite possibly this will undermine the democratic consensus upon which the western economies are based.

# References

Babeau, A. (1985), *La fin des retraites?*, Paris, Hachette.

Binney, E.A. and Estes, C. L. (1988), 'The retreat of the state and its transfer of responsibility: the intergenerational war', *International Journal of Health Services*, XVIII, pp. 83–96.

Binstock, R. H. (1983), 'The aged as scapegoat', *The Gerontologist*, XXIII, pp. 136–43.

Bourgeois-Pichat, J. (1988), 'Du XX$^e$ au XXI$^e$ siècle: l'Europe et sa population après l'an 2000', *Population*, XLIII, pp. 9–42.

Casey, B. and Bruche, G. (1983), *Work or Retirement? Labour Market and Social Policy for Older Workers in France, Great Britain, the Netherlands, Sweden and the USA*, Aldershot, Gower.

Conrad, C. (1988), 'Die Entstehung des modernen Ruhestandes: Deutschland im internationalen Vergleich 1850–1960', *Geschichte und Gesellschaft*, XIV, pp. 417–47.

Crown, W. H. (1985), 'Some thoughts on reformulating the dependency ratio', *The Gerontologist*, XXV, pp. 166–71.

Easterlin, R. A. (1987), 'The new age structure of poverty in America: permanent or transient?' *Population and Development Review*, XIII, pp. 195–208.

Eversley, D. and Köllmann, W. (eds) (1982), *Population Change and Social Planning: Social and Economic Implications of the Recent Decline in Fertility in the United Kingdom and the Federal Republic of Germany*, London, Edward Arnold.

Falkingham, J. (1989), 'Dependency ratios re-examined', *Journal of Social Policy* (April).

Flora, P. (1986a), 'Introduction', in P. Flora (ed.), *Growth to Limits*, vol. 1, pp. xi–xxxi.

Flora, P. (ed.) (1986b), *Growth to Limits: The Western European Welfare States Since World War II*, 5 vols, Berlin and New York, Walter de Gruyter.

Garms-Homolová, V., Hoerning, E. M. and Schaeffer, D. (eds) (1984), *Intergenerational Relationships*, Toronto and Lewiston, New York, C. J. Hogrefe.

Gaullier, X. (1988), *La deuxième carrière: ages, emplois, retraites*, Paris, Editions du Seuil.

Holzmann, R. (1988), *Reforming Public Pensions: Background, Pressures and Options*,Paris, Organisation for Economic Co-operation and Development.

ILO (International Labour Office) (1987), *Demographic Development and Social Security (Report II)*, Geneva, ILO.

ISSA (International Social Security Association) (1987), *Conjugating Public and Private: The Case of Pensions*, Studies and Research no. 24, Geneva, ISSA.

Johnson, P. (1989), 'The structured dependency of the elderly: a critical note', in M. Jefferys (ed.), *Growing Old in the Twentieth Century*, London, Routledge.

Laslett, P. (1989), *The Coming of the Third Age*, London, Weidenfeld & Nicolson.

Lazear, E. P. (1979), 'Why is there mandatory retirement?', *Journal of Political Economy*, LXXXVII, pp. 1261–84.

Longman, P. (1987), *Born to Pay: The New Politics of Aging in America*, Boston, Houghton Mifflin.

Luhmann, N. (1981), *Politische Theorie im Wohlfahrtsstaat*, Munich and Vienna, G. Olzog.

Phillipson, C. (1982), *Capitalism and the Construction of Old Age*, London, Macmillan.

Pifer, A. and Bronte, L. (eds) (1986), *Our Aging Society*, New York, W. W. Norton.

Preston, S. H. (1984), 'Children and the elderly: divergent paths for America's dependents', *Demography*, XXI, pp. 435–57.

Rein, M. and Rainwater, L. (eds) (1986), *Public and Private Interplay in Social Protection: A Comparative Study*, London and Armonk, New York, M. E. Sharpe.

Schmähl, W. (ed.) (1989), *Redefining the Process of Retirement in an International Perspective*, Heidelberg, Springer.

Schulz, J. H. (1988), *The Economics of Aging*, 4th edn, Dover, Massachusetts, Auburn House.

Schulz, J. H. and Myles, J. (1989), 'Old age pensions: a comparative perspective', in R. Binstock and E. Shanas (eds), *Handbook of Aging and the Social Sciences*, 3rd edn, New York, Van Nostrand Reinhold.

Townsend, P. (1981), 'The structured dependency of the elderly: a creation of social policy in the twentieth century', *Ageing and Society*, I, pp. 5–28.

Walker, A. (1980), 'The social creation of poverty and dependency in old age', *Journal of Social Policy*, IX, pp. 49–75.

Waring, J. M. (1975), 'Social replenishment and social change: the problem of disordered cohort flow', *American Behavioral Scientist*, XIX, pp. 237–56.

# Part I

## Welfare, Age and Generation

# 2

# Demographic Change and Intergenerational Transfers in Industrialised Countries

John Ermisch

To what extent do changes in fertility and mortality affect the transfer of resources between generations? In the first half of this article, a simple framework is used to illustrate the types of transfers and to show how this question may be answered when *all* intergenerational transfers are taken into account. The framework uses the concept of stable populations, which is often used by demographers to suggest answers to questions involving complex population dynamics. In this context, it is possible to estimate the direction of *net* intergenerational transfers (from younger to older ages or vice versa). Recent estimates are reported for contemporary Britain, Japan and the USA, and their sensitivity to different demographic regimes is examined.

When fertility exhibits strong swings, as it has done in industrialised countries, and mortality is constantly improving, the age distribution of the population changes dramatically over time. In addition, economic institutions, like state pensions systems, have been altered. In these circumstances, although the simple framework is suggestive, it is not possible to measure how demographic changes affect *all* intergenerational transfers. The second half of the article does, however, examine how demographic changes have affected two important intergenerational transfers made through the state: public education expenditures and state pensions. As the latter are shown to be particularly influenced by age distribution changes, prospective demographic pressures on state pensions are given particular attention.

## Generations and transfers

A generation is a group of people born in the same year (or set of consecutive years). In a world of stable population (in which the age distribution is constant, but the population may be growing or declining) and stable social institutions, intergenerational transfers are merely flows of resources between people of different ages. In this hypothetical world, all generations would experience the same net transfers at each age. Thus, there would not be transfers of *lifetime* resources from one generation to another, and most questions of inter-generational justice disappear. When social institutions change (e.g. a pension scheme is introduced or its coverage expanded) and age distributions alter, some generations may be net beneficiaries of transfers from other generations, thereby giving rise to intergenerational transfers of lifetime resources and issues of equity between generations. While such transfers are probably more interesting, they are almost impossible to measure.

The hypothetical world of a stable population and society is, therefore, an informative starting point for examining how demographic changes affect inter-generational transfers. Only in this simple case can any comprehensive measure of intergenerational transfers be produced, in contrast to measures of particular transfers which could easily be offset by other transfers in the opposite direction.

Transfers are defined in a more general way than in national income accounting conventions. When an age group consumes more or less than its labour income, an 'intergenerational transfer' of resources is said to take place. This definition is in keeping with the original analysis of the effects of intergenerational transfers by Samuelson (1958), and it encompasses transfers of resources that pass through markets or the family or government.

Transfers of resources between generations can take a number of forms. They can be made through market transactions. For instance, young persons can borrow from older persons (directly or through financial institutions), as would be the case in the life cycle theory of consumption. In that theory, persons are net borrowers when they are young, and net lenders when middle-aged; thus transfers go from older generations to younger ones. Beyond retirement age, persons finance consumption by selling their assets, causing transfers to go from younger to older generations.

Transfers can also be made through government programmes of expenditure, taxation and borrowing. The most obvious one is retirement pensions, but publicly financed expenditures on education and on health and borrowing by the public sector also represent transfers between generations. Retirement pensions on a 'pay as you go' basis are transfers from younger to older generations, while education expenditures represent transfers in the opposite direction.

Transfers are also made by the family. Parents expend resources in raising their children. They may also make gifts and bequests to them, and they may lend them money directly. Children may help support their parents in old age.

With various transfers going in different directions, it is difficult to state whether net transfers flow from younger to older generations or from older to younger. The direction of net transfers depends on the particular institutions, government programmes, customs and individual behaviour of the population, but the main focus here is the important influence that the age distribution of the population has on it. The age distribution is obviously the outcome of the history of fertility and mortality (and, in open countries, migration), and in a stable population it depends on the levels of these.

Because people consume more than they produce at some ages, while the reverse is true at other ages, the age distribution affects net transfers. What is not so clear, and indeed may appear somewhat paradoxical, is that it affects lifetime consumption as well. This is clearer if we think of a society with no capital goods. Its 'social budget constraint' states that, summing over all ages, consumption must equal production. The weights on age-specific consumption and production in the social budget constraint (i.e. the age distribution of the population) vary for different fertility and mortality schedules. As they vary, the transfers of resources between age groups (generations) change because the relative sizes of age groups who consume more than they produce and vice versa are altered, and this also changes the constraint on consumption. As a consequence, a person's consumption opportunities over the life course are affected by the age distribution of the population in which the person lives.

In our simple world of stable population and society, the direction of net intergenerational transfers can be summarised as the difference between the average age of consumption and the average age of production. Lee (1980) shows that purely as a consequence of intergenerational transfers lifetime consumption opportunities will increase with the rate of population growth if the average age of consumption exceeds the average age of production. Thus, in the case of a comparison of stable populations with different growth rates, the effect of a difference in growth rates on lifetime consumption is intimately related to the direction of net transfers: if transfers go from younger to older generations, then a higher population growth rate increases lifetime consumption.

Because, as a consequence of these intergenerational transfers, a person's lifetime consumption opportunities depend on the fertility of the entire population, childbearing has effects that go beyond the individual family. In this sense, the transfers constitute an externality associated with childbearing.

## Measures of the direction of net transfers

Measurement of the direction of net transfers is virtually impossible unless some simplifying assumptions are made. Measurement is made in the context of a theoretical model which assumes that the age profiles of consumption and production have a fixed shape (but could rise over time at a constant rate), and that the population age distribution is stable. Following Lee (1985), the analysis is placed in a household setting, in which the age profiles of consumption and production refer to the age of household heads rather than to individuals. The household setting has both theoretical and empirical advantages, as Lee (1980) and Lee and Lapkoff (1988) explain. A particular empirical advantage is that household expenditure on children does not have to be apportioned among children of different ages.

In the estimates reported here, details of which are in Ermisch (1989), the household consumption profile includes three classes of expenditure. The first and largest is private household expenditure on goods and services. The other two categories are publicly funded expenditure on education and publicly funded health and personal social services expenditure.

Since the focus is on expenditure on goods and services, 'production' excludes work in the home, although it may be equally productive. A rationale for this focus is the rarity of transfers of services produced at home between households.

With this focus on production through paid employment, there are three main components in computing production by the age of the household head. The first is the set of age-earnings profiles for men and women. Market production also depends on the extent of participation in paid employment, which depends on the age profiles of participation in part-time and full-time paid employment by men and women. Finally, paid employment by children between the ages of 16 and 19, before they leave home (according to the household formation rules used here), must also be included.

The sum of all three components of earnings for Great Britain are shown in Figure 2.1 as the mortality-adjusted age profile of production, or resources, along with the mortality-adjusted consumption profile. The sharp, saw-toothed bulge in household earnings during the household heads' forties reflects the earnings of their teenaged children before leaving home.

Assuming no productivity growth over generations, so that the interest rate (and population growth rate) is zero, the average ages of household consumption and production in contemporary Britain are estimated to be 46.3 and 41.3 respectively; a 2 per cent per annum rate of productivity growth and interest rate yields average ages of consumption and production of 41.7 and 38.7 respectively. Thus, net transfers go from younger to older generations. Figure 2.1 indicates how this result comes about. It shows production exceeding consumption at most ages below 60, but particularly among heads aged 40–55, while the opposite occurs at ages above 60. The conclusion about the direction of net transfers would be strengthened if the life expectancy of the elderly improved or if the age of retirement continued to fall.

The mortality-adjusted profiles of Japanese consumption and production are shown in Figure 2.2, which is comparable to Figure 2.1 for Britain. The net flow of Japanese transfers to older generations is readily apparent, with production substantially in excess of consumption at ages 20–60 and the reverse at higher ages. The difference between the average ages of consumption and production for Japan is substantially larger than for Britain, ranging from 4 to 6.5 years. Japan's fertility rate is similar to Britain's but its mortality is lower. Does the larger difference between average ages of consumption and production in Japan

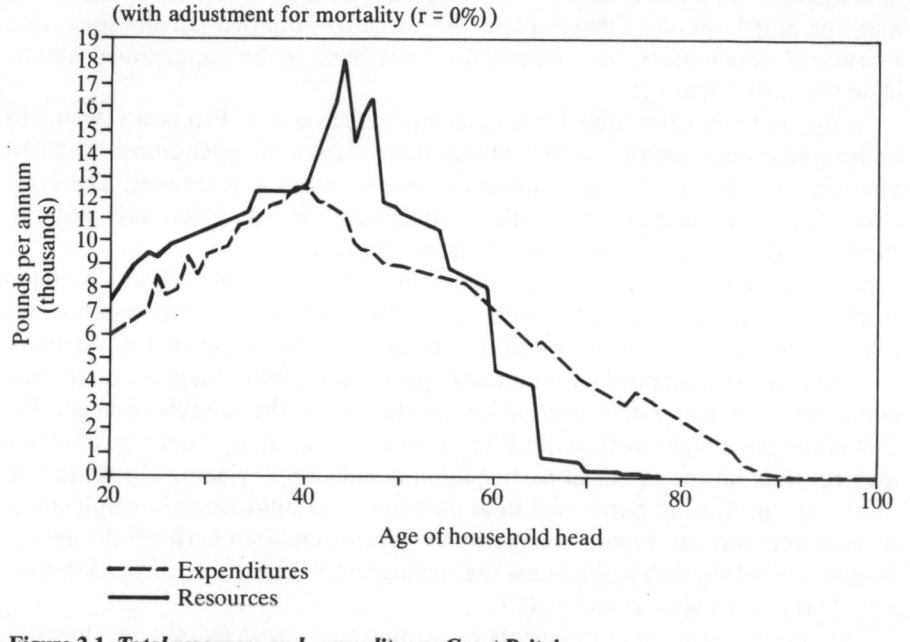

Figure 2.1 *Total resources and expenditures, Great Britain*

mainly reflect differences in social and economic institutions between the two countries, or is a difference in life expectancy responsible?

Japan has the highest life expectancy in the world. A Japanese woman aged 20 can expect to live 61.3 more years, while a 20-year-old British woman can only expect to live 58.2 more years, according to the recent lifetables. If the 1985 Japanese lifetable is substituted for the British one in the calculation of the average ages of consumption and production, the difference in these ages is very close to that obtained for Japan, suggesting that almost all the difference between Japan and Britain can be accounted for by lower mortality in Japan.

Analysis by Ermisch (1989) suggests that even with moderately higher fertility, such as that experienced in the baby boom of the 1960s, and higher mortality, such as that in the late nineteenth century, transfers go from younger to older generations in an industrialised society like Britain. It appears that the social and economic institutions of modern industrial society are sufficiently orientated towards making transfers from younger to older generations to make the *direction* of net transfers invariant to moderate differences in fertility and mortality.

These estimates agree with American estimates by Lee and Lapkoff (1988), both in direction and magnitude. When only the production and consumption of market goods and services are considered, as is the case in the British and Japanese calculations, their estimates indicate that average age of consumption exceeds the average age of production by 4.4 years. When use of time in the

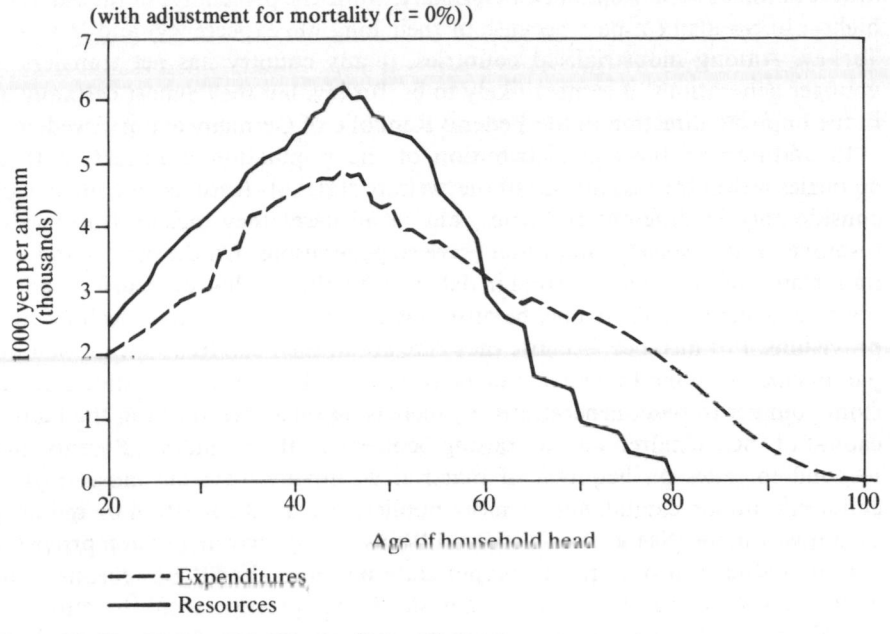

Figure 2.2 *Total resources and expenditures, Japan*

production of household services and in education are also included in the analysis, but leisure, which cannot be transferred between people, is excluded, their estimates show the average age of consumption exceeding the average age of production by 3 years. Lee and Lapkoff's estimates also indicate that transfers still go from younger to older generations when leisure time is incorporated in the calculation. In conjunction with the computations for Britain and Japan, these results suggest that the finding of a net flow of transfers from younger to older persons in industrialised countries is robust.

In other northern and western European countries, life expectancies are similar to Britain's and, with the exception of Ireland, fertility is similar or lower. In conjunction with institutions resembling (in a broad sense) those of Britain, these comparisons suggest that the direction of net transfers is also from younger to older generations in other countries of northern and western Europe. Indeed, the very low fertility in the Federal Republic of Germany, Denmark, the Netherlands, Switzerland, Austria, Sweden and Italy suggests that this direction is much more likely in these countries, since the young heads of household have fewer children to support.

Between 1960 and 1984, changes in fertility and mortality have reduced the proportion of the population aged under 15 and raised the proportion aged 65 and over in all industrialised countries except Ireland (see Table 2.1). Thus, population dynamics have been shifting net transfers in favour of older generations. The proportion of children in the population is highest in Turkey and lowest in the Federal Republic of Germany, while the percentage of the elderly is highest in Sweden (in part because of their long life expectancy) and lowest in Turkey. Among industrialised countries, if any country has net transfers to younger generations, it is most likely to be Turkey, but they almost certainly go in the opposite direction in the Federal Republic of Germany and in Sweden.

In addition to the age distribution of the population, transfers in these countries reflect the institutions of the 'welfare state'. Its features, of course, vary considerably in different countries, but in all cases they include transfers of resources within society, and often between generations. On the other hand, the importance of the welfare system in determining the net flow of transfers should not be exaggerated. There may be offsetting family responses to the welfare state provisions. For instance, because they care about their children's future welfare, parents may respond to higher state pensions, which entail a larger state transfer from younger to older generations, by increasing their investment in the human capital of their children and by raising bequests to their children. Parents may respond to taxes on bequests of material wealth by investing more in their children's human capital, and to more publicly provided education by reducing such investments (See Becker, 1981 and Willis, 1988). Private pension provision may be reduced in response to higher state pensions. For these reasons, state intergenerational transfers may give a misleading impression of the direction and magnitude of intergenerational transfers, and despite the strong assumptions made in computing the measure of net transfers discussed above, it does provide a more comprehensive measure.

The expansion of the welfare state is, nevertheless, an important post-war development, and because its provisions are geared to identifiable demographic groups, such as the elderly and children, it has affected the pattern of inter-generational transfers in many industrialised countries. The second half of the article examines the extent to which population dynamics and changing institutions have affected transfers between generations made through the state.

## Demographic change and transfers through the welfare state

The set of arrangements that has come to be called the welfare state primarily redistributes resources by taxing some people in order to provide services or transfer payments to others, although it also operates through regulation of markets (e.g. equal opportunities in labour and housing markets). Transfers are generally accomplished through progressive or proportional tax systems in conjunction with the services or transfers based on 'need' or contingent on circumstances, like unemployment, the presence of children, or retirement.

In the previous section, the impact of intergenerational transfers in a hypothetical world in which the pattern of transfers had been established for a long time and the population was stable was considered. But the post-war expansion of the welfare state suggests that members of some generations may benefit much more than others from the welfare state provisions. For instance, the extension of pension rights in many countries to people, such as those retiring during the 1960s and 1970s, who had made limited contributions to state pension schemes represented a large transfer to the older generations from the generations working during these years. In contrast, most of these latter generations have contributed to their pensions throughout their working career; thus they will tend to have much lower ratios of (discounted) benefits to contributions than the previous generations of pensioners. This is probably an example of intergenerational transfers involving transfers of *lifetime* resources between generations, although we cannot be sure because of transfers outside the pension scheme that may offset those made inside the scheme.

Not all transfers through the welfare state show up, like pensions, as direct public expenditure. In some countries there are insurance schemes for medical care, and in many countries benefits for children are provided through tax allowances. Tax concessions are also often used to encourage the provision of welfare services by charities, and subsidies for self-provision of housing are offered through the tax system in many countries.

Nevertheless, direct public expenditure on education, health services, pensions, unemployment benefit and other income maintenance programmes, and social services is a very important part of the welfare state. The Organisation for Economic Co-operation and Development uses the term social expenditure to describe these, and it is the fastest-growing component of public expenditure in the OECD countries.

About 80 per cent of social expenditure in OECD countries is on education, health services and pensions, and another 6 per cent is on family benefits. From the nature of these expenditures, it is clear that many services and transfers in the welfare state are channelled to specific age groups, especially children and the elderly. Despite this and the shifts in age distribution shown in Table 2.1, changes in the age structure of the population played a relatively minor role in the expansion of intergenerational transfers through the welfare state in industrialised countries.

Table 2.2. shows the contribution to the growth in social expenditure (in constant prices) attributable to changes in population age structure in two large categories of social expenditure entailing intergenerational transfers: education and pensions, which together account for over half of social expenditure in OECD countries. Expenditure on health services may also entail inter-generational transfers, but the OECD calculations fail to disaggregate health service expenditure by age groups. Disaggregated calculations for the United Kingdom (see Ermisch, 1985) indicate that 20 per cent of the increase in real health service expenditure between 1961 and 1981 was attributable to changes in the age structure.

Changes in demographic structure appear to have made a substantial contribution only to the growth in pension expenditure, 30 per cent of which (on average) is attributable to the growth in the population aged 65 or over. The demographic contribution to changes in expenditure on education is generally

**Table 2.1** *Age structure of the population in industrialised countries*

| | % population aged 0–14 | | | | % population aged 65+ | | | |
|---|---|---|---|---|---|---|---|---|
| | 1960 | 1973 | 1984 | 2000 | 1960 | 1973 | 1984 | 2000 |
| *Northern Europe* | | | | | | | | |
| Denmark | 25.2 | 22.9 | 18.8 | 16.1 | 10.6 | 12.9 | 14.9 | 15.4 |
| Finland | 30.4 | 22.9 | 19.5 | 17.6 | 7.3 | 10.0 | 12.4 | 14.1 |
| Ireland | 30.5 | 31.1 | 29.7 | 27.5 | 10.9 | 11.0 | 10.6 | 9.1 |
| Norway | 25.9 | 24.2 | 20.4 | 17.2 | 10.9 | 13.3 | 15.5 | 15.3 |
| Sweden | 22.4 | 20.7 | 18.3 | 15.3 | 11.8 | 14.5 | 16.9 | 17.2 |
| United Kingdom | 23.3 | 23.9 | 19.5 | 19.0 | 11.7 | 13.6 | 14.8 | 15.3 |
| *Western Europe* | | | | | | | | |
| Austria | 22.0 | 23.9 | 18.6 | 17.8 | 12.2 | 14.5 | 14.2 | 15.1 |
| Belgium (a) | 23.5 | 22.8 | 19.4 | 17.5 | 12.0 | 13.8 | 13.8 | 15.8 |
| France | 26.4 | 24.4 | 21.5 | 19.0 | 11.6 | 13.2 | 12.9 | 14.7 |
| FRG | 21.3 | 22.4 | 15.6 | 15.9 | 10.8 | 13.9 | 14.7 | 16.7 |
| Luxembourg | 21.4 | 20.8 | 17.6 | 16.1 | 10.8 | 13.0 | 13.2 | 15.2 |
| Netherlands | 30.0 | 26.4 | 20.0 | 16.5 | 9.0 | 10.5 | 11.9 | 13.7 |
| Switzerland | 24.0 | 22.7 | 17.8 | 15.5 | 10.2 | 11.8 | 13.8 | 16.7 |
| *Southern Europe* | | | | | | | | |
| Greece | 26.1 | 24.4 | 21.3 | 20.1 | 8.1 | 11.7 | 13.3 | 16.1 |
| Italy | 24.9 | 24.0 | 19.4 | 17.9 | 9.0 | 11.3 | 12.9 | 16.1 |
| Malta | | | | 20.2 | | | | 12.4 |
| Portugal | 29.2 | 28.4 | 24.6 | 22.4 | 8.0 | 9.9 | 10.5 | 12.3 |
| Spain | 27.3 | 27.6 | 23.9 | 21.5 | 8.2 | 9.9 | 11.8 | 13.6 |
| Turkey | 41.2 | 41.1 | 37.0 | 31.9 | 3.7 | 4.7 | 4.2 | 5.5 |
| Yugoslavia | 30.5 | 27.4 | 24.8 | 20.5 | 6.3 | 7.8 | 9.0 | 12.6 |
| *Eastern Europe* | | (1970) | (1980) | | | (1970) | (1980) | |
| Bulgaria | 26.1 | 22.8 | 22.1 | 20.6 | 7.5 | 9.6 | 11.9 | 15.1 |
| Czechoslovakia | 27.4 | 23.0 | 24.3 | 21.3 | 8.6 | 11.3 | 12.5 | 12.2 |
| GDR | 21.1 | 23.4 | 19.5 | 19.3 | 13.7 | 15.5 | 15.9 | 13.7 |
| Hungary | 25.3 | 20.8 | 21.9 | 18.4 | 9.0 | 11.5 | 13.4 | 14.9 |
| Poland | 33.5 | 26.9 | 24.3 | 21.7 | 5.8 | 8.3 | 10.1 | 12.0 |
| Romania | 28.2 | 25.9 | 26.7 | 23.4 | 6.7 | 8.6 | 10.3 | 12.5 |
| USSR | 30.7 | 28.6 | 24.3 | 23.5 | 6.8 | 7.8 | 10.0 | 11.9 |
| | | (1975) | (1985) | | | (1975) | (1985) | |
| USA | 31.0 | 25.2 | 21.9 | 21.8 | 9.2 | 10.5 | 11.7 | 12.0 |
| Japan | 30.2 | 24.3 | 21.8 | 18.5 | 5.7 | 7.9 | 10.0 | 15.1 |

*Note*
(a) 1983, not 1984.

*Sources:* Eastern Europe and all projections: United Nations (1986), *World Population Prospects: Estimates and Projections as Assessed in 1984*, New York, UN; all other figures: OECD (1986), 'Labour force statistics 1964–1984', Paris, OECD; OECD (1973), 'Labour force statistics 1960–1971', Paris, OECD.

**Table 2.2** *Impact of demographic change on the growth of social expenditure in industrialised countries*

| Country | | Annual percentage growth in real expenditure (a) | | Per cent attributable to demographic change (b) | |
|---|---|---|---|---|---|
| | | 1960–75 | 1975–81 | 1960–75 | 1975–81 |
| France | Education | – | 1.0 | – | –60 |
| | Pensions | 7.7 | 8.7 | 25 | 9 |
| FRG | Education | 7.2 | 1.6 | 8 | –56 |
| | Pensions | 6.3 | 2.1 | 49 | 43 |
| Italy | Education | 4.6 | 3.9 | 7 | –5 |
| | Pensions | 9.6 | 7.7 | 27 | 32 |
| United | Education | 5.0 | –2.0 | 12 | 20 |
| Kingdom | Pensions | 5.9 | 4.5 | 27 | 22 |
| Finland | Education | 3.0 | 1.7 | –20 | –76 |
| | Pensions | 11.1 | 5.5 | 25 | 45 |
| Ireland | Education | 7.4 | 4.5 | 18 | 31 |
| | Pensions | 8.2 | 6.6 | 9 | 17 |
| Netherlands | Education | 4.3 | 1.1 | 16 | –45 |
| | Pensions | 10.3 | 5.2 | 26 | 38 |
| Norway | Education | 6.9 | 3.6 | 10 | –14 |
| | Pensions | 12.1 | 4.6 | 17 | 41 |
| Sweden | Education | 3.4 | 2.1 | 6 | –14 |
| | Pensions | 8.7 | 6.9 | 26 | 25 |
| Japan | Education | 5.7 | 4.1 | –4 | — |
| | Pensions | 12.7 | 13.7 | 27 | 27 |
| USA | Education | 6.1 | 0.4 | 18 | — |
| | Pensions | 7.2 | 4.4 | 25 | 57 |
| Canada | Education | 8.4 | 1.0 | 16 | — |
| | Pensions | 8.3 | 6.8 | 29 | 49 |
| Australia | Education | 8.9 | 1.2 | 24 | — |
| | Pensions | 8.5 | 4.0 | 26 | — |
| New Zealand | Education | 5.2 | –0.9 | 37 | — |
| | Pensions | 5.2 | 7.7 | 37 | 32 |

*Notes*
(a) Average compound growth rate in expenditure at constant prices.
(b) Rate of growth in client population divided by growth rate of real expenditure; client populations are: persons aged 0–24, and population aged 65 and over.

*Source:* OECD (1985), 'Social expenditure, 1960–1990: problems of growth and control', Paris, OECD, Tables 6 and A.

much smaller (the 'negative demographic contributions' to education expenditure change shown in Table 2.2 reflect a fall in the population aged 0–24 in conjunction with a rise in education expenditure), although it should be noted that taking persons aged 0–24 as the client population for education in the calculations of Table 2.2 may understate the contribution of age structure changes to education spending. Thus, on the basis of past experience in state intergenerational transfers, demographic changes have only had a major influence on transfers between workers and pensioners, which is the main focus of this book, and even in this case, most of the increase in pension expenditure is attributable to better pensions and pension coverage rather than to more pensioners.

## Prospective demographic change and pensions

Demographic pressures on pension expenditure over the remainder of this century are very moderate in most industrialised countries, Japan being an important exception. But pressures for more spending on pensions will build up considerably during the first three decades of the next century, as the baby boom babies approach retirement age. Furthermore, the structure and practice of many state pension systems do not allow much scope for economic growth to ease the pension burden on the working population. This can be seen from a simple model of a 'pay-as-you-go' pension scheme, which is the most common type of scheme in industrialised countries.

In a pay-as-you-go scheme, pension expenditure, which equals the product of benefits per pensioner (b) and the number of pensioners (P), must be balanced by contributions from the working population. These contributions are equal to the product of the size of the working population (L), the average earnings of each worker (w) and the (employer's plus employee's) contribution rate (c). This identity implies that

$$\frac{b}{w} = c \left( \frac{L}{P} \right).$$

Many pension schemes effectively index the pension to earnings; in other words, they try to maintain the pension as a proportion of wages, thereby permitting pensioners to participate in real income growth as well as protecting them against inflation. Thus, b/w is effectively held constant. It is, therefore, clear that the fall in the number of workers per pensioner (L/P) must be offset by a rise in the contribution rate. For instance, if fertility were to remain at its present levels, in the Federal Republic of Germany the worker-to-pensioner ratio declines by almost 60 per cent between 2000 and 2030, and in Great Britain it falls by 40 per cent over this period (see Hauser, 1982 and Ermisch, 1985).

The long-term movement in the ratio of persons aged 65 and over to the population of working age (aged 15–64) is illustrated in Table 2.3 (using the 'medium variant' population projections of the United Nations, which are

**Table 2.3** *Ratio of persons aged 65+ to those aged 15–64 in industrialised countries*

|                  | 1960 | 1980 | 2000 | 2025 |
|------------------|------|------|------|------|
| *Europe*         | 15.1 | 20.3 | 21.8 | 29.1 |
| *Northern Europe* | 17.5 | 23.1 | 22.8 | 30.0 |
| Denmark          | 16.5 | 22.3 | 22.4 | 34.9 |
| Finland          | 11.5 | 17.7 | 20.6 | 33.7 |
| Ireland          | 19.4 | 18.3 | 14.3 | 17.2 |
| Norway           | 17.6 | 23.4 | 22.7 | 32.2 |
| Sweden           | 18.1 | 25.4 | 25.5 | 35.8 |
| United Kingdom   | 17.9 | 23.5 | 23.3 | 29.7 |
| *Western Europe* | 17.1 | 22.1 | 23.1 | 33.6 |
| Austria          | 18.3 | 24.2 | 22.5 | 31.1 |
| Belgium          | 18.5 | 21.9 | 23.6 | 31.8 |
| France           | 18.8 | 21.9 | 22.2 | 30.7 |
| FRG              | 16.0 | 23.4 | 24.8 | 36.5 |
| Luxembourg       | 16.0 | 20.0 | 22.2 | 34.3 |
| Netherlands      | 14.8 | 17.4 | 19.6 | 35.4 |
| Switzerland      | 15.2 | 20.8 | 24.6 | 39.1 |
| *Southern Europe* | 12.9 | 18.1 | 21.7 | 26.9 |
| Greece           | 12.6 | 20.5 | 25.3 | 28.0 |
| Italy            | 14.2 | 20.8 | 24.3 | 30.9 |
| Malta            | 13.0 | 16.0 | 18.3 | 33.0 |
| Portugal         | 12.7 | 16.5 | 18.8 | 24.1 |
| Spain            | 12.8 | 17.0 | 21.0 | 24.0 |
| Turkey           | 6.4  | 8.0  | 9.1  | 13.1 |
| Yugoslavia       | 10.0 | 13.5 | 18.9 | 27.1 |
| *Eastern Europe* | 12.9 | 18.3 | 19.6 | 26.3 |
| Bulgaria         | 11.3 | 18.0 | 23.5 | 26.5 |
| Czechoslovakia   | 13.4 | 19.7 | 18.4 | 25.4 |
| GDR              | 21.0 | 24.7 | 20.5 | 28.5 |
| Hungary          | 13.8 | 20.8 | 22.3 | 30.1 |
| Poland           | 9.5  | 15.4 | 18.1 | 27.0 |
| Romania          | 10.3 | 16.3 | 19.5 | 22.8 |
| USSR             | 10.8 | 15.3 | 18.3 | 23.5 |
| USA              | 15.5 | 17.1 | 18.1 | 27.5 |
| Japan            | 9.0  | 13.4 | 22.6 | 32.9 |

*Note*
USSR and Turkey are not included in the regional or continental totals.

*Source:* United Nations (1986), 'World population prospects: estimates and projections as assessed in 1984', New York, UN.

probably on the high side concerning future fertility levels in industrialised countries, thus on the low side concerning this ratio). With the exception of Ireland, this ratio has risen substantially throughout the industrialised countries. But during the remainder of this century this ratio rises very little in most countries, and in six countries there will actually be a reduction in the number of elderly per person of working age.

In Japan however, this ratio increases by almost 70 per cent between 1980 and 2000, reflecting the sharp fall in Japanese fertility during the 1950s and the large improvements in life expectancy among the Japanese. Japan is undergoing the most rapid population ageing ever experienced, and the (changing) pension scheme is subject to strong demographic pressure in consequence. During the first three decades of the next century this elderly dependency ratio is projected to increase dramatically again in most of the industrialised countries, including Japan.

The reciprocal of the elderly dependency ratio is the number of persons of working age per elderly person. It tends to move similarly over time to the number of workers per pensioner ($L/P$) of our simple pension model. Table 2.3 shows that in the Netherlands, Finland, Switzerland and Denmark large declines in the number of persons of working age per elderly person are expected, reaching levels below three by 2025. In Sweden, the Federal Republic of Germany and Luxembourg also, less than three persons of working age per elderly person are projected for 2025. At present labour force participation rates, this amounts to less than two workers per pensioner.

A compensating rise in the contribution rate is required if the pension is to be maintained as a proportion of earnings. In many schemes, like Germany's and Britain's, although it is not strictly dictated by legislation, indexation effectively tends to maintain this proportion. Faster economic growth, which raises earnings, also raises the pension promised in the scheme. Thus, faster economic growth does not reduce the burden of pensions on the working population; their contribution rate must rise to match the fall in the ratio of workers to pensioners. In order to reduce the burden, the level of pension benefits must be reduced relative to earnings ($b/w$ must fall), but this generally entails a major change in the nature of the pension scheme. Alternatively, changes in retirement age must increase the number of workers relative to pensioners ($L/P$ must be increased).

The steep rise in the contribution rates to historically unsurpassed levels under present state pension schemes could force changes at short notice because of resistance by the working population to the payment of such large contributions. For instance, the projected increase in the contribution rate in Great Britain during the first three decades of the next century is equivalent to a reduction in the rate of growth of real disposable earnings of 0.4 percentage points (for example, from 1.5 to 1.1 per cent per year) if the incidence of the contribution rate were fully on employees. In a sluggish economy that would be a significant reduction in real income growth. The British state pension contribution rate (employer's plus employee's) would reach 30 per cent during the mid-2030s, in contrast to 20 per cent today (Ermisch, 1985). Moreover, among the northern and western European countries other than Ireland, Japan and the USA, the decline in the ratio of persons of working age to elderly persons between 2000 and 2025 is expected to be the smallest in Britain. Thus, we would expect much more dramatic contribution rate increases in these other countries, particularly the Netherlands, Finland, Switzerland, Denmark, Sweden and the Federal Republic of Germany. For instance, in the Federal Republic of Germany, the projected contribution rate (employer's plus employee's) would be 35 per cent in 2035 compared with 18 per cent in 1982 (Hauser, 1982 and Schmähl, this volume).

Resistance by the working population to paying these increasingly high contribution rates appears to be a matter of legitimate concern. After the turn of the century, or even before, periodic political strife over pensions is likely to be in store for most, if not all, industrialised countries. If worker resistance leads to a reduction in pension benefits for those retiring during the 2020s and 2030s, the baby boom generations will have received a poor return from state pension schemes. They will have contributed from their earnings throughout their lives, but will end up receiving a lower proportion of earnings in benefits than did members of previous generations. In other words, through the pension scheme they would have transferred lifetime resources to other generations.

Clearly, this potential pension problem arises because of the relative generosity of pensions promised in present schemes. Making these pension promises appeared cheap in the 1960s and 1970s when the ratio of workers to pensioners was high, but it becomes much more costly to deliver on these promises in the future when the small post-1970 generations must pay the pensions of the large baby boom generations. The implicit intergenerational contracts that are sometimes attributed to pay-as-you-go pension schemes are strained when the generations differ considerably in size.

These calculations of the 'burden' of the elderly assume no adjustment in retirement practices. One way in which the potential intergenerational conflict may be resolved is by a reversal of the trend towards earlier retirement which has been encouraged in the recent era of unemployment. The improved standard of health which is probably associated with the improvement in life expectancy experienced in the post-war years would permit an extension of working life, particularly if new forms of work organisation permit greater flexibility of working hours with partial pensions for partial retirement, as pioneered in Sweden. Recent problems of pension finance in some countries (e.g. the USA) arose because of the maturing of pension schemes, or the 'ageing of state pensions'; the very large pressures on state pensions in the next century arise from the 'ageing of populations' in mature pension schemes.

## Conclusions

Recent estimates strongly suggest that net transfers are from younger to older generations in contemporary industrialised countries, and the ageing of populations in industrialised countries has been shifting net transfers in favour of older generations. With regard to the expansion of intergenerational transfers through the state, demographic changes have only played a major role in the increase of transfers from workers to pensioners. The rapid ageing to be experienced early in the next century, as the baby boom babies retire, is likely to put considerable pressure on pay-as-you-go pension schemes that transfer resources to the elderly.

## References

Becker, G. S. (1981), *A Treatise on the Family*, Cambridge, Mass., Harvard University Press.

Ermisch, J. F. (1985), *Economic Implications of Demographic Change*, Manchester, Manchester Statistical Society.

Ermisch, J. F. (1989), 'Intergenerational transfers in industrialized countries: effects of age distribution and economic institutions', *Journal of Population Economics*, forthcoming.

Hauser, R. (1982), 'How to guarantee West German public pension payments during the next fifty years', *Zeitschrift für die gesamte Staatswisseschaft*, CXXXVIII, pp. 440–68.

Lee, R. D.(1980), 'Age structure, intergenerational transfers and economic growth: an overview', *Revue Economique*, XXXI, pp. 1129–56 (November).

Lee, R. D. (1985), 'Population growth and intergenerational transfers in a household setting', Working Paper of the Graduate Group in Demography, Berkeley, University of California.

Lee, R. D. and Lapkoff, S. F. (1988), 'Intergenerational flows of time and goods: consequences of slowing population growth', *Journal of Political Economy*, XCVI, pp. 618–51 (June).

Samuelson, P. A. (1958), 'An exact consumption-loan model of interest with or without the contrivance of money', *Journal of Political Economy*, LXVI, pp. 467–82 (December).

Willis, R. (1988), 'Institutions and population growth: a theory of the equilibrium interest rate in an overlapping generations model', in R. D. Lee, W. B. Arthur and G. Rodgers (eds), *Economics of Changing Age Distributions in Developed Countries*, Oxford, Oxford University Press.

# 3

# The Welfare State and Generation Conflict: Winners and Losers

## David Thomson

### Equity as a temporal issue

Buried deep in the literature of theoretical public economics resides an important body of thought on the nature and meaning of the welfare state. The ideas are often arcane and highly abstract, the expression of them terse and intimidating to the uninitiated. The preoccupations – the impact of welfare redistributions upon savings behaviour, capital accumulation and long-run economic growth – have never been mainstream social policy issues, though they perhaps should be. And as a result the debates about welfare and its evolution which are conducted by historians, sociologists, demographers, social administrators and policy analysts remain largely untouched by these insights and premonitions.

This is a pity, for a number are critical to current social policy issues, most especially the ageing of modern societies. A key point of the political economists has been that the essence of all major social welfare activities is a redistribution of resources between generations, and not between rich and poor as is so commonly assumed. Generation should in consequence be a prime variable in welfare analysis, and the theorists have suggested a range of possible outcomes to watch for (Burbridge, 1987).

Some argue that taking resources from members of one generation and giving them to others can, at least in theory, be achieved equitably and to the advantage of all, though this would depend upon the level of redistribution attempted and upon surmounting difficulties during the early years. Others have been less sanguine. In a famous but short-lived debate in the 1950s, Samuelson (1958) and Lerner (1959) questioned whether a redistribution system such as that evolving in modern societies could ever be fair to different generations. The image of the chain-letter was invoked – would not the welfare state behave like the childish craze for a no-cost win to which many fall victim just once in their youthful years, profiting the scheme's initiators at the expense of the gullible who join later? Thirty years on the metaphor is looking disturbingly apt.

The debate proved inconclusive. A focus upon generation, and the likelihood that collective social security programmes would mean vastly different and contradictory things to successive generations within the same society, represents a path not taken in our intellectual life – and we are all the poorer for this. Political economists seemed to lose interest in generational questions and the potential for fundamental conflict which these presented, and social scientists failed to pick them up.

This comment deserves some qualification. From time to time generation has been acknowledged as a factor in modern history, most especially in the welfare literature of the United States and Australia – interesting that this should occur in two of the least-developed of modern welfare states (Easterlin, 1980, 1987; Harrington, 1984; Jones, 1983; Mendelsohn, 1983; Parsons, 1984; Preston, 1984). More recently hints of a generation perception have begun to appear in some demographic studies (Ermisch and Joshi, 1987; Hugo, 1986), and philosophers have not ignored the issue (Daniels, 1988; Parfit, 1984; Sikora and Barry, 1978; Wynne, 1980). Yet despite this generational perspectives remain unexplored, and few attempts have been made to examine them as significant forces shaping modern societies.

In what follows I want to eschew the familiar approaches of the historian and social scientist and take up the challenge thrown out by the political economists of twenty or thirty years ago. Our question is, 'Can the historian see significant evidence of sustained, cumulative and structured generation conflict in the operations of the modern welfare state?' There is little to be gained any more in studying the welfare states simply as battlegrounds between rich and poor, employer and employee, and our other synonyms and apologies for class. We are all agreed that they have not been strong on redistribution between the affluent and impoverished, and that they are probably a good deal weaker on this now than they were a couple of decades ago. At the same time the measurable amount of redistributive activity expands, and it is time that we took on board the significance of these two trends.

Redistribution between rich and poor has not been the prime concern of populations as they erected their welfare states in the third quarter of the twentieth century, or struggled to maintain them in the fourth. Instead, the welfare states represented a daring experiment in the large-scale shifting of resources between generations, as a means of easing the hardships that occur at various points in the human life cycle. They amount to an exercise in group life insurance, and not an assault upon the wealthy – for that their populations have shown remarkably little taste, whatever the rhetoric might suggest to the contrary. Success or failure in spreading resources across time must be the core of our analysis, though not of course to the exclusion of other variables. Two broad types of interacting redistribution are in operation in modern societies, and a willingness to assist the poor is predicated upon the larger success in securing successive generations against risk and insecurity. Redistribution across class, we might suggest, is 'piggy-backed' upon successful redistribution between generations, and if successive generations do not feel so secured they will not tolerate major welfare activities for the benefit of the poor.

The argument here, from an observer of recent decades who asks questions about generations, is that the modern welfare states are failing to behave equitably over time, and that with this failure comes the present loss of faith in the welfare state experiment. Further, the inability or unwillingness to operate intergenerational exchanges fairly is now revealed on such a scale as to seriously endanger the continued consensus for collective welfare programmes. The key factors in this troubled evolution of the welfare states, however, have been political rather than more purely demographic or economic.

During their short lives the welfare states have seen the range and scale of their prizes and penalties alter so repeatedly and radically as to create persisting generations of lifetime 'winners' and 'losers' – successive cohorts of citizens who because of their varied birthdates are accumulating contrary experiences of what it means to live in a modern welfare state. This is of critical importance to all discussions of ageing and the elderly. In asking, as our societies are now doing increasingly, what rights to assistance the aged might enjoy, or what duties to help the non-aged lie under, or whether more or less redistribution in favour of the elderly is desirable or practicable or just or wise, an unprepared citizenry grapples with unfamiliar and uncomfortable questions.

At present the aged seem still to be viewed as 'children', as a group who have things done to them or for them but who are not part of the active decision-making, responsibility-bearing or obligation-bound adult population. This is likely to change, for what the historical analysis suggests is that the generation now middle-aged and entering old age is the 'welfare generation', the cohort who have been the prime beneficiaries of the welfare state throughout their adult lives. Their lifetime financial contributions to the programme of pooled resources which is the essence of the welfare state have been small, and their claims much more considerable. Those who preceded them into old age found the welfare state of more limited worth – and those who follow are being asked as a generation to invest a great deal more than they will ever receive in return. How to make this palatable or politically saleable will be a major test for us all.

In short, the very nature of aged populations is changing, in ways not comprehended in our present debates, and along with this come shifts in relations between generations. Members of the welfare generation are now arriving at old age with assets, expectations and histories of benefit quite unlike those of their predecessors, and it remains to be seen whether the young who are expected to make growing transfers to them will feel bound to do so. At the end of the twentieth century the implicit welfare contract which binds members of successor generations is up for renegotiation – and the aged stand right at the centre of this, with a great deal to lose.

In a brief article it will not be possible to tackle many of the questions begged by this argument. Ethical issues and the macroeconomics of it all will have to be left to one side – indeed, many of the more obvious reactions and objections must lie as if unanticipated. The concern is to outline the processes and steps by which the welfare states are being transformed, but two preparatory matters crucial to a fuller understanding of that analysis cannot be ignored. One is the nature of what we might term the implicit welfare contract between generations. My contention, to be explored in other places, is that while altruism and a spirit of selflessness need not be dismissed as a part of this, the core unspoken belief underlying a welfare state is one of reciprocity and consistency, of the citizen-taxpayer's right to some future services of a scale and nature comparable to those now being offered to others (Thomson, 1989a, 1989b).

The modern welfare state, it is often noted, provides a relatively secure, risk-free environment for the citizen – but what is much less remarked is that it does so by imposing enormous risks of another kind. A young person reaching adulthood any time after 1970 faces the prospect, as previous generations have not done, of handing over a third or more of lifetime earnings for redistribution by a political process over which he or she exercises minimal control. Most of this money will be given as cash or services to persons of some other age or life-phase – persons old, or young, or sick, or out of work – and the contributor is required to have faith that when he or she enters those phases and meets the same conditions, the rules observed by the society will still be the same, with others then feeling obligated to make their surplus income available in like manner. This acceptance of high risk creates a trust that is being sorely tried in the final quarter of this century. The history of the modern welfare states is of societies acting without sufficient regard for and often in direct contradiction of these inherent intergenerational contracts.

The second matter that cannot pass unremarked is the process by which certain generations have been able to 'capture' the welfare state, permitting them to remodel it over time in step with their own ageing priorities. In particular, it will need to be explained why the 'welfare generation', the young adults of the first twenty-five years of the modern welfare state, have been able in the last twenty years to refashion what were once youth-centred welfare states into mechanisms for benefiting the aged ahead of others. My account would emphasise a number of factors and the overall influence of self-interest, though not self-interest in an overt or even conscious manner. There is no suggestion here of a deliberate and knowing campaign to violate the welfare contract or defraud future generations: the process of reforming the welfare state has been more subtle, more incremental, more accidental.

For one thing, a lack of thought as to the nature of the crucial understandings that bind generations has helped produce policies which undermine these unarticulated agreements. Second, the modern welfare states maintain annual accounts of their income and dispersions, but never data on lifetime costs and benefits, so that we now possess few means of assessing how these societies have handled the trust reposed in them by successive generations. A third factor has been an inevitable conflict between the demands of the welfare contract for consistency and reciprocity over very long periods of time, and of the political systems with which we try to operate those contracts – systems which emphasise action for the most immediate of reasons, which must balance a budget or appease a lobby or win an election this year rather than decades hence.

A rapid growth in expectations and a mounting willingness to press them is another influence at work here. Our systems for pooling resources were established, quite unexpectedly, at the beginning of a quarter-century of sustained economic growth. This coincidence – let us call it that for now – is usually seen as one of immense good fortune, but may yet be viewed as a curse which permitted inordinate expectations of the welfare state to take root and flourish. For two or three decades major portions of the population experienced welfare states which seemed to know no limits, which met mounting demands with apparent ease and at a price much less than the immediate benefit. At the end of this growth phase a population habituated to expansion and little cost was, not surprisingly, unwilling to accept that there were limits after all, that the welfare state is ultimately a zero-sum state in which larger shares for some must mean less for others, or that past benefits imposed obligations to pay now. A revision of the welfare state, and especially a collapsing of expensive youth-benefiting programmes, was a more tempting option.

A failure of leadership also played a part. During the 1970s these societies failed to produce political or intellectual leaders who would insist upon the obligations and the restraint of self-interest which are inherent in maintaining the welfare contract. The adversarial nature of modern democracies may make it impossible for such leaders to emerge and have effect. Changes in the composition of the electorate could perhaps have played a part, though it must be pointed out at once that analyses of the ages of electors suggests no strong link here: the 'ageing of the welfare state' has not followed an obvious ageing of the electorate.

Perhaps most critical of all was the lack of a powerful constituency for preserving the youth-states which many of the early welfare states were in essence. Everyone over the age of about 40 has a clear interest in maintaining or enhancing the pensions and the services of the aged, since all are already beneficiaries or can envisage themselves as such within a short space of time. But support for youth-favouring programmes is necessarily much more transitory, diverse and unaware of itself. Those who will want a low-interest first-home loan a few years hence are currently still at school, without a vote, and not thinking of themselves as potential mortgage seekers. In the climate of the 1970s and 1980s, with resources for redistribution being outstripped by demands, it was much easier to quietly eliminate one by one the many benefits for the young, while expanding those of more interest to the ageing. But in doing so these states unwittingly called into question the whole notion of a commitment between generations.

The remainder of this essay surveys the diverging welfare states in which successive generations find themselves living, using the experience of my own country as a representative illustration of a much wider process. Some will insist that the New Zealand story is unique, not paralleled elsewhere, even unbelievable. This cannot be accepted – the pattern described is widespread in the late twentieth century, indeed is perhaps inherent in the very nature of the welfare state. I would be delighted to be proven wrong, to be shown convincing examples of modern societies behaving with consistency and restraint so that successive generations enjoy an equal incentive to maintain the implicit contract. But at present we do not see them: perhaps others will be stung by the generalisations into companion studies.

## Creating the youth-state

New Zealand made the decisive break from the old 'minimal welfare state', with its limited range of low-slung safety nets and its minuscule taxation demands, in the late 1930s following the election of its first Labour government. The modern welfare state erected then and expanded in subsequent decades was a cunning construct, though this was probably not so much deliberate as a result of competing political demands and of reactions to the desolation of the Depression years. In particular, the new welfare state managed to bind into a welfare compact persons of all ages, that is, of all generations then alive, by promising gains now or in the near future, and at little evident cost. No large group was required to pay heavily in anticipation of some very distant reciprocal treatment – faith in collective security was not tried too severely.

There is a popular belief that the modern welfare state has a prime function to cater for the aged, and this the new state certainly did, though to a much more limited degree than is now recalled. In New Zealand's case a scheme of non-contributory, means-tested old-age pensions had been in place since 1898, and this was expanded and liberalised in the late 1930s. The age of eligibility for both men and women was lowered to 60 years; weekly payments were raised considerably; incomes and assets testing were eased; and a new if limited contributory universal superannuation scheme was introduced. All this, combined with promises of more spending upon health, gratified the elderly, and more importantly, perhaps, served to assure the then-middle-aged, the group who were expected to fund much of the new welfare state, that they could look forward soon to some definite return upon their investments.

But while these moves helped win the older half of the electorate to an expanded social security programme, it was young adults who were to be the major beneficiaries of the changes. Expanded state spending upon family benefits, family health services, housing and education absorbed a much larger portion of total national resources than did redistributions towards the aged. In the year 1951, for example, social security and health benefits to the aged amounted to about 3 per cent of GDP. But this was dwarfed by the more obvious expenditures upon young adults and their children: 3 per cent of GDP was invested in building homes for young families; 2 per cent was spent on education, 2.2 per cent on cash benefits for families, and just under 1 per cent on war pensions, most of which again went to the young (NZ Department of Statistics, annual, *National Income*).

Moreover, these constituted only the more immediately measurable of the expenditures upon young adults – they also gained through health expenditures, a new range of child welfare services, free dental, general practitioner and hospital services for their children (services not free to all age groups), war veterans' rehabilitation schemes which put thousands of young men through university or trade training, into homes or businesses or on to farms, and many more. Substantial income taxation exemptions for young children and non-earning spouses, worth perhaps the equivalent of a further 2 per cent of GDP in 1951, helped to make them the first 'welfare generation', the first generation of major welfare beneficiaries though they never thought of themselves as such (Thomson, 1989b). Access to these benefits was made free of means testing in all but a few circumstances. One effect of this was that those on middling and higher incomes became key recipients of welfare-state largesse, to the persisting chagrin of left-wing observers. But another result, one perhaps vital to the survival of the welfare consensus, was to bind in all members of the community behind the pooling and redistribution of resources by political action, a binding in of powerful social elements which has disappeared in more recent years.

This balance of benefits heavily in favour of the young persisted throughout the 1950s and 1960s – long enough, that is, to create what we might speak of as a generation of beneficiaries. The process reflected the peculiar origins of the modern welfare state as a reaction to the ravages of depression and war in the 1930s and 1940s. It was shaped by a desire for nation rebuilding – for promoting population growth after the falling fertility and the 'race suicide' panics of the 1930s, for removing the malnutrition, slum housing, stunted growth, and physical and mental underdevelopment revealed during depression and war, for fostering investment and growth, for releasing the potential of the youth of the nation.

The particulars of this story are peculiar to New Zealand, but the general pattern is not. The timing and the pace of welfare expansion will have created different generational imbalances in each modern state, yet the similarities are also striking. Analysis of public spending upon programmes which benefit citizens of different ages, together with a study of taxation rates and exemptions, suggests a comparable erection of youth-states in the early post-war years in most developed nations (Flora and Heidenheimer, 1981; OECD, annual).

## The ageing of the welfare state – restructuring social security

A critical turning was reached around 1970, when the implicit contracts between generations were put to their first serious test, and found wanting. The first welfare generation were by then entering middle-age, and had little further use for youth-fostering programmes. Indeed, to maintain them would have brought heavy costs, since the large 'baby boom' cohorts were by now reaching early adulthood and so seeking assistance in establishing their own families and careers. According to the intergenerational understanding this should not have mattered: having passed through a major phase of benefit, and being now in a life-phase in which surpluses were most to hand, the welfare generation could have been expected to step aside, pass on a comparable array of benefits to those who followed them in turn, and accept as the middle-aged before them had done the role of major funders of the welfare state.

But while the contract may have required this cession of place as prime beneficiaries, practical politics did not. Neither the welfare generation, nor those older than them who were now in old age and who felt, perhaps understandably, that they had earned a right to a more generous old age after funding the early years of the welfare state, revealed an interest in sustaining the youth-state. A welfare state remoulded to ageing interests held more appeal. The steps in this revision of purpose and function have been many and varied. A few are well known, although more have passed quite without remark. We can begin by looking at changes in social security, since these are the most obvious, readily measurable, and by far the most widely discussed, although, while they are of great symbolic importance, their impact has perhaps been less than that of moves in other spheres.

During the last twenty years the universal family benefit paid in New Zealand to all who care for dependent children has been eroded in value. By the 1980s it was worth just one-third as much as it had been in the 1950s relative to average gross or net earnings – and similar things have happened elsewhere. In some countries, Canada and Sweden for instance, the process of erosion was halted temporarily in the 1970s with major revisions of support for young families, but a steady whittling away has been more standard: no examples have yet come to light of family allowances which have retained their true 1950s or 1960s worth relative to incomes. In a number of instances eligibility for family allowances has been restricted (Field, 1980; Flora and Heidenheimer, 1981; Guest, 1985; Ismael, 1985, 1987; Jones, 1983; Lister, 1982; Mendelsohn, 1983).

Records of national expenditures upon child allowances reveal almost everywhere a shrinking of the portion of GDP invested by the state in families (Flora et al., 1983; OECD, annual). In Scandinavia, for example, the fraction of GDP devoted to family allowances and related family services grew rapidly in the 1950s and more especially in the 1960s, but since the early 1970s there has been no growth in Denmark or Norway, some expansion followed by retreat in Sweden, and unequivocal gains in Finland alone which started the period well behind the others in this regard (Nordic Council, annual). In New Zealand the fraction of GDP involved is now one-third of what it was thirty years ago.

All of this contrasts strikingly with the concurrent enhancement in the universal payments made on account of age – a development which gives the lie to the familiar apology that poor national economic performances have forced states to contract their welfare undertakings. The pensions paid to the elderly of the 1960s and earlier were no longer acceptable to a new generation of the ageing.

For one thing, the weekly value of the age benefit has grown. New Zealand now operates a non-contributory, unfunded universal old-age pension system known as National Superannuation, with a flat-rate taxable payment being made regardless of income or assets. During the last thirty years the universal family allowance has increased by 400 per cent at face value, prices by 800 per cent, wages by 900 per cent – and the net age benefit by 1,600 per cent: most of the change has occurred since 1970. From the 1940s to the early 1970s this pension was equivalent in value to 26–28 per cent of the total net income of the median 'standard family' (a young man aged 25 to 34 in full-time employment, his non-earning wife, and two small children for whom family benefits were received). In the 1980s it has moved beyond 40 per cent. Similar, if less striking rises in the relative worth of old-age pensions have been reported in the 1970s and 1980s in Europe, North America and Australia (Clark *et al.*, 1984; Council of Economic Advisers to the US President, 1985; Fiegehen, 1986; Harrington, 1984; Health and Welfare Canada, 1986; Jones, 1983; Mendelsohn, 1983).

Moreover, a rise in the worth of individual payments forms just one aspect of the change – in a variety of ways access to social security for the aged has been liberalised during the past twenty years. In New Zealand in this period the age of entitlement to a full pension has been lowered for both sexes from 70 years to 60; all assets and incomes testing has been eliminated, as have requirements to retire; pension rates have been fully indexed to movements in average male net earnings; and indexation to the cost of living has also been introduced, should this in any year prove more favourable to the aged than is indexation to earnings. Not surprisingly the fraction of GDP absorbed by state pensions to the aged has doubled in the last ten years, while the elderly as a portion of the population have grown very little.

It is possible that this easing of entitlement to age benefits since 1970 may have gone further in New Zealand than in some other places, but the trend is one of the most widely remarked of all international welfare trends of this era. Records of the fraction of GDP devoted to this purpose provide one measure of the trend. Since the mid-1960s, for example, the portion expended upon the aged and disabled had doubled in Norway, and trebled in Denmark, Finland and Sweden (Nordic Council, annual), and in Canada, Australia and the United States a comparable doubling in little more than a decade has been reported.

The contrary movements in allowances for the old and the young has been striking, and are not confined to social security spending alone. Various pieces of data hint strongly that the overall disposition of government spending has lately been tipped in favour of the elderly. Education spending, for instance, has in many instances shrunk as a fraction of GDP, even while the demands mount for a highly trained workforce for the twenty-first century. In Britain the percentage of GDP expended in this way has shrunk by about 20 per cent in the last decade as it has done in West Germany, while in Denmark and Sweden it has remained more constant (OECD, annual).

Meanwhile public expenditure upon health, a service of much more direct concern to an ageing electorate, has everywhere expanded. Between 1971 and the mid-1980s the fraction of GDP absorbed in this grew by 56 per cent in New Zealand, 27 per cent in Britain, 50 per cent in Germany, 60 per cent in Sweden, and so the examples run on (OECD, annual). Within this expansion further shifts of resources towards the aged may also have taken place, although this is reported upon by few nations. In Britain, for example, around 45 per cent of National Health Service spending is now consumed by persons of retirement pension age (Central Statistical Office, annual, *Social Trends* 18). Wroe's (1973) estimates of the early 1960s and 1970s put the comparable fraction at around 28 per cent, and the Phillips Committee in the 1950s suggested a smaller fraction still, although the three sets of estimates are not strictly comparable in character (Committee on the Economic and Financial Problems of Provision for Old Age, 1954). Hospital in-patient records indicate similarly the growing dominance of the health services by the aged, a shift that goes well beyond what simple demography might determine.

The elimination of much public expenditure on housing perhaps constitutes the most significant of all the moves to collapse the welfare state for the 'post-welfare generations', although the complexities of housing investments and subsidies are immensely difficult to fathom, let alone compare internationally. An account of the recent New Zealand experience may serve to illustrate a possible wider trend here, as well as to reveal the scale of the incremental changes involved – and perhaps to stimulate others into similar studies.

Slum clearance and the furnishing of quality homes fit for young families formed one of the dominant social welfare thrusts in New Zealand from the mid-1930s. Public housing assistance from that date took two main forms. First, the Labour government began a programme to erect single-unit houses with substantial gardens for subsidised rental to low- and modest-income young families. By the 1960s around 10 per cent of the nation's housing stock consisted of these 'state houses', although by then some had already been sold into private ownership. In the 1950s at least 1 per cent of GDP was invested each year in this construction work: the degree of further state investment through undercharging on rentals and the like is unknown. But the amount spent on erection alone was not insignificant, being equivalent to all public spending on the elementary school system, or three-quarters of the health vote, or one-half of spending on retirement pensioners.

Second, and much more importantly, the state provided an array of low-interest mortgages, interest-free loans and non-repayable grants to young adults wishing to buy their own homes, private ownership being by far the dominant housing form in the country, with 80 per cent of households achieving private ownership by around age 40. A median-income standard family in 1961 seeking a new home of average price would have been given an interest-free grant equivalent to 20 per cent of the total price, and a thirty-year mortgage to cover the remaining 80 per cent, the interest rate being about one-half of the current 'open market' rate. This assistance was available largely without means testing: only a few of the most affluent of young adults would have faced any restriction upon access to these government subsidies.

The result was a massive state investment in private ownership, and since none of the capital gains realised had to be returned to the state, and since mortgage conditions were not reviewable as personal income or market interest rates rose, major disguised grants of state money to private individuals were taking place. In the late 1950s and the early 1960s low-cost loans to young private homebuyers absorbed 2 to 3 per cent of GDP per annum, about as much as the entire public expenditure upon education or the national health bill.

During the 1960s and more especially in the mid-1970s the state decided to scale down assistance to those seeking housing, unless they were aged, and with this has gone one of the most important elements in the welfare state of the young. State housing construction has been greatly reduced, with the fraction of GDP involved in the 1980s being just one-fifth of what it had been twenty or thirty years earlier. Moreover, much of the public housing stock has been sold into private ownership, and the rentals charged upon the remainder have been lifted to 'market levels' so that the element of direct subsidisation involved is now minimal.

A comparable contraction has taken place in help to private owners. Interest-free grants have been cut; state mortgages now cover a shrinking fraction of the cost of a basic first home; and the interest rates charged have risen, not unexpectedly, to 'market levels'. (No income tax relief is available upon mortgage interest payments in this country.) Perhaps more critical has been the tightening of means testing, a key feature of the 1970s and 1980s welfare state of the young, known by the euphemism of 'targeting', so that all but the lowest-income groups have been removed from eligibility for state benefits. The fraction of GDP invested in state loans to private buyers was by the early 1980s just one-third of what it had been twenty years earlier: the actual degree of subsidy involved, given the change in interest rates and the like, was perhaps one-fifth to one-tenth of its former levels. And all this has occurred, it will be recalled, as the population of young adults has grown very markedly in size.

Modelling exercises permit some measure of the changes involved. Until the early 1970s a standard family of median income, after making use of all the government grants, income tax exemptions and low-interest loans then available to it, could have purchased a standard 110-square-metre first home by devoting 12 to 15 per cent of its total net income to mortgage repayments. An identical young family making an identical purchase in the early 1980s would have to devote 40 per cent to the same end (Thomson, 1989b). And this is the most conservative of estimates possible. During those twenty years New Zealanders in general did not inhabit a static quantity or quality of housing, as the model family is assumed to have done; the per capita increase in room numbers was 36 per cent, for example. The housing expenditures of older households fell during this same period as a fraction of their total spending.

Not surprisingly young adults have had to adapt their behaviour to the new realities, not only by accepting older or smaller or more derelict homes, all of which trends have been noted, but also, I suggest, by marrying later, delaying the births of their children, having fewer children, the young mother going back into paid employment sooner, and the like. The changes in youth behaviour have more complex reasons than this, of course, and they cannot be pursued here. It may have been a quite fortuitous coincidence that family patterns amongst the young should have adapted as and when they did, thus permitting young adults to meet the mounting costs of membership of the late-twentieth-century welfare state. But a suspicion grows that these changes in behaviour may have been in large part a response to the reshaping of social policy priorities and costs which has been evident in the last twenty years. The young, whatever their income levels, have been learning some important lessons about their welfare state in the 1970s and 1980s - that it does not deliver, and that it certainly has no intention of giving them what older fellow citizens once enjoyed.

My guess - it can be little more at this stage - is that a similar change is taking place elsewhere, though the nature of the move will be quite particular to each nation and its housing provisions. Newspaper reports of growing youth homelessness, the crowding of families in inadequate shelter, and of the mounting barriers to first-home purchase have become commonplace in Britain, North America and Australia as well as New Zealand. Government reports, and the frequency of attempts to ease some of the more acute difficulties of young home seekers, reflect an official awareness of the problems, if nowhere of their historic origins or structural nature. A contraction of public investment in housing is evident in the national accounts of various countries. In Britain the combined investments of central and local government in public housing averaged more than 4 per cent of GDP throughout the 1970s, peaking at nearly 6 per cent in 1975 when it was comparable in scale to all public spending on health or retirement pensions: by 1987 it stood at 1.3 per cent (Central Statistical Office, *Annual Abstracts*). OECD data on government housing outlays suggests almost everywhere a decline in this spending since the early 1970s.

Cuts in housing expenditure need not of course be taking place solely to the loss of the young. But the suspicion is that overall public expenditures on free or subsidised services has shifted from areas which most benefit the young to those favoured by the aged. British statistics on 'final incomes' provide some of the best evidence of this hidden redesigning of the modern welfare state: writers in other countries hint at similar moves (Council of Economic Advisers to the US President, 1985; Flora and Heidenheimer, 1981; Guest, 1985; Harrington, 1984; Ismael, 1987; Jones, 1983; Mendelsohn, 1983; Preston, 1984; Ross, 1981; Scotton and Ferber, 1978).

By making use of Family Expenditure Survey data the resources of single pensioner households, the poorest of elderly households in which little income is available other than from government pensions, can be compared with incomes of an array of other household types. The key finding is that while the 'disposable incomes' of this poor minority have been improving steadily over the last twenty years in relation to all other groups, 'final incomes' (counting use of public services as well as cash incomes) have moved much more rapidly in favour of the aged. This indicates their growing share of the benefits of public services not ostensibly tied to any particular group. For example, in the mid-1960s households consisting of two adults and two children had on average nearly five times the 'final income' of the average single retirement pensioner, but by the early 1980s they had just three times as much (Central Statistical Office, *Annual Abstracts*; UK Department of Employment, annual).

## Reshaping taxation

A study of public expenditures suggests a possible widespread process of redesign, with two different welfare states now being in effect at the same time – a modern welfare state offering a wide range of benefits through all of life's phases for the initiators of the welfare state, and a minimal, means-testing welfare state of the old safety-net type for their successors, large and potentially very disruptive portions of whom can expect little of a positive nature from the welfare state throughout their lives. But this creation of incompatible lifetime experiences extends well beyond the realm of public expenditures. Amongst others, changes in taxation have reinforced the process, for the first welfare generation have experienced a state of negligible personal costs by comparison with that facing their successors. A sharp rise in income taxes – the membership fee of the welfare state, we might call them – has been a universal experience of the last twenty years. Less noticed but related has been a progressive elimination of exemptions that once served to keep taxes away from young adults. The scale of the change has passed largely without comment.

Consider the example of New Zealand again. A young single man of median earnings in the 1950s or early 1960s faced an income tax bill (including social security contributions) equivalent to 15 per cent of his gross earnings. Should he have had a standard family to support taxes fell to 9 per cent, and were matched exactly by the value of the two family benefits received – in other words, the family would have enjoyed a nil 'effective income tax rate' throughout the years of childraising. Families with below-average earnings, or three or more children, would have secured even greater gains, and if the housing, health, education and other welfare benefits to a young family are taken into account also, the effective income tax rate of the standard family becomes highly negative. Because the majority of young adults of that era had families of three or more children, the result was a minimal tax contribution by the whole cohort or generation. The effective income tax rate for all who were aged 25–34 years in 1951, for example, was just 4 per cent of gross income: ten years later the same group, now aged 35–44 years, was paying 2 per cent of gross income in effective income tax, and in return received a wide range of free health, welfare and education services for themselves and their children, together with all of the other benefits of life in a modern society.

The experiences of their successors are much less favourable. During the last twenty years income tax rates have risen sharply, but more importantly exemptions have been reshaped so as to throw many more of the costs of funding the welfare state upon young adults, thus reducing the burdens of those in middle age. In New Zealand, as in Britain, Australia, Canada and elsewhere, income tax exemptions for non-earning spouses or children have been whittled away or eliminated altogether, giving all young adults of the 1970s and beyond a similar experience.

A young New Zealand man of median income by 1981 faced an income tax demand of 27 per cent of his gross earnings: supporting a standard family would have reduced this to 23 per cent, while the two family benefits received amounted to just 5 per cent of his gross income. This left an 18 per cent effective income tax charge, in place of the nil effective one of twenty years earlier, and the extras now available by way of public expenditures were greatly reduced. The overall 'generational tax rate' was four times what it had been for their predecessors at the same stage of life in the 1950s, and closer to eight times the comparable rate in the early 1960s. The trend yet again – perhaps ultimately very dangerously for the welfare state's survival – has been to target a limited range of exemptions to low-income groups alone, with the result that medium-and higher-income young adults learn that the welfare state has very little interest in them, except as funders of the benefits of earlier generations.

Furthermore, these changes represent just one aspect of the shift in taxes away from older persons. For example, the elimination of high marginal tax rates, a widespread development of the 1980s, has been of much more limited benefit to younger adults since incomes in all modern societies peak between ages 40 and 60. A more recent trend has been to curtail tax deductibility on insurance and superannuation contributions: Britain some years ago ended life insurance tax exemptions for all new policies while preserving it for existing ones; New Zealand has eliminated deductions for all employee contributions to pension and superannuation schemes after these had been in place for several decades; and Australia is revising its taxation of superannuation funds. The intention is to increase the tax take: the unintended message driven home is that the benefits of one generation are not to be available to their successors. Another common trend has been the substantial decline in the portion of direct taxes paid by the self-employed and by companies, leaving most now to be paid by individual wage and salary earners: because the self-employed and shareholders predominate in middle age this means that a larger share of the total tax demand has been moved towards the young.

So, too, do changes in employment, most especially the rise in female employment. In New Zealand in the early years of the new welfare state women on average held paid employment for very few years, even in middle age. But women of the post-welfare generations are spending most of their lives in paid employment, with small breaks for childraising, and so are spending a few decades paying 30 or more per cent of their earnings in income taxes. The result over a lifetime is that the taxation contributions of the women who succeed the welfare generation are many times larger than those of their predecessors just a decade or two older. This point, and the possible political significance of highly inconsistent experiences of contribution, seems to elude all who advocate yet more employment amongst women as a means of sustaining the current welfare state for the aged.

The question of possible social class differences is being ignored throughout this article – deliberately, so as to highlight an alternative analysis of society. However, it is not overlooked in the larger research project from which this report is drawn. Each of the developments being discussed here, including changes in social services, taxation, earnings and housing assistance, is being tested for its impact upon individuals and families at various points in the income range. It is not possible to record here the complexities of that study, but two brief comments might be noted.

First, even though means testing is being used increasingly to direct assistance to low-income groups alone, the experiences of the whole generation of young adults remain common in many respects. For example, the relative costs of buying a first home appeared to rise three times between the 1960s and the 1980s for a young family of median income. At the same time a complex of changes in taxes, access to social welfare benefits, new rules on eligibility for government loans, and the grading of mortgage interest rates according to income ensured that high-income young families also faced a threefold increase in costs. So too did families on modest incomes – those at the twenty-fifth percentile point in the income range. Low-income families (at the tenth percentile) faced a fivefold increase in costs, despite efforts to deliver special housing and tax assistance to them. In other words, the changes proved broadly similar across a wide band of incomes, and for this reason it is plausible to speak of a shared generational experience. The experiences of generation, we might argue, are proving at least as consistent as those of class.

Second, a consistency of experience across all income groups or 'classes' may be less important politically than what is happening to specific powerful sections of the population. In particular, young white males are a group well able to voice their concerns with effect, and it is the lessons being learnt by this group that lie at the heart of the analysis here. If they conclude that our systems of collective action work to their disadvantage then we must expect pressing demands for change – and it is perhaps no matter for surprise that the attraction to the politics and economics of the New Right appears especially strong amongst this group.

## Employment, debt and investment

The forging of the two diverging welfare states is being advanced in a multitude of other ways, each of which serves to give successive generations very different experiences of the risks involved in the welfare contract. Our discussion of these must here be brief and speculative, simply because as a community of scholars we have yet to consider them seriously for their impact upon generations. But they should not pass unremarked for that reason – the powers of the state are being employed in a variety of ways to advance the interests of some generations ahead of others.

Mortgage lending furnishes an obvious illustration of this. Because older persons in general lend money, and younger ones borrow, changes in interest rates or the conditions of lending have potentially powerful effects in shifting resources between one generation and another. Revision of government lending has already been discussed, but comparable moves in the private sector have not. In New Zealand the state imposed a series of restrictions upon lending institutions, their activities and interest charges during the first thirty years of the modern welfare state. In part this was a reaction to depression and wartime experiences, in part an enthusiasm for Keynesian intervention, and in part a deliberate decision to assist the young. Statute and regulation combined with a popular consensus which favoured borrowers ahead of lenders to ensure that subsidised government loans should be available to the young, and that no mortgage terms could be altered once the loan had been taken up.

But during the 1970s and more rapidly in the 1980s this consensus has been replaced by a legal regime and social climate dominated by the demands of lenders: the beneficiaries of the earlier consensus have appeared unwilling to maintain it when it is no longer to their advantage to do so. In the last decade interest rates have been lifted and held well above inflation rates, and more importantly, mortgage conditions are now altered several times a year if necessary, at the sole discretion of the lender, so as to ensure a continuing positive rate of return. Economists and politicians offer a range of explanations as to why we must now put the interests of lenders ahead of borrowers: the effect upon generations is nevertheless one further element in the 'ageing of the welfare state'.

The management of inflation is potentially significant here also because differing rates of inflation may well affect successive generations inconsistently. The standard argument of governments in the 1980s is that inflation must be halted at all costs, amongst other reasons because it makes housing so expensive for the young: if the price is greatly increased unemployment amongst the young then this is but a sad necessity. Another interpretation might be that inflation has been and still is 'managed' in the interests of the welfare generation rather than the society as a whole.

In the 1970s, when inflation in New Zealand accelerated rapidly, that generation were in middle age, with earnings that moved up faster than did prices, with houses whose capital value rose sharply, and mortgages which dwindled to insignificance because protected by the 'unalterability' consensus. Conventional wisdom has it that the elderly fared less well, but this is also open to question (Clark *et al.*, 1984). In the 1980s the middle-aged and elderly have seen their pensions indexed against inflation, but not their interest earnings. And security of interest earnings is preserved best by low inflation, the priority of the 1980s.

The halting of inflation, somewhat ironically, can be a very mixed blessing to the young. One of the things making the gamble of buying a home worth the mounting costs has been the expectation that rapid inflation would raise the capital value of the asset, and perhaps reduce the scale of payments relative to income – but the way societies now fight inflation runs counter to these hopes. All of this is, of course, largely conjectural: where the interests of successive generations might lie in the management of inflation as they move through life's phases has yet to be explored, but the likelihood of advantages and losses must at once be recognised.

The allocation of employment constitutes another of the obvious but less measurable shifts in the experiences of successive generations. Large-scale youth unemployment has been a widespread phenomenon of the last decade, and this was an experience unknown to most of the first welfare generation. The question is whether this is simply a matter of bad luck – a consequence of being born into too large a generation, or of entering the labour market upon the eve of a downswing in the economic cycle (Easterlin, 1980, 1987) – or of something more, of being the victims of policies and practices over which societies do exercise some control and choice.

Contrasts here between the depressions of the 1930s and the 1970s are fascinating. In that earlier period societies reacted by insisting that the middle-aged and elderly share the risks and misfortunes. In New Zealand, for instance, pensions were cut between 1932 and 1935, and mortgage repayments were deferred, frozen, written down and waived altogether through legislation and regulation, in the interests of keeping young families in their homes and businesses. Older lenders protested, but the society revealed its values very clearly (Thomson and Macdonald, 1987). Unemployment was also shared much more evenly so that youth rates were not out of keeping with those of older workers: British unemployment statistics reveal a similar pattern (Eichengreen, 1987).

But in the depression of the 1970s and 1980s the emphases have been reversed. It is as if modern societies have decided that when rationing of a scarce supply of jobs becomes necessary, protecting the lifetime employment experiences of older workers has a priority ahead of all else. Again, it will be argued that the youth unemployment of today is an accident rather than a construct, less a structural feature of welfare states as they age than an unplanned outcome of a welter of protective employment practices which have grown up in recent decades. These include unionisation, the growing dominance of white-collar work, lifetime employment contracts, 'tenure', 'last-on-first-off' hiring and firing policies, superannuation arrangements and many more.

These issues cannot be debated here, and for our present purposes it is enough to note two points. First, our current rationing of jobs is predictable and explicable, given the pattern of political ageing now apparent in modern societies. Second, the result regardless of cause is that successive generations are pushed still further apart, in terms of what they know life in a welfare state to mean.

In a variety of other ways the employment experiences of the generations are diverging still more. For one thing, the earnings of young men (aged 20–24 for example) in full-time work have fallen relative to those of men in their forties and fifties, in New Zealand's case from around 85 per cent in the 1950s and 1960s to 65–70 per cent in the 1980s (NZ Department of Statistics, five-yearly, *Census of Population*). In Australia and North America similar patterns are apparent (Australian Bureau of Statistics, irregular; Easterlin, 1987; US Bureau of the Census, annual). Second, the treatment of older and younger adults whose lifetime employment experiences are interrupted is proving very different – severance payments and the like for older workers have no parallels amongst the young, who have in many countries in recent years seen their unemployment payments curtailed through various means (Jones, 1983; Ismael, 1985, 1987; Ross, 1981). Third, the concept of lifetime secured employment or 'tenure' is vanishing, from public as well as private employments; those who began their working careers in the 1960s or earlier will enjoy the security of these and the superannuation, sickness and other fringe benefits which accompany them, while those who follow to perform the same tasks will not.

Fourth, the removal of many benefits for young trainees works to give latecomers to the welfare state less reason to look favourably upon it. The decline in the value of student bursaries, the removal of assistance schemes for entrants to the public service, the ending of trainees' salaries for teachers and many other groups, plans to introduce or increase parental contributions towards the support of children in higher education, the instituting of student loans schemes or of graduate taxes in countries where these have been unknown, all teach important lessons about the meaning of the welfare state to different generations. So too, it might be noted, do all moves towards charging for the use of public services – paying for services once free puts those who experienced the earlier regime and those who did not into two different states.

Fifth, employment-related superannuation schemes are now being altered against the interests of the young. In the late twentieth century many state and private occupational pension schemes (as well as health insurance ones) have been revealed as seriously underfunded; the rate of contribution in earlier years was not enough to afford the present beneficiaries the level of payment they now seek and are given. The general reaction to this has been to increase the amount of subsidisation out of current income through direct cross-subsidisation from government funds, to raise the percentage contributions from current employers and employees, and to use high interest rates to draw money into the super-annuation funds (Burbridge, 1987; Council of Economic Advisers to the US

President, 1985; Coward, 1974; Health and Welfare Canada, 1986; OECD, annual). Increased returns from these supposed insurance plans arc not promised later in life to today's contributors in recognition of their higher level of payment. The immediate effect is to keep programmes solvent: the longer-term effect is a likely erosion of faith in our willingness or ability to operate private or public collective security programmes fairly across long stretches of time.

One further inconsistency of experience might be noted. The first welfare generation lived in states which invested heavily in the future, both in terms of capital and of human stock, and the resources they now enjoy in later life are a direct product of having been succeeded by a larger generation. The young adults of the late twentieth century live in societies of very much lower long-term investment. A number are also amassing large budget and external deficits which have serious implications for the lifetime consumption to be expected by those who will still be here some decades hence. Capital stocks are being run down, as is revealed when capital formation rates are measured against GDP. In almost all OECD countries these have fallen substantially during the last decade, with declines of 25 per cent and more not uncommon.

Perhaps of greater, because less readily reversible, impact will be the sharp fall in fertility which has been evident in all modern states since the later 1960s. The possible connections between this and the concurrent ageing of the welfare state cannot be debated here, but the trends do have a clear significance for successive generations. Low investments since 1970 have freed a greater portion of the total resources for redistribution towards the ageing, and have few long-term consequences for those who will not be citizens of the twenty-first century: the same cannot be said for the young adults and children of today.

## Troubling issues for the 1980s

In the last decade of the century the modern welfare states enter a particularly difficult phase of their history, and their responses to it may well determine whether the large-scale pooling and redistribution of resources through political action becomes a permanent feature of human society, or passes as an interesting but failed experiment in social organisation. The piecemeal erosion of the welfare state of the post-welfare generations has thus far proceeded with-out much comment, though its reality is not unsensed by younger adults. This period of quiescence cannot be expected to last, for at least two develop-ments are pushing forward questions of redistribution between young and old.

Demographic change is not one of the more immediately pressing factors, though longer-term trends are highly significant. In most modern societies the next two decades will bring little change in the overall 'dependency ratio' of elderly to younger adults, even though the change thereafter will be very rapid. The implications of that pending shift for policies today will be discussed in a moment, but before that it might be noted that some new measures of demographic balance are going to be needed as societies come to debate generational issues.

Conventional analysis focuses upon the experience of the society at a few particular moments, and suggests that between 1900 and 1980 elderly 'dependency burdens' doubled, with a further 50 per cent increase to follow between 1980 and 2030. However, the lifetime experiences of individuals or birth cohorts will be of much greater change. Given the lengthening of life and the decline in fertility which have occurred, the average individual will face lifetime obligations towards aged persons which in the early twenty-first century are five to ten times what they had been a century before (Thomson, 1989a). Rising demands by the aged may compound this trend: even if they do not rise the demographic process will render the experiences of obligation to predecessors and successors highly incompatible. The welfare contract of consistency and reciprocity presupposes successor generations of constant size and longevity. This is manifestly not the experience of generations in the welfare state era, but this point will not become acute during the next decade.

Much more important will be a changing perception of the affluence of the ageing members of the first welfare generation. A prevalent image of the elderly is still of impoverishment, but in the 1980s this no longer accords with the facts. Scholars in the United States have been amongst the first to note this; the average aged US citizen now has an income and a personal expenditure on a par with that of non-aged persons, and somewhat ahead of that of some younger age groups with responsibilities for childraising. Perhaps even more telling of the change is the finding that the aged now seem to engage in growing amounts of saving, at an age when people were once presumed to run down their capital in order to maintain consumption (Council of Economic Advisers to the US President, 1985; Harrington, 1984; Levy, 1987).

Similar developments have become apparent elsewhere. In New Zealand, for example, an analysis of incomes and expenditure data shows that the average elderly person now receives and spends considerably more than do those in their twenties and thirties, when resources for households of different age are divided on a per capita basis. Even when we employ more sophisticated 'adult-equivalence' scales, taking account of economies of scale in shared households and the lower demands of young children, the conclusion is still that while the middle-aged have been moving ahead fastest in the last decade, the elderly have now equalled or bypassed the incomes and expenditures available per adult in households where the head is aged under 40. The single-income young family of two children now has 20 per cent less real purchasing power than it did in 1960, the elderly household 100 per cent more (Thomson, 1989b). Growing rates of saving amongst the elderly, alongside falling ones amongst the young, are also hinted at strongly in these records. And few of the welfare generation have yet reached old age: much more marked changes can be expected during the coming decade. These realities and the obvious manifestations of affluence which accompany them are beginning to impinge upon public consciousness.

The trend in Britain is comparable, though it lags a few years behind the moves elsewhere. In the mid-1960s the average disposable income (total cash income after taxes and welfare benefits) for all households of two adults and two children was five times as great as that of 'special retirement pensioner households', units which included only the poorer half of elderly persons. This gave those in the younger households a per capita income 1.25 times that of the poorer of pensioners; by the mid-1980s the multiple was 0.9, that is, less than the incomes of the aged. (If we employ standard 'adult-equivalence' scales here the change is from 2.0 to 1.5.) In terms of 'final income', after usage of free public services is also taken into account, the per capita measure of average resources shows a fall for the young from 1.2 to 0.8 of the average income of a poorer pensioner (2.0 to 1.3 on an adult-equivalence basis).

This is the case, it will be recalled, even after a growing number of two-adult-two-child households have shifted from one to two incomes as young women have increasingly taken on paid employment. In relation to the incomes and expenditures of the non-elderly in general the aged of today stand about where they did twenty years ago (Thomson, 1986), but by comparison with large groups of young adults the aged have advanced considerably. My analyses of Australian and Canadian data suggest parallel trends, and the findings make comprehensible such developments as the stalled or worsening infant mortality rates of Britain and elsewhere, the lack of improvement in youth and young adult mortality in the last decade, and the marked lengthening of life in the older ages which has become evident in a number of societies in recent years (Central Statistical Office, *Annual Abstracts*; NZ Department of Statistics, irregular, *Life Tables*; UN, annual, *Demographic Yearbook*).

All of this will call into question our standard justifications for redistribution towards the aged. A degree of intergenerational inconsistency in benefits and contributions could be accepted by all as fair and right, when the present resources of the beneficiaries were clearly less than those of the contributors, but this argument is losing much of its force. A reassessment of generational roles and obligations cannot be avoided as populations become more aware of the new disposition of resources.

The final critical development of the late 1980s and the 1990s is the crushing of youthful expectations. During the 1970s and much of the 1980s, as the welfare states were remoulded and their worth to younger persons diminished, the fiction was maintained and believed that an upturn in fortunes for the young would still come – that job prospects and career opportunities would improve, that an array of benefits would be available as they raised children, and most importantly that in old age a substantial return on a lifetime of investment would be assured. But as the 1980s have passed it has become increasingly difficult to sustain this essential faith that in the long run it will all be worthwhile.

For one thing, talk of our demographic futures has become more open and realistic, in some cases fostered by governments seeking to prepare younger citizens for a dashing of pension promises. Growing numbers of young adults are now realising that, quite aside from what governments might offer or they themselves demand, the legacy of low investment in the 1970s and 1980s will inevitably mean severe limits to the redistributions that can be demanded from a small successor generation a few years hence. A growing awareness is spreading that unless future generations of the young prove willing to pay taxes on a scale seen nowhere in the present century, the young adults of today cannot expect as they reach old age a treatment comparable to that which they are now giving the aged, let alone a return commensurate with their many times greater lifetime contributions.

Furthermore, governments at the end of the 1980s are beginning to say, in effect, that there is no intention of honouring the welfare contract later in the lives of the present young adults. Plans for raising retirement ages, introducing stiffer means testing for state pensions, lowering the relative levels of state benefits through non-indexing for price or wage movements, and raising the contribution levels for the rest of the working life are all now being mooted widely, but they are to come into effect only after the welfare generation has passed on. What societies must and will find themselves discussing soon is why the young adults of today can be expected to play the part assigned to them by history, that of willing funders of a lifetime welfare state which they themselves will never inhabit. Upon a resolution of this hinge all questions concerning the elderly.

# References

Australian Bureau of Statistics (irregular), *Income Distribution*, Canberra, ABS.

Burbridge, J. (1987), *Social Security in Canada: An Economic Appraisal*, Toronto, Canadian Tax Foundation Paper no. 79.

Central Statistical Office (annual), *Annual Abstract of Statistics*, London, CSO.

Central Statistical Office (annual), *Social Trends*, London, CSO.

Clark, R., Maddox, G. L., Schrimper, R. A. and Sumner, D. A. (1984), *Inflation and the Economic Well-being of the Elderly*, Baltimore, Johns Hopkins University Press.

Committee on the Economic and Financial Problems of Provision for Old Age (Phillips Committee) (1954), *Report*, London, HMSO.

Council of Economic Advisers to the US President (1985), *Annual Economic Report of the President*, transmitted to the Congress, February 1985, Washington.

Coward, L. (1974), *Mercer Handbook of Canadian Pension and Welfare Plans*, Toronto, CCH Canadian Ltd.

Daniels, N. (1988), *Am I My Parents' Keeper? An Essay on Justice Between the Young and the Old*, New York, Oxford University Press.

Easterlin, R. (1980), *Birth and Fortune*, New York, Basic Books.

Easterlin, R. (1987), 'The new age structure of poverty in America: permanent or transient?', *Population and Development Review*, XIII, pp. 195–208.

Eichengreen, B. (1987), *Juvenile Unemployment in Interwar Britain: The Emergence of a Problem*, Discussion Paper no. 194, London, Centre for Economic Policy Research.

Ermisch, J. and Joshi, H. (1987), *Demographic Change, Economic Growth and Social Welfare in Europe*, Discussion Paper no. 179, London, Centre for Economic Policy Research.

Fiegehen, G. (1986), 'Income after retirement', *Social Trends*, XVI, London, Central Statistical Office.

Field, F. (1980), *Fair Shares for Families*, Occasional Paper no. 3, London, Study Committee on the Family.

Flora, P. and Heidenheimer, A. (eds) (1981), *The Development of Welfare States in Europe and America*, New Brunswick, New Jersey, Transaction Books.

Flora, P., Kraus, F. and Pfenning, W. (1983), *State, Economy and Society in Western Europe, 1815-1975*, London, Macmillan.

Guest, D. (1985), *The Emergence of Social Security in Canada*, Vancouver, University of British Columbia Press.

Harrington, M. (1984), *The New American Poverty*, New York, Firethorn Press.

Health and Welfare Canada (1986), *Overview: The Income Security Programmes of Health and Welfare Canada*, Ottawa, Health and Welfare Canada.

Hugo, G. (1986), *Australia's Changing Population*, Melbourne, Oxford University Press.

Ismael, J. (ed.) (1985), *Canadian Social Security Policy*, Kingston, McGill-Queens University Press.

Ismael, J. (1987), *The Canadian Welfare State: Evolution and Transition*, Calgary, University of Alberta Press.

Jones, M. (1983), *The Australian Welfare State*, Sydney, Allen & Unwin.

Lerner, A. (1959), 'Consumption-loan interest and money', *Journal of Political Economy*, LXVI, pp. 512-18.

Levy, F. (1987), *Dollars and Dreams: The Changing American Income Distribution*, New York, Russell Sage Foundation.

Lister, R. (1982), 'Income maintenance for families with children', in R. Rapoport (ed.), *Families in Britain*, London, Routledge & Kegan Paul.

Mendelsohn, R. (1979), *The Condition of the People: Social Welfare in Australia*, Sydney, Allen & Unwin.

Mendelsohn, R. (1983), *Australian Social Security Finance*, Sydney, Allen & Unwin.

NZ Department of Statistics (annual), *National Income and Expenditure*, Wellington, NZDS.

NZ Department of Statistics (five-yearly), *Census of Population and Dwellings*, Wellington, NZDS.

NZ Department of Statistics (irregular), *Life Tables*, Wellington, NZDS.

Nordic Council (annual), *Yearbook of Nordic Statistics*, Stockholm, NC.

Organisation for Economic Co-operation and Development (annual), *National Accounts*, Paris, OECD.

Parfit, D. (1984), *Reasons and Persons*, Oxford, Clarendon Press.

Parsons, D. (1984), 'On the economics of intergenerational control', *Population and Development Review*, X, pp. 41-54.

Preston, S. (1984), 'Children and the elderly: divergent paths for America's dependents', *Demography*, XXI, pp. 435-57.

Ross, D. (1981), *The Working Poor: Wage Earners and the Failure of Income Security Policies*, Toronto, Canadian Institute of Economic Policy.

Samuelson, P. (1958), 'An exact consumption-loan model of interest with or without the social contrivance of money', *Journal of Political Economy*, LXVI, pp. 467-82.

Scotton, R. and Ferber, H. (eds) (1978), *Public Expenditures and Social Policy in Australia*, Melbourne, Longman Cheshire.

Sikora, R. and Barry, B. (eds) (1978), *Obligations to Future Generations*, Philadelphia, Temple University Press.

Thomson, D. (1986), 'The overpaid elderly?', *New Society*, pp. 3-4 (7 March).

Thomson, D. (1989a), 'The intergenerational contract - under pressure from population ageing', paper to the Sixth World Conference of the International Society for Family Law, Tokyo, 7–11 April 1988, published in J. Eekelaar and D. Pearl (eds), *An Ageing World –Challenges and Dilemmas for Law and Social Policy*, Oxford, Oxford University Press and Tokyo, Nihon Kaju Shuppon.

Thomson, D. (1989b), *Selfish Generations: The Ageing of the Welfare State*, Wellington, Allen & Unwin.

Thomson, D. and Macdonald, B. (1987), 'Mortgage relief, farm finance, and rural depression in New Zealand in the 1930s', *New Zealand Journal of History*, XXI, pp. 228–50.

UK Department of Employment (annual), *Family Expenditure Survey*, London, HMSO.

United Nations (annual), *Demographic Yearbook*, New York, UN.

US Bureau of the Census (annual), *Current Population Reports*, Washington, Government Printing Office.

Wroe, D. (1973), 'The elderly', *Social Trends*, III, London, Central Statistical Office.

Wynne, E. (1980), *Social Security: A Reciprocity System under Pressure*, Boulder, Colorado, Westview Press.

# 4

# Justice and Transfers Between Generations

## Norman Daniels

The ageing of society forces major changes in the institutions responsible for social well-being. As the 'age profile' of a society – the proportion of the population in each age group – changes, social needs change.[1] As society ages, proportionally fewer children need education, fewer young adults need job training, but more elderly need health care and income support. Changing needs find political expression. Strong voices press for reforms of the institutions which meet these needs. At the same time, advocates for existing institutions and their beneficiaries resist change. The result is a heightened sense that the old and the young are in conflict, competing for a critical but scarce resource, public funds that meet basic human needs.

Underlying this common perception of competition between the old and the young, underlying the call for 'generational equity' in our ageing society, there lurks a challenging 'new' problem: what is a just or fair distribution of social resources among the different *age groups* competing for them? My approach to this problem, the prudential lifespan account, involves our imagining that we can prudently allocate a lifetime fair share of a particular resource, such as income support or health care, over the whole lifespan. Then, what counts as a prudent allocation between stages of a life will be our guide to what counts as a just distribution between age groups. But an institution which solves the age-group problem must also solve another problem of distributive justice that is on the minds of those who call for generational equity: the problem of *equity between birth cohorts*. In this article I shall distinguish these two problems and suggest how they can be simultaneously solved for schemes that transfer such goods as income support and health care over the lifespan. Worries of the sort raised by David Thomson (this volume) that one cohort will skew the transfer system to its own advantage will be addressed briefly in the final section. I will begin by distinguishing the age-group and birth-cohort problems of distributive justice.

## Age groups and birth cohorts

In what follows the term 'age group' will refer to people who fall within a certain age range or are at a certain stage of life. For the most part, I will be concerned with justice between the young and the old. I will often simplify the problem by taking those over 65 to be the *old* (or the *elderly*) and taking those of working age, between 16 and 65, to be the *young*. Even if I mainly talk about justice between the old and the young, I seek a solution to the age-group problem which generalises to other age-group distinctions.

The elderly are an age group which includes all people over age 65. But the current elderly also belong to a particular birth cohort, namely the cohort of people born prior to 1923. We may also say that the elderly are 'the older generation'. But 'birth cohort', 'age group', and 'generation' mean different things. To answer the question about justice between age groups, we must distinguish between these notions.

At a given moment, people in a particular age group also belong to a particular birth cohort. Over time, an age group comprises a succession of birth cohorts. Twenty years ago, the elderly included only pre-1903 birth cohorts. Today, they include all pre-1923 birth cohorts. Age groups do *not* age. Over time, new and different birth cohorts simply move into an age group. In contrast, birth cohorts *do* age. They pass through the stages of life, and so, at different times, fall into different age groups. The 1903–23 birth cohorts were among the young in 1968; now they are among the old.

A birth cohort is a distinct group of people with a distinctive history and composition. The question, 'What is a just distribution of social goods between birth cohorts?' thus carries with it the assumption that we are focused on the differences between distinct groups of people. For example, special questions of fairness may arise because of particular facts about the socio-economic history and composition of particular birth cohorts. The notion of an age group abstracts from the distinctiveness of birth cohorts and considers people solely by reference to their place in the lifespan. Consequently, our question about justice between age groups also abstracts from the particular differences between the current elderly and the current young that arise because of the distinctive features of the birth cohorts which happen to make up those age groups. We are concerned with a common problem about justice between the old and the young that persists through the flux of ageing birth cohorts.[2]

It is tempting, in our actual roles as voters or public planners or taxpayers or adult children or elderly parents, to think only about justice between the current young and the current old. After all, each of us identifies with one group or the other. It is easy, that is, to lose sight of the more abstract, timeless question about age groups and to slip into the more immediate question about justice between particular birth cohorts. How is *my* cohort faring under these policies? Will my cohort – will I – do as well with social security or Medicare as the current elderly? How will 'we' do compared to 'them'?

The question about justice between birth cohorts is an important one; indeed, it is foremost in the minds of many who ask for 'generational equity', as we have seen. I will argue that it is not as philosophically central as the age-group problem, though it poses a critical practical problem. This claim about the priority of the age-group problem is controversial and requires a defence. Indeed, some will insist that there is never any question of justice between the young and the old except one that is about justice between particular cohorts – *these* young and *these* old. They eliminate the age-group problem in favour of the birth-cohort problem.

I think there are two moral problems, not one. Insisting, for example, that different cohorts should be treated equitably or fairly does not tell us just what transfers society ought to guarantee between the young and the old. Knowing that what we do for one cohort must be equitable compared to what is done for another does not help us to learn what we should do for either as they age. Answering the age-group question properly, however, may teach us what to do for each birth cohort over time.

Another point suggests that these problems are distinct. The question about age groups is centrally connected to certain other issues of justice in a way that the question about birth cohorts is not. For example, worries about age bias and age discrimination abstract from any consideration about birth cohorts. In asking whether people over 65 should be required to retire, or whether they should be denied access to life-extending medical services such as dialysis, as they are in Great Britain (Aaron and Schwartz, 1984), we are not asking a question which in any way turns on differences between birth cohorts. We are asking a question about the treatment of different age groups. Similarly, other moral issues, such as questions about filial obligations, are raised about the young and the old in general. These issues too abstract from questions about particular birth cohorts. These points of difference between the problems motivate my decision to give priority to the age-group problem and to treat the special issue of justice between birth cohorts as a problem to be addressed after we understand what justice between the young and old involves.

The term 'generation' is ambiguous in several ways. A question about 'justice between generations' can thus mean any of several things. A generation may be equivalent to a birth cohort, as in 'the generation born in the 1960s'. Much of the discussion of 'generational equity' which we encountered when surveying perceptions of competition between the young and the old was really a discussion of equity between birth cohorts. We may also mean by 'generation' groups of cohorts which do not exist at the same time. This reference to non-proximate cohorts is intended when we discuss the problem of obligations to future generations, which is sometimes called the problem of justice between generations. Thus we might ask what current generations owe to future generations with regard to preservation of the environment. Finally, we may mean by 'generation' what I have called an age group. Thus, if we are concerned with the perennial struggle between generations, we are talking about the conflict that persists over time between the old and the young, through the succession of birth cohorts. I will restrict my use of 'generation' to contexts in which we talk about justice to non-proximate, future (or past) generations, and I will pay little attention to this problem of justice. It is worth noting that the kind of competition between age groups which concerned us earlier does not arise in the problem of justice between generations. Age groups co-exist, co-operate, and compete in the same political and moral setting. Future generations are at the mercy of current ones – indeed, as Parfit (1984) shows, what present generations do determines who will be the members of future generations, not merely what happens to them.

The question about age groups poses a distinct problem of distributive justice, though it is not, by any means, the whole of the problem of distributive justice. Any answer to it, including the one I develop, will consequently be only a fragment of a more complete theory of distributive justice. But even if the age-group question poses a distinct problem of justice, we do not necessarily perceive it distinctly. Rather, we perceive the problems raised by the ageing of society as a tangle. We confuse the loose ends of distinct problems of justice with each other. We can now, however, unravel some of the strands. For example, some of the concerns in the United States about enhanced benefit programmes for the elderly and reduced programmes for children touch centrally on issues of justice between age groups, though the underlying question is never clearly formulated.[3] Other concerns, especially those which focus on the future solvency of Medicare and social security, are primarily a response to the birth-cohort question, though they may be voiced as problems about distribution between the old and the young or between generations. My point is that these distinctions are not merely semantic but signal substantively different issues about which we are often confused.

Our tendency to confuse these questions is not simply the result of collective stupidity. Rather, the confusion results primarily from our perception of competition between groups. We see the age-group question in competitive terms and it is easy to slip from that vision into the question about cohorts. It, too, is then quite naturally posed in competitive terms. I suggested earlier that the real question about age groups can be solved only if we look at the problem in a radically different way. Now I will suggest what this new look involves.

## The prudential lifespan account

The key to solving the problem of justice between age groups is acknowledging the humbling fact that we age. To see why this banal fact is so important, consider what I shall call the Inequality Objection. Principles of distributive justice tell us what inequalities in the distribution of important goods are morally permissible. Specifically, important principles of distributive justice prohibit our using 'morally irrelevant' traits of individuals, like race, religion or sex, as a basis for differential treatment in the distribution of important social goods, such as educational or job opportunities, civil liberties, health care, income and wealth. In distributive contexts we must consider only morally relevant facts about individuals: talents and skills in hiring and promotion, health status in medical settings, performance (including special deficits or gifts) in educational institutions, and poverty, disability, and employment status in income support schemes. But just as race or sex is a morally irrelevant trait, so too is age. Justice demands that we treat people equally, ignoring their morally irrelevant traits, such as race or age.

This Inequality Objection turns on two distinct claims, one about the moral relevance of age, the other about inequalities between persons. The first claim is that, because age, like race or sex, is a morally irrelevant trait, it cannot be used in ways that promote inequalities between persons. It is not self-evident, however, which particular traits are morally relevant or irrelevant to distribution. It takes substantive moral argument to establish what is relevant in particular distributive contexts. I postpone the problem of deciding whether age is ever morally relevant.

The Inequality Objection fails because age is different from race or sex. Remember the banal fact: we grow older, but we do not change race or sex. If we treat the young one way and the old another, then over time each person is treated both ways. The advantages (or disadvantages) of *consistent* differential treatment by age will equalise over time. An institution which treats the young and the old differently will, over time, still treat people equally. Whereas differential treatment by race or sex always generates inequalities between persons, differential treatment by age does not necessarily. Therefore, even if age is a morally irrelevant trait, using it in certain distributive contexts will not generate an inequality in life prospects for morally irrelevant reasons – because it generates no inequality at all. (Of course, I am assuming that the policy is stable over time and that all people go through the whole age range. This idealisation ignores 'start-up' problems that arise when we begin such policies.) The basic question remains: *which* unequal treatments of age groups are just or fair?

The prudential lifespan account of justice between age groups builds on this basic point: from the perspective of institutions that operate over a lifetime, unequal treatment at different stages of life may be exactly what we want. As we age, we pass through social institutions responsible for distributing important social goods to us, such as income and health care, in accordance with various distributive principles. Since our needs vary at different stages of our lives, we presumably want these institutions to be responsive to these changes. It is prudent to design institutions so that our entitlements, our legitimate claims to goods and services, reflect our changing needs. Because goods and services are not available in unlimited quantities, we must be prudent about which ones we claim at certain stages of our lives lest we deprive ourselves of important benefits at others. In general, budgeting prudently enables us to take from some parts of our lives in order to make our lives as a whole better. Specifically, this may take the form of 'saving' resources by deferring their use from one stage of life to another.

In the United States, we defer income from our working lives to our post-work retirement period, which has generally been after age 65, in two main ways. We may contribute tax-sheltered income to group and individual pension plans during periods in our lives when our earnings are high, drawing on them when we retire and our income is lower. This tax policy is a social subsidy which provides incentives for us to accumulate vested assets. We also defer income from our working lives to our retirement period by paying a payroll tax. This tax revenue from the employed is used to fund the social security benefits of currently retired workers. In this scheme there are no *vested* savings, and the income transfer from young to old also involves some income redistribution to poorer retirees. But, if the social security system remains stable, young workers will be entitled to claim benefits when they age and retire. There is an intergenerational compact which has the effect of transferring resources from an individual's working years to his retirement years, ensuring that basic needs can be met over the whole lifespan. Moreover, it transfers income in a way that is relatively well-protected against inflation and the uncertainties of predicting individual lifespan (Parsons and Munro, 1978), even though the system may need adjustments to allow for shifts in birth and economic growth rates.

Our health-care system has a similar 'saving' function, though we do not often notice it. This saving function is more apparent when there is a comprehensive national health service or insurance scheme. To see it in the United States, however, we must think of our private and public insurance schemes as one set of institutions, adding Medicare and Medicaid on to our system of largely employer-funded health-care insurance. We then notice that employed workers – young and middle-aged adults – pay the overwhelming share of all health-care costs. On the average, their annual health-care insurance premiums – partly in the form of employer benefits, partly in the form of their own payments, partly in the form of payroll taxes – far exceed their actual health-care costs. There is a transfer of health-care resources to children and, even more dramatically, to the old. Indeed, those over age 65 use health-care funds at roughly 3.5 times the rate of those under 65 (Gibson and Fisher, 1979), though it is a relatively small proportion of high-cost users among the elderly who account for this statistical increase (Zook and Moore, 1980).

In effect, society is community-rated as one risk pool, despite great differences in the health status of different age groups. The relatively healthy adult working population pays a premium that exceeds what is actuarially fair to it. Age groups are treated differently. The old pay less and get more, the young pay more and get less.

Viewed from the perspective of an institution that operates over our lifespan, however, the 'unfairness' of this inflated premium is an illusion. What is crucial about the health-care system is that we pass through it as we grow older. The system transfers resources from stages of our lives in which we have relatively little need for them into stages in which we do. We pay for health care we do not use in our middle years, but we receive health care we do not pay for in childhood and old age. We feel we pay through the nose as working adults, but we are free-loaders in youth and old age.

Two basic points thus emerge from our discussion of the unequal treatment of different age groups. First, such unequal treatment does not mean that persons are treated unequally over their lifespan. Second, such unequal treatment may have effects which benefit everyone. These two points provide the central intuition behind the prudential lifespan account of justice between age groups. The lifespan account involves a fundamental shift of perspective.

We must not look at the problem as one of justice between distinct groups in competition with each other, for example, between working adults who pay high premiums and the frail elderly who consume so many services. Rather, we must see that each group *represents* a stage of our lives. We must view the prudent allocation of resources through the stages of life as our guide to justice between groups. From the perspective of stable institutions operating over time, unequal treatment of people by age is a kind of budgeting within a life. If we are concerned with net benefits within a life, we can appeal to a standard principle of individual rational choice: it is rational and prudent that a person take from one stage of his or her life to give to another in order to make his or her life as a whole better. If the transfers made by an income-support or health-care system are prudent, they improve individual well-being. Different individuals in such schemes are *each* made better off, even when the transfers involve unequal treatment of the young and the old.

We cannot, however, treat people unequally by race or sex within institutions that transfer goods and achieve the same, unproblematic results. We would be treating different *persons* unequally, benefiting some people at the expense of others – even if the transfers promoted aggregate well-being and in that sense made society as a whole, or on the average, better off. Thus taking from one race in order to benefit another, or to benefit society as a whole, is morally highly problematic. Taking from some to give to others crosses the boundaries between persons, and distributive schemes which cross personal boundaries in this way risk failing to respect the importance of persons. We cannot simply generalise the principle of rational choice for individuals, which applies to stages of a life, and convert it into a principle of social choice, which applies to different persons.[4]

If we can determine what form of prudential reasoning we should use to design institutions that allocate resources over our lifespan, then we may specify which transfers between age groups actually improve prospects for everyone. We will be using what is prudent over a lifespan to determine a result which neither young nor old can object to as unfair to them. Prudence is our guide to justice here because of what is distinctive about the age-group problem.

We cannot, however, rely on prudential reasoning by fully informed rational agents, the standard model of the welfare economist, to carry out our task.[5] First, we must restrict the scope of the appeal to prudential reasoning. We must assume that we are appealing to prudence only within the frame provided by a set of principles which govern distributive justice between persons. Prudential reasoning by fully informed persons cannot tell us about what is just when we transfer goods in a way that irreducibly crosses the boundaries between persons. Put more simply, for prudent budgeting, a budget is needed, but what the budget is must depend on what is just, on what people are entitled to. An important aspect of framing our problem is to insist that we are concerned with institutions that operate over the whole lifetime; hence we must blind our prudent planners to their age. We must also modify the form of prudential reasoning for other reasons. If we set a fully informed consumer the task of budgeting his fair share of health care over his lifetime, we would have to restrict him to choices made at an early point in life. Otherwise, jumping from plan to plan would lead him to exceed his fair share. But then we seem to bias plans in favour of the prudence of the young and ignore the prudence of the old.

More careful thought about what lifetime prudential planning requires leads us to a solution to this problem of bias. If we are concerned about well-being over a lifetime, we must make sure that at each stage of our lives we have available to us from our fair share resources which can serve as all-purpose means for pursuing whatever our plan of life at that stage happens to be. The device of putting our rational deliberator behind a 'veil of ignorance' that blinds him to any knowledge of his particular conception of what is good, and asking him to think instead about well-being in terms of an index of such all-purpose means, gives us a way of making the reasoning about lifetime well-being appropriately neutral.[6]

Simply stated, then, we can solve the age-group problem by considering what principles for the design of institutions prudent planners would choose to govern the institutions they pass through as they age. These planners must make their choices, however, from behind a veil of ignorance that keeps them from knowing their age or their conception of what is good in life. They can judge their well-being only by reference to an index of primary social goods. Moreover, the principles they choose must fall within the frame imposed by more general principles of distributive justice. This is a very abstract formulation of the method for solving the age-group problem; I will apply this approach to the problem of income support in the next section. (My discussion of how this approach is used to allocate health care over the lifespan is in Daniels, 1988, chs 4–6; see also Daniels, 1985, ch. 5).

## The prudential lifespan account and income support

Before discussing the birth-cohort problem, I want to comment briefly on the implications of the prudential lifespan account for the distribution of income between age groups. How would it be prudent, from the perspective of our hypothetical rational deliberators, to allocate income over the lifespan? The answer to this question should tell us what distribution of income between the young and old is fair. It should tell us how institutions should be designed to facilitate income transfers between age groups.

Our deliberators operate within the 'frame' I described in the preceding section. They must suppose that *fair shares* of income are to be allocated over the lifespan and that they must live through each stage of the scheme they devise. I have also argued that those prudent deliberators should not be the fully informed agents economists usually employ in their models. Rather, these deliberators do not know the details of their plan of life and must instead reason about their well-being by reference to an index of all-purpose or primary social goods, including income and opportunity. The argument for this constraint is based on an appeal to the classical theory of rational prudence. To demonstrate an equal concern for all parts of their lives, the prudent deliberators should not base their choices on the details of the plan of life they happen to hold at the time of choice. Since we revise plans of life, often in fundamental ways, as we age, we must avoid biasing our choices in favour of preferences we happen to have at a given stage of life. In effect, for the purpose of solving this problem of justice, prudent deliberators are barred from thinking about how to maximise their happiness or the overall satisfaction of their desires. Instead, they maximise their well-being as measured by an index of primary social goods, though we shall here let income stand as proxy for the whole index.

Under these constraints, prudent deliberators would have to reason as follows. They cannot expand their lifetime income share by allocating it in certain ways, e.g. by setting aside income early in life and investing it heavily in their own human capital or otherwise. Such investment strategies are already accommodated within the notion of a (lifetime) fair income share, or so I am supposing. Similarly, they cannot argue in favour of allowing inequalities in income levels between stages of their life provided that such inequalities work to make them maximally well-off (as measured by income) during the stages of life in which they are worst-off. It is important to see why this familiar, Rawlsian argument will not work here (cf. Rawls, 1971).

This form of reasoning is used by the hypothetical contractors in Rawls's Original Position. They choose Rawls's Difference Principle to govern income inequalities *between* persons. Co-operation among people with unequal shares may generate a larger social product, e.g. through certain incentives. This larger product, though divided unequally, can make the worst-off individuals better off (as measured by the index) than they would have been had they insisted on equal shares. But this reasoning is blocked by the assumption that lifetime shares of income are already fixed as fair shares. Inequalities in income levels between stages of life work only as a zero-sum game, making one period of life better off at the expense of another period or stage in life.

If we knew that a plan of life for an individual contained preferences which at all stages of life would make the unequal distribution preferable, because it would increase lifetime satisfaction, then that would be a better distribution for that individual. But we cannot know that plans of life will cohere in this way, and in general they do not. It is this fact which led us earlier to block out information about plans of life in order not to bias planning in favour of what the young think is prudent. So the prudent course of action would be to allocate resources in such a way that income (standing proxy for the complete index of primary goods) would remain roughly equal over the lifespan. (I say 'roughly equal' because we will want to adjust income in a way to be explained.) The Income (or Standard of Living) Preservation Principle, as I shall call it, ensures that institutions facilitate income transfers over the lifespan in such a way that the individual has available to himself, at each stage of life, an adequate income to pursue whatever plan of life he may have at that stage of life. Of course, 'adequate' is here relative to his lifetime fair income share.

To apply the Income Preservation Principle to our income-support system, we need an important qualification. Income must be adjusted if it is to count as a measure of well-being at different points in the lifespan, for we are really interested in *standard of living*. Specifically, we must adjust income to accommodate some general facts about how income *must* be spent by individuals, that is, facts about the needs for income at different stages of life *given institutional arrangements in the United States*. For example, if income spent on raising children, including advancing their educational opportunities, is at least in part inelastic and represents a 'durable good' which produces benefits to parents over the lifespan, then we should adjust pre-retirement income levels by subtracting some portion of income spent on children. Similarly, if out-of-pocket individual expenditures on health care rise substantially with age, as they typically do in the United States, then we must adjust the income of the elderly to account for both Medicare payments and out-of-pocket costs. We are interested in the relationship between income and standard of living, because equal income levels at different stages in life may not represent equal standards of living.

A similar retreat from unadjusted measurements of income is made by economists when they want to measure the effects of our income-support system on well-being over the lifespan. When economists discuss the adequacy of income-support levels under social security, they invoke the notion of a *replacement ratio*, which is a ratio of *some* measure of retirement income to *some* (perhaps different) measure of pre-retirement income (see Boskin and Shoven, 1984, p. 2). Difficult methodological issues, which are not always morally or ideologically neutral, surround the decision to use a particular measure of income in calculating replacement ratios. For example, these ratios are very sensitive to whether we use peak-earning-year income levels or average-earning-year levels. Similarly, they are very sensitive to whether or not we adjust income levels to exclude certain child-rearing expenses or health-care expenses, on the grounds that these uses of income are inelastic responses to needs which should not be pooled with other straightforward 'consumer' uses of income.[7]

The Income Preservation Principle appears to favour a replacement ratio of one between pre- and post-retirement income. To determine whether our income-support system is in compliance with this principle, we would have to resolve these empirical disputes, which is not my task here. Moreover, the contribution of social security benefits to overall post-retirement income varies with income level. Social security benefits comprise a decreasing share of post-retirement income as income levels increase. Thus the application of the Income Preservation Principle to the design of the social security system is further complicated by its differential contribution to income support for different economic subgroups. Since social security is embedded within a more comprehensive public and private system of income transfers between age groups, including a full array of individual and group pensions and other sources of income, we cannot apply the principle to social security in isolation.

The prudential lifespan account in general suggests that post-retirement income levels (or standard of living) should approximate pre-retirement income levels (or standard of living), across the board for all levels of fair income shares. Is this principle satisfied in the United States? We can answer this question only in part. There is some evidence that our income-support system, lumping together social security and other sources of pension income, preserves standard of living on the average. Aaron (1982, p. 70) summarises evidence which suggests 'that the elderly on the average are able to sustain consumption during retirement about equal to the average consumption they could achieve over their lifetime'. There are, however, important subgroups of the elderly, e.g. widows or the very old, whose income levels fall well below their lifetime averages.[8] In any case, the principle our prudent deliberators would choose applies only to *fair income shares*. We have not addressed the question of whether income distribution in the United States is in general just. There are good reasons to think it is not, but I cannot address this complex moral and empirical question here without abandoning my subject. Thus we cannot say whether the Income Preservation Principle generally holds in our system.

One point about the income redistributive effects of social security is relevant, however. Different economic subgroups within each birth cohort fare differently in terms of benefit ratios. Lower-income groups enjoy higher benefit ratios than upper-income groups, which gives the appearance of an income transfer between subgroups within a cohort. Of course, the real transfer is between high-income groups in later cohorts and low-income groups in earlier ones. Assuming stable institutions operating over the lifespan, this is equivalent to transfers between subgroups within cohorts.

The point that is relevant here is that such income redistribution – which *seems* to go beyond the mere savings function of social security – may nevertheless be necessary if the Income Preservation Principle is to be satisfied. That principle governs the whole system of transfers between age groups – all public and private income-support measures. Some degree of 'progressive' taxation and 'progressive' benefit structure within social security itself may be needed to correct for 'regressive' measures elsewhere in the system of transfers between age groups. Thus a social security system that provided less income redistribution when considered by itself might, when seen as part of the total income transfer system, actually increase income inequalities over the lifespan.

Thus the redistributive function of the social security system can keep the whole income-support system from violating the Income Preservation Principle more widely.

This point is important because some critics of the social security system believe it should not be used to carry out multiple functions, that is, to provide for income redistribution as well as savings or annuities. They believe it 'sneaks in' redistributive effects under the guise of its savings function. But regardless of whether the public is adequately informed of the redistributive effect, it is important to see that the redistributive function may result only in a more acceptable *savings* outcome. That is, it may only *appear* to be redistributive, while it is actually correcting for biases which would make it more difficult to satisfy the Income Preservation Principle in the total income-support system. When some critics of the social security system (see Boskin *et al.*, 1986) point to significant differences in replacement ratios and to transfers within cohorts, we should not be tempted to ask: is this pattern equitable or just? We cannot answer this question about social security in isolation from the rest of the income-support system. We must look at the overall effect on the standard of living as a whole to see whether this part of the system acts in ways that conform to the Income Preservation Principle. This point is independent of whether or not our overall income distribution is just or fair.

## Justice between birth cohorts

In what follows, let us assume that we have a solution to the problem of justice between age groups. If the prudential lifespan account is correct, the Income (Standard of Living) Preservation Principle should govern institutions involved in income support and the Age-Relative Fair Equality of Opportunity Principle should govern the design of our health-care system. We must still ask how different birth cohorts fare when they pass through institutions intended to meet the requirements of justice between age groups. What does justice require in the treatment of birth cohorts? What kinds of inequalities in the treatment of birth cohorts are still equitable or fair? In particular we want to know when benefit ratios are equitable (where the *benefit ratio* is the ratio of benefits received to contributions made).

In general, how different birth cohorts will fare in these institutions over their lifespans will depend both on features of the institutional design and on such important social variables as demographic changes and variations in rates of real economic growth. For example, a pay-as-you-go system (like our social security system) relies on direct transfers between birth cohorts. It is particularly sensitive to changes in birth rates or the ratio of retirees to contributors. An income-support system that relies more directly on vested savings by each cohort is less sensitive to these changes, but it is more sensitive to others. It may provide less protection against inflation or increases in life expectancy, and it may leave each birth cohort to benefit or suffer from important fluctuations in economic conditions during crucial working years. In what follows, I shall focus attention on the ways in which our pay-as-you-go social security and Medicare systems accentuate *inequalities* between birth cohorts in the face of projected demographic changes. This discussion of the kinds of issues involved is meant to be illustrative, not comprehensive.

It will help to compare what I am calling the birth-cohort problem with a problem that resembles it in some ways, the problem of obligations to future generations. Both of these problems involve questions about net transfers of resources from one group of persons – one cohort or generation – to another. In this regard, they both differ from the age-group problem. Transfers from one age group to another can be thought of as allocations within a life rather than between persons. The problem of obligations to future generations can be expressed in this way: does justice require one generation (birth cohort) to refrain from depleting resources – both the environment (non-renewable resources) and accumulated capital – so that later generations can have the means to live a decent life? This formulation is sometimes expressed as the question: is there a *Just Savings Principle* between generations?

Approaches to the problem of a Just Savings Principle are controversial. As Rawls (1971) formulates the problem, it is primarily a matter of *preserving* adequate capital and non-renewable resources so that successive generations are in a position to maintain institutions of justice. How much must be saved if successive generations are to be able to construct a framework of institutions that provide them with a just distribution of such primary goods as liberty, opportunity and income? It is to solve this problem that Rawls invokes the device of a thick veil of ignorance. We do not know which generation we will be in when we are choosing our principles of justice. Moreover, he imposes a motivational constraint on parties making the hypothetical contract: they are concerned about the well-being of a generation or two in each direction (from grandparents to grandchildren). Contractors under such constraints, he argues, would prudently grant each generation an equal claim on resources necessary to maintain institutions of justice. In this way, the just savings rate acts as a constraint on other principles of justice, such as the Difference Principle. Thus no society can maximise the well-being of its worst-off members unless it has set aside the resources required by the Just Savings Principle.

Other philosophers have approached the problem differently. Brian Barry (1978) suggests that if people in one generation have concerns about the well-being of those in another, such as their children or grandchildren, then because the well-being of such descendants depends on the kind of world they live in, the welfare of the next generation should be thought of as a public good. Coerced saving would be required to preserve that public good. He thinks it problematic, however, that what justice requires towards future generations is contingent on what sentiments people in current generations happen to have. This argument is like Rawls's in making justice dependent on either actual or hypothetical sentiments towards children. Barry (1978,p. 243) also suggests a quite different argument. Justice requires that we preserve equality of opportunity, and this means we must preserve a range of opportunities for future generations comparable to the range we currently enjoy. Barry's argument, however, supposes that the principle of equal opportunity applies across generations. This supposition, however, is part of what is at issue when we ask about obligations to future generations: are we obliged to protect *their* opportunity? Barry's argument appears to beg the question.

I will offer no solution to the problem of a Just Savings Principle, not only because I do not have one, but also because I think we can separate the question about equity between birth cohorts from it. Our problem about birth cohorts arises in the context of institutions which transfer income or aid-in-kind between age groups so that their *consumption* will yield just income-support and health-care distributions over the lifespan. The problem of what each cohort must refrain from consuming so that later cohorts can live decent lives arises regardless of whether birth cohorts experience unequal benefit ratios. The birth-cohort problem that concerns us is not a special case of the problem of finding a Just Savings Principle. A Just Savings Principle would not necessarily tell us how to solve the birth-cohort problem, but I believe we can solve the latter without having the former.

Our birth-cohort problem should be approached separately, as follows. Each cohort wants institutions which solve the age-group problem effectively. This is true because each cohort ages and has an interest in solving the age-group problem. But institutions or transfer schemes that solve the age-group problem operate under considerable uncertainty. There is uncertainty about population and economic growth rates, as well as about technological change, which further affects productivity. Errors are likely to abound, and inequalities in benefit ratios between cohorts will arise as a result. But institutions which can solve the age-group problem must remain stable over time. They must weather the political struggle that will result as a result of unjustifiable or unacceptable inequalities in benefit ratios. Such institutions will be able to survive the struggle among co-existing birth cohorts only if each feels it has a stake in preserving them. (This point is made more ominously by Thomson, this volume.)

Notice that there is an important difference here between our birth-cohort problem and the problem of a Just Savings Principle, at least where the latter is concerned about obligations to distant, future generations. Current generations have a power over distant future ones that contiguous cohorts cannot exercise over each other. Each birth cohort will have an interest in preserving institutions which solve the age-group problem – and such solutions will thus be stable over time – only if there is an underlying commitment to strive for *equity* in benefit ratios.

The practical target for this commitment we can take to be *approximate equality* in benefit ratios. Nevertheless, uncertainty obtains. Unplanned and unpredicted changes in population growth rates or productivity (and real wages) will affect rates of return on the taxes (both individual and employer) which are paid. Economists have shown that in a pay-as-you-go social security system, in which no reserves accumulate, there is an implicit rate of return on tax payments that equals the sum of the rate of growth of the labour force and the rate of increase in wages (see Aaron, 1982, p. 76; cf. Samuelson, 1958 and Aaron, 1966). As a workforce grows larger and richer it *can* pay taxes sufficient to finance benefits for retirees which are greater than the taxes the retirees paid while working. As population and economic growth rates change, however, there will be changes in the implicit rates of return for different cohorts. Moreover, the question remains, who should benefit from such changes as increased productivity? Should some of the benefits go to retirees, or should they be kept – in the form of lower social security tax rates – by the workforce? Similarly, if growth rates drop, should the burden of such decreases also be borne by retirees?

The argument has been made that some portion of increased productivity should be shared with earlier cohorts now not in the workforce (cf. Spengler and Kreps, 1963). Their contributions, say in the form of investments in education or research, may have contributed to the increased productivity of later cohorts. Conversely, if productivity declines, say because there has been too much consumption and not enough investment in education or research or protection of natural resources, then earlier cohorts ought to share the burden of economic decline.

The framework on which these points rest, however, emphasises *desert* as a distributive principle. Rewards or entitlements should be proportional to contribution one has made. This framework has other implications, however. If productivity increases because of the special energy of the current workforce, then current retirees would seem to have no claim on increased benefits. If productivity drops, not because earlier cohorts invested foolishly, but because the current workforce grows lazy or mismanages foreign affairs, then current retirees do not deserve to share in the losses. Must benefit ratios depend on disentangling these sources of change? It is hard to see how a stable system could incorporate such factors in its scheme of benefits.

We might try to cut through some of the complex issues of desert by appealing, as I did earlier in this section, to the interest each cohort has in providing for stable institutions that solve the age-group problem. Cohorts must co-operate to achieve such stability. But co-operation will require some *sharing of risks* across cohorts. In general, the burdens of economic declines and of living through unfavourable retiree/employee ratios must be shared, as must the benefits of economic growth and favourable retiree/employee ratios. This suggests again that approximate equality in benefit ratios should be a practical target of public policy, if not a hard and fast rule.

We operate an income-support system in a *non-ideal* context. It will always encounter various sorts of 'interstitial' equity considerations which are generated by both great uncertainty and political expediency (cf. Barry, 1965, ch. 9). A good example is the tremendous windfall in benefit ratios offered to the early entrants into the social security system in the United States. They paid taxes for very little of their working lives, but received lifetime benefits. Nevertheless, attempting to lower that ratio might have undermined political support for the social security system as a whole; that in turn would have meant forgoing the introduction of an institution which was arguably necessary to solve the age-group problem. Similarly, in the United States, no reserve fund was ever generated which was significant enough to cushion the effects of recent declines in real wages or projected declines in the ratio of retirees to workers. Politicians were afraid to raise tax rates without pairing the increases with benefit increases. And conservative politicians feared that socialism would follow if large capital funds were controlled by the government (cf. Derthick, 1979). (Ironically, it is now conservative politicians who tend most sharply to criticise the unequal benefit ratios later cohorts have.) The point is that some compromises with approximate equality in benefit ratios will have to be made for periods of time in order to establish an institution which on the whole makes the system more just, in this instance by helping to solve the age-group problem.

## Intergenerational equity and the social security system

Institutions that distribute important social goods over the lifespan, such as the social security system and Medicare, must be governed by principles that solve both the age-group and birth-cohort problems. To solve the age-group problem, I have initially ignored the birth-cohort problem. But institutions which ideally solve the age-group problem operate under varying demographic and economic conditions and under considerable uncertainty about these variations. These factors lead to inequalities in the way birth cohorts fare. Nevertheless, birth cohorts have an interest in achieving stable solutions to the age-group problem. To achieve such institutional stability there must be a commitment to securing equitable treatment of different cohorts. If one cohort seeks terms too much in its favour, say when it is young, it will very likely pay the price when it is old; similarly, if it seeks too much when it is old, it will risk rebellion from the young. Therefore, I have suggested that approximate equality in replacement ratios should be the practical target of public policy regarding 'mature' institutions. Since, however, different cohorts must be willing to share risks, they must also tolerate errors, or departures from approximate equality.

In this section I will be concerned with criticisms of the US 'pay-as-you-go' income-support system which derive from concerns about equity between birth cohorts. It is worth a reminder, however, that I am not here concerned with all the criticisms which fall under the umbrella notion 'generational equity'. For example, some critics complain that the elderly are faring well in public budgets at the expense of children, sometimes appealing to crude notions of equity, such as equal per capita expenditures of public funds. My prudential lifespan account solves the age-group problem while avoiding this competitive perspective. Other critics complain that we are putting too many resources into 'consumption' by the elderly and too little into investments in human and other capital, and we are not adequately protecting the environment and other resources needed for future productivity. I have not addressed these important issues, which deserve full discussion. My concerns in this section are only with the birth-cohort problems that fall under the 'generational equity' umbrella.

I will consider two quite different types of argument that appeal to concerns about equity between birth cohorts. The first type of argument, represented widely in the literature on the US social security system, focuses on the unequal benefit ratios which are projected for the 'mature' social security system over the next three or four decades. Those who complain about the projected ratios seem to agree with my contention that we should seek approximately equal benefit ratios as a solution to the birth-cohort problem, but they believe that no modifications of the current system can really achieve an equitable, stable solution and that we should abandon the pay-as-you-go transfer scheme between cohorts in favour of schemes which rely on transfers within cohorts, e.g. those resting on vested savings. In general these arguments, which rest on economic and demographic claims, share the view that intercohort transfer schemes are intrinsically flawed because they cannot avoid birth-cohort inequities. The second type of argument is largely political. Represented by Thomson's argument (this volume), it admits that 'ideally' there might be an acceptable design for an intercohort transfer scheme that simultaneously solved the age-group and birth-cohort problems. The difficulty is that the world is not ideal and that it *may be* – indeed, *has been* and perhaps *always will be* – politically tempting for a cohort that benefited from transfers in its direction while young to revise the transfer scheme in ways that favour its later years as well. I shall consider the implications of both types of argument for the approach I have sketched.

Arguments of the first sort point to significant inequalities in benefit ratios enjoyed by different cohorts passing through the US social security system. The important inequalities are not those that involve 'windfall' benefits for early entrants in the system when it is first being established. I have already suggested that such inequalities may have to be accepted as the cost of making the system acceptable. More serious issues are raised by the claim that there will be significant intercohort inequalities within our mature social security system. For example, Russell (1982; cited in Aaron, 1982, p. 74) calculates a real internal rate of return for cohorts of workers who reach age 65 between 1960 and 2000 that ranges from 2.6 to 4.9 per cent. (The internal rate of return is the discount rate that would equate benefits with the sum of employer and employee taxes.) Similarly, Leimer and Petri (1981; cited in Aaron, 1982, p. 74) used different assumptions to project real internal rates of return for workers at age 22 ranging from 3.7 per cent for workers who entered the labour force in 1960 to 2.5 per cent for workers entering in 2000. These calculations about internal rates of return must be reconciled with projections made by other researchers who find that young workers now in the workforce and future entrants will pay more in taxes than they will receive in social security benefits (see Boskin and Shoven, 1984 and Aaron, 1982, p. 75). These projections all depend on important methodological assumptions, especially an assumed real discount rate of 3 per cent (that is, the value of future taxes and benefits is discounted at a real rate of 3 per cent). As Aaron points out (1982, p. 75), these projections are compatible with calculations of positive internal rates of return, provided the internal rates of return are lower than the discount rate.

One conclusion we might draw from these claims about inequalities in benefit ratios is that we should modify the pay-as-you-go scheme. We should allow it to accumulate a large reserve pool of assets that can later be used to increase benefit ratios for cohorts who would otherwise suffer low returns as a result of demographic shifts. This proposal – a version of which is incorporated in the 1983 financing reforms to the Social Security Act – is perfectly compatible with the approach I have sketched to the age-group and birth-cohort problems. This is 'fine-tuning' the transfer scheme so that it aims at approximate equality in benefit ratios while prudently allocating income (standard of living) over the whole lifespan.

Some argue for a stronger conclusion from the projections about benefit ratios. They claim that the current system discourages savings or has other features which imply that the rate of return to younger cohorts is less than could be achieved from other ways these cohorts might invest in their own futures. What is urged is some form, partial or complete, of withdrawal from the current scheme in favour of an approach that makes each cohort rely on itself to solve the age-group problem.

I have responded to these claims in some detail elsewhere (Daniels, 1988; see also Aaron, 1982); here I just want to make some general points. First, as Aaron (1982, p. 78) has pointed out, we should not confuse a general theorem of growth theory, that we should invest where we can get the best return, with conclusions about the specific means for enhancing investment. Dismantling our pay-as-you-go system is not necessarily the appropriate means for increasing returns on investment. Second, we should be wary of straightforward comparisons of rates of return of different investment strategies. Important features of the benefit package provided by social security, such as its indexing to protect against inflation, are not replicable in any private market.[9] Social security solves a standard problem facing annuities: we do not have to decide just how much to save given the uncertainty about how long we will live. Therefore we cannot easily match this feature with alternative investments. Third, real rates of return in alternative markets are quite variable. A system which relied on such investments, e.g. through vested assets of retirees, might make each cohort subject to more significant risks than those involved in the fluctuating ratios of retirees to workers. Fourth, there are important benefits to be gained from a public transfer system between age groups, such as social security, which cannot be realised through private alternatives. For example, there are benefits that result from reducing the dependency of retirees on private family resources. A public system of transfers to the elderly frees adult children to pursue the well-being of their own children and is less demeaning to, and generally preferred by, the elderly. Social security stabilises family life by minimising the risks that would attend private transfers (cf. Kingson *et al.* 1986, p. 24). Thus our current system accomplishes social goals which would not be met by proposals to 'privatise' the system.

Not all criticisms of social security which emphasise generational equity call for dismantling the system in favour of more extensive reliance on private savings and pensions. But it is not an accident that some who favour 'privatising' the system are also attracted to the talk about generational equity. Libertarians, for example, believe that all coercive welfare redistributions are unjust. On this view, individuals are entitled to the results of free exchanges they make, whereas redistributions take the results of such exchanges without the consent of all parties. Accordingly, libertarians support the concept of a minimal state, one which refrains from interventions in markets, especially interventions which coercively transfer goods from one set of individuals to another. These libertarian views would lead those who hold them to complain about generational inequity. Net transfers from one birth cohort to another, administered through a coercive taxation scheme, constitute a type of non-voluntary welfare redistribution. Unequal benefit ratios, to the extent that they reflect net transfers of resources between cohorts, are a special case of the injustice or inequity that results from all coerced welfare redistributions. Thus a catchword, like 'generational equity', can unite people who actually have quite different concepts of justice or equity in mind. A concern for generational equity, in the sense of equity between cohorts, does not necessarily imply an interest in 'privatising' social security or Medicare.

Let us turn now to the second, more political type of argument. This is the claim that birth cohorts cannot be trusted to abide by a transfer scheme which ideally solves the age-group problem through intercohort transfers, because, as it ages, it may use its increasing political power to revise the scheme in favour of its old age, benefiting heavily at both ends of the lifespan. We should distinguish a modest and a strong version of this argument. The modest version is that, as Thomson (this volume) argues, we have seen massive evidence that a particular cohort has been greedy in just these ways in New Zealand, and that similar distortions have occurred in transfer schemes elsewhere. But this recent history does not imply that such a pattern will generally be the case: it might depend on rather special circumstances in which that cohort found itself. The strong version of the argument says that the pattern is quite general, perhaps inevitable. Here, more long-term historical evidence might be cited, or a comprehensive argument (e.g. from public choice theory) might be made to the effect that large-scale, state-managed transfer schemes are sitting ducks for the self-interested behaviour of ageing cohorts, as their political power increases. For example, Epstein (1988) has argued that the willingness of elders to transfer resources to their own offspring will not generalise to their willingness to transfer resources to the offspring of others included in such state-managed schemes.

Both the modest and strong versions of this argument challenge one of the premises of my own account. I emphasised that each cohort has an interest in finding a stable solution to the age-group problem. If it is better for the age-group problem to be solved by intercohort co-operation, because such co-operation better shares the risks of changing economic and demographic growth rates, then each cohort has an interest in sustaining a transfer scheme that includes the assurance of approximately equal rates of return. The political arguments suggest that a cohort that benefited in its early years from transfers to it that were intended to be part of a stable, prudent scheme would have an overriding interest in revising the transfer scheme in its favour as it aged. That is, given the opportunity, self-interest will drive a cohort to undermine a fair scheme, taking unfair advantage of the less powerful cohort that follows it.

We should notice, of course, that not all cohorts have behaved in such a narrowly self-interested way. Presumably the investment in the young that characterised the early welfare state in New Zealand was an investment made by an older cohort. The political argument must imply that such 'errors' of altruism or other-regarding behaviour are not likely to be repeated. If later cohorts learn from history, they will not trust in the stability of ideally fair intercohort schemes.

But what is the alternative? If we avoid schemes that depend on intercohort transfers like the social security system, then we still have to answer the question: how can social institutions facilitate adequate types and rates of saving? That is, we are back to the age-group problem, but we must now solve it by relying only on the resources of one cohort. Moreover, we are ruling out an important advantage offered by a system which involves intercohort transfers, namely that it tends to share risks more widely over time. We cannot take advantage of the fact that an equitable form of risk-sharing would be much more desirable than the results of this form of privatising. Concerns about intergenerational equity should not drive us away from promising solutions to the age-group problem, since we cannot escape that problem in any case.

The political argument ignores another fundamental point. Avoiding schemes which involve intercohort transfers in order to avoid unequal benefit ratios does not mean that different cohorts will fare equally well once each is solely responsible for its own well-being over the lifespan. Some cohorts may pass through economic hard times just when they most need to be setting resources aside for their own futures; others may be blessed by favourable rates of productivity, economic growth rates, and dependency ratios. Inequalities will abound. It is not at all obvious that inequalities of benefit ratios in intercohort schemes will generate more intolerable forms and degrees of inequality than the inequalities that result when each cohort must depend on its own resources and good luck. It may be the case that, given uncertainties over long periods of time, such as the lifespan of a cohort, cohorts would be better off co-operating, despite the risk that some cohorts may try to abuse transfer schemes, than they would be facing the risks that come without co-operation. The problem becomes one of institutional design and the securing of long-term commitment to schemes that are fair.

The political argument against intercohort schemes may also prove too much. Solutions to the age-group problem that rely solely on intracohort transfers are also subject to the greedy meddling of more powerful cohorts. Reliance on vested saving schemes, for example, creates only the illusion of cohort security, for tax and other policies can be revised in ways that favour one cohort over another and destroy the value of such savings. Thomson's article (this volume) has the great virtue of refocusing our attention away from income support and health care and on to the wide variety of types of intercohort transfers that do take place. It is simply not possible to retreat to 'private' schemes which are immune to the revisions of their terms. All entitlements seem subject to the political argument, and so it is not really just an argument against intercohort co-operative schemes.

The 'ideal' solution I have sketched to both problems is not merely utopian. It can serve as a basis for moral and political criticism of attempts by particular cohorts to undermine just transfer schemes. If there were broad recognition of the fact that it ought to be the target of long-term public policy, then it might be easier to counter self-centred efforts of particular cohorts. The account would give a clear basis for critical assessment of proposals to reform the rates or types of transfers involved in an existing scheme: it would hold them up to a principled set of criteria, namely those embodied in the prudential lifespan account and in the requirement that benefit ratios be approximately equal. There is, after all, more than one way to learn from history. Rather than learn that no cohort can trust another, we should seek to make more explicit the principles around which cohorts can seek the benefits of co-operation.

## Acknowledgement

I would like to thank Oxford University Press for allowing me to draw heavily in this article on material from my book *Am I My Parents' Keeper? An Essay On Justice Between the Young and the Old* (New York, 1988).

## Notes

1 See Russell (1982) for a detailed study of the effects of the baby boom generation as this demographic bulge has passed through schools, entered the workforce, and faces retirement.

2 This is *not* to say that in general, e.g. in the social sciences, we can talk about the old and the young in abstraction from the different experiences these groups have which derive from differences between cohorts. The 'experience of old age', for example, will vary from birth cohort to birth cohort, depending on facts about each cohort's education and prior history. See Featherman (1983).

3 Preston (1984, p.452) confuses the issue when he contrasts 'individual' and 'collective' perspectives.

4 This point is the core of Rawls's (1971,1982) criticism of utilitarianism; cf. Daniels (1979) and Parfit (1973, 1984).

5 A full argument for the points summarised here is given in Daniels (1988, ch.3).
6 The reasons for appealing to this veiled form of prudence derive, however, from the requirements of prudence alone. Arguments about the ideal nature of persons, like those in Rawls's (1971, 1980) justification of his contractarian approach to the general problem of distributive justice, are not needed here, as we are concerned with a narrower problem. For a more complete discussion of the nature of the prudential reasoning involved in my argument, see Daniels (1988, ch.3).
7 See Boskin and Shoven (1984) for an excellent discussion of the methodological issues and some calculations of the effects on replacement ratios of using different income measures.
8 See Boskin and Shoven (1986) for a detailed study of pockets of poverty among the elderly.
9 Aaron (l982, p.76) notes that a careful selection of securities can yield a portfolio that behaves as if it were indexed. He points out that it may not continue to do so, and that its real rate of return would be close to zero, which is well under the normally used real discount rate of 3 per cent.

# References

Aaron, H. J. (1966), 'The social insurance paradox', *Canadian Journal of Economics and Political Science*, XXXII, pp. 371–7 (August). Cited in Aaron (1982, p.76).

Aaron, H. J. (1982), *Economic Effects of Social Security*, Washington, DC, Brookings Institution.

Aaron, H. J. and Schwartz, W. (1984), *The Painful Prescription*, Washington, DC, Brookings Institution.

Barry B. (1965), *Political Argument*, London, Routledge & Kegan Paul.

Barry, B. (1978), 'Circumstances of justice and future generations', in B. Barry and R. I. Sikora (eds), *Obligations to Future Generations*, Philadelphia, Temple University Press, pp. 204–48.

Boskin, M. J. and Shoven, J. B. (1984), 'Concepts and measures of earnings replacement during retirement', Working Paper no. 1360, Washington, DC, National Bureau of Economic Research.

Boskin, M. J. and Shoven, J. B. (1986), 'Poverty among the elderly: where are the holes in the safety net?', Washington, DC, National Bureau of Economic Research.

Boskin, M. J., Kotlikoff, L. J., Puffert, D. J. and Shoven, J. B. (1986), 'Social security: a financial appraisal across and within generations' (unpublished).

Daniels, N. (1979), 'Moral theory and the plasticity of persons', *Monist*, LXII, 3, pp. 265–87.

Daniels, N. (1985), 'Family responsibility initiatives and justice', *Law, Medicine and Health Care*, XIII, 4, pp. 153–9.

Daniels, N. (1988), *Am I My Parents' Keeper? An Essay on Justice Between the Young and the Old*, New York, Oxford University Press.

Derthick, M. (1979) *Policymaking for Social Security*, Washington, DC, Brookings Institution.

Epstein, R. A. (1988), 'Justice across the generations', paper given at the Conference on Intergenerational Justice, University of Texas, Austin.

Featherman, D. L. (1983), 'The life-span perspective in social science research', in P. B. Blates and O. G. Brim, Jr (eds), *Life-Span Development and Behavior*, New York, Academic Press, vol. 5, pp. 1–59.

Gibson, R. M. and Fisher, C. R. (1979), 'Age differences in health care spending, fiscal year 1977', *Social Security Bulletin*, XLII, 1, pp.3–16.

Kingson, E. R., Hirschorn, B. A. and Harootyan, L. K. (1986), *The Common Stake: The Interdependence of Generations: A Policy Framework for an Aging Society*, Washington, DC, Gerontological Society of America.

Leimer, D. R. and Petri, P. A. (1981), 'Cohort specific effects of social security policy', *National Tax Journal*, XXXIV, pp. 9–28 (March). Cited in Aaron (1982, p.74).

Neugarten, B. (ed.) (1982), *Age or Need? Public Policies for Older People*, Beverly Hills, Sage Publications.

Parfit, D. (1973), 'Later selves and moral principles', in A. Montefiori (ed.), *Philosophy and Personal Relations*, London, Routledge & Kegan Paul, pp. 137–69.

Parfit, D. (1984), *Reasons and Persons*, Oxford, Oxford University Press.

Parsons, D. O. and Munro, D. R. (1978), 'Intergenerational transfers in social security', in M. J. Boskin (ed.) (1978), *The Crisis in Social Security: Problems and Prospects*, 2nd edn, San Francisco, Institute for Contemporary Studies, pp.65–86.

Preston, S. H. (1984), 'Children and the elderly: divergent paths for America's dependents', *Demography*, XXI,4, pp.435–57.

Rawls, J. (1971), *A Theory of Justice*, Cambridge, Massachusetts, Harvard University Press.

Rawls, J. (1980), 'Kantian construction in moral theory', *Journal of Philosophy*, LXXVII, 9, pp. 515–72.

Rawls, J. (1982), 'Social unity and the primary goods', in A. K. Sen and B. Williams (eds), *Utilitarianism and Beyond*, Cambridge, Cambridge University Press, pp. 159–85.

Russell, L. (1982), *The Baby Boom Generation and the Economy*, Washington, DC, Brookings Institution.

Samuelson, P. (1958), 'An exact consumption-loan model of interest with or without the social contrivance of money', *Journal of Political Economy*, LXVI, 6, pp. 467–82.

Spengler, J. and Kreps, J. (1963), 'Equity and social credit for the retired', in J. Kreps (ed.), *Employment, Income, and Retirement Problems of the Aged*, Durham, North Carolina, Duke University Press, pp. 198–229.

Zook, C. J. and Moore, F. D. (1980), 'High-cost users of medical care', *New England Journal of Medicine*, CCCII, 18, pp. 996–1002.

# 5

---

# But Why Is There Social Security?

---

## Denis Kessler

The creation of social security schemes and the development of pension schemes in most developed countries, just before or after the Second World War, is still a puzzling phenomenon. Why was it suddenly necessary to force people to join social insurance schemes covering the risk of old age? A growing amount of literature on the subject has focused on the effects of social security, on saving for instance, but, surprisingly, the study of the effects of social security has not been accompanied by a careful examination of the basic reasons which led to the introduction of social insurance schemes in the first place.

Our contention is that the economic and social effects of social security would be better understood if the factors underlying the creation of social security schemes were clearly determined. Moreover, future developments within social security and pension schemes, notably in the context of an ageing population, are difficult to predict if we do not really know why they actually exist. Indeed, the mere existence of social insurance schemes is still an open question. This article does not attempt to answer it but explores some hypotheses relative to the question of the existence of social security and pension schemes.

We will explore four main hypotheses relative to household and firm behaviour: (1) the myopia hypothesis; (2) the life cycle hypothesis; (3) the intergenerational altruism hypothesis; and (4) the implicit long-term employee-employers contract hypothesis. After a brief presentation of each of these four models, we will assess their likely impact on saving, intergenerational transfers and labour market equilibrium. We will then check whether or not each of these models is consistent, first, with the existence of mandatory old-age insurance schemes, and second, with their historical development.

## The myopia hypothesis

### Myopia, saving and retirement

According to this first model of behaviour, the time horizon of individuals or households is rather limited. They look only a few years ahead, and in some cases only a few months ahead. They react mostly to current phenomena or variables, such as current income, and ignore long-term events. They do not especially care for the well-being of coming generations. They do not make any significant intertemporal arbitrages and accumulate a little saving out of their current income merely for short-term precautionary motives. Such myopic individuals leave only unplanned bequests to their heirs, if they leave a bequest at all. They are keen on borrowing to finance current consumption and may well underestimate the burden of future repayments. Due to their usual lack of collateral and their limited assets, such individuals are often liquidity- and credit-constrained. They may well have liquidity and even solvency problems when some unanticipated events occur, and many unanticipated events are likely to happen due to their short-sightedness.

### Myopia and old-age insurance schemes

What are the effects of introducing social security and pensions in a world of myopic households? First, such myopic individuals do not make labour-leisure arbitrages over the life cycle. They do not allocate their lifetime in such a way as to maximise their utility. In other words, they do not plan ahead in order to voluntarily choose to retire later. They will remain on the labour market (or continue working when independent) as long as they can. In the same spirit, these myopic individuals will not save during the active part of their life in order to finance their off-labour market phase, namely retirement.

Are social security and pensions necessary in a world of myopic individuals? The answer is yes and no. The answer is positive, since these myopic individuals may well end up in a difficult situation if unable to work when old (for reasons of sickness or due to labour market tensions). Since they do not own a large amount of assets, these myopic individuals may well end up in poverty. If people are myopic, it seems obvious that they will undersave and that the amount of personal saving will not be optimal. The consequent old-age poverty has undesirable social effects (the so-called social externalities), and the government (or municipalities) will have to intervene to care for the elderly poor. Indeed, without a compulsory social insurance scheme, it is feared that people would not protect themselves, and in this case the consequences would require public or private assistance for humanitarian reasons. The corresponding transfers would be financed by taxes or charitable contributions. A situation where those who do protect themselves must also assume financial responsibility for those who do not is, in terms of the distribution and level of well-being, second-best compared to a situation where everybody is forced to insure himself or herself.

But the answer may be negative. In a myopic world, one can suppose that the government will also be myopic. Why should the government be far-sighted if most or all individuals are myopic? In a world full of myopic individuals, intertemporally inconsistent behaviour entails problems, notably poverty, that do not have an easy collective solution.

The myopic hypothesis helps explain why there are social security and pension schemes. Such institutions are designed to force people to protect themselves so as to avoid ending their life in poverty. The fact that people would not save, or would save only for short-term purposes, in the absence of social security and pension schemes explains why it seems that the introduction and quick expansion of such schemes did not have any impact on discretionary saving.

**Myopia and the historical development of old-age social insurance schemes**

The question which arises is the following: the myopia behavioural hypothesis appears to be consistent with the *existence* of social security. But how can we explain the fact that social security schemes operating on the pay-as-you-go principle, as well as most pension schemes, appeared just before or after the Second World War?

It does not seem reasonable to make an *ad hoc* assumption that people became more myopic at that specific historical period, thus making necessary the introduction of a forced saving scheme. The only reasons we could advocate are, first, that people did not grasp the implications of the sharp increase of their life expectancy, and second, that labour market conditions deteriorated for aged workers due to the rise in the rate of unemployment. Nonetheless, the myopia hypothesis appears a little weak as an explanation of historical events.

# The life cycle hypothesis

The core of the explanation of consumption and saving behaviour is the life cycle hypothesis. Let us note that this hypothesis was formulated by Modigliani forty years ago, roughly at the time when social security was implemented and pension funds expanded.

**The life cycle model**

According to this hypothesis, individuals seek to allocate their resources over their life cycle, according to their preferences, in order to maximise their utility. In the most common case, consumption at each period provides a specific utility; there exists a positive rate of time preference; and the preferences are homothetic. In this case, if the interest rate equals the rate of time preference (or if the intertemporal elasticity of substitution is nil), consumption over the life cycle is constant, and wealth-age profiles present a characteristic hump shape with a maximum at the age of retirement. The profile of consumption is then independent of the profile of resources, at least when capital markets are perfect. The age-income profile is supposed to be given, and the retirement age is fixed exogenously.

In other words, according to the life cycle hypothesis, it is assumed that people save primarily to finance their retirement period, and do not intend to leave bequests. In this case also, bequests would be involuntary and, according to Modigliani (1987), the bulk of existing assets would be life cycle assets, not inherited assets. It should be pointed out that in the usual life cycle hypothesis, individuals are presumed to have a finite horizon (their own lifetime) and to anticipate rather correctly their age of death.

### Life cycle and old age insurance schemes

If all individuals behaved as assumed by the life cycle hypothesis, it is easy to see that there is no need a priori for social security or pension schemes. People follow a forward-looking model of behaviour that allows them to have resources and hence consume (and live) at any age. It is therefore somewhat surprising that it is this model which is used to analyse the effect of social security on saving (see the extensive literature following Feldstein's article published in 1974, notably Danziger *et al.*, 1981, Kessler *et al.,* 1981 and Kessler, 1983). Is it possible, then, to keep the basic life cycle model framework and still explain the creation of social security and pension schemes? Two issues can be raised here.

The first issue deals with the assumption of quasi-certainty of life duration. If individuals do not know their precise age at death, they will face some problems in determining the optimal amount of saving. Assuming that an individual dies before he is expected to, he will leave a positive unplanned bequest proportional to the difference between his expected and actual age of death. This bequest could have been consumed had he known perfectly his life duration. He has in fact oversaved. In the opposite case, where he lives longer than expected, he might end up without any resources to consume and has hence undersaved.

Two cases can then be distinguished. First, individuals know that there is an uncertainty related to their age of death. They can decide to insure themselves in order to overcome the disutility resulting from this uncertainty. In this case, there is a need for a private annuity insurance market, not for mandatory social security and pension schemes. The problem is, of course, to know if a private annuity market can function in an optimal way, and overcome the problem arising, for instance, from adverse selection.

Second, individuals could systematically underestimate their life expectancy. Their subjective probabilities of survival are inferior to their actual probabilities. This underestimation leads them to make suboptimal consumption and saving plans, and to systematically underinsure themselves, since they have an imperfect appreciation of the risk they face. In this case, the reasons for creating a social security scheme are clearer. It is necessary to force people to insure themselves because they cannot individually appreciate the risk of living longer than expected. (There is some empirical evidence that such underestimation of life expectancies does exist; see Hamermesch, 1985.)

The second issue deals with another uncertainty which is not linked to the age of death but to some crucial characteristics of the environment. Let us assume again that, according to the life cycle model, individuals save in order to finance their retirement period. This programme, optimal at the time when it was designed and decided, might subsequently appear less than optimal if the characteristics of the environment change. Two crucial, and linked, variables are the inflation rate and the interest rate. If we exclude the case where individuals earn, save and consume the same good, they will have to trade financial or physical assets for consumption goods when aged to finance their retirement period. The value of the exchange between financial and physical assets and consumption goods will depend upon the rate of inflation, the change in the assets' price structure and the rate of interest.

Imagine in a dynamic setting that an individual has accumulated throughout his working period an amount of wealth corresponding exactly to his consumption needs in retirement. Assume that, due to unanticipated price movements, the relative value of financial assets falls. Aged individuals, even if they follow a strict and optimal life cycle model of behaviour, will find themselves in a difficult situation. The problem then is to see how individuals form expectations about future interest rates or relative price developments. In case of unexpected events, due eventually to exogenous shocks, individuals will be unable to finance their consumption expenditures.

### Life cycle behaviour and the historical development of old-age social insurance schemes

If we assume that basically households behave according to the life cycle hypothesis, two factors could contribute to explaining why it has become necessary in the middle of the twentieth century to implement social insurance schemes.

First, one can argue that the very important rise of life durations due to declining mortality rates throughout the twentieth century helps to explain the increasing need to force people to insure themselves against a risk they systematically underestimate but which the government can know at the aggregate level.

Second, the economic and financial environment encountered severe problems in the 1920s and 1930s, and the crisis has largely contributed to making the creation of a social security scheme necessary, especially if we consider that it operates on a pay-as-you-go basis. The functioning of capital markets has not allowed individuals to finance their consumption when aged through an anterior saving effort. Therefore another scheme is necessary in which there is an instantaneous transfer between working and non-working populations, and where the value of the transfer does not depend upon erratic movements in capital markets.

In conclusion, in a world full of people behaving as in the simple life cycle model, with perfect capital markets and no uncertainty, there is no a priori need for social security and pension schemes. It can be argued that these schemes exist because of the actual characteristics of the environment (lifetime uncertainty, imperfect capital markets, imperfect information, etc.) and not because of actual consumption and saving behaviour.

## The intergenerational transfer hypothesis

Let us now turn to a third behavioural hypothesis. This third hypothesis, which rests explicitly upon the existence of important voluntary transfers between succeeding generations, appeared in the economic literature after the myopia and the life cycle hypotheses. Individuals are supposed to be more far-sighted and more patient, less individualistic and more altruistic, than in the myopic or life cycle approaches.

This hypothesis stems from the empirical observation that a large number of financial flows occur between individuals belonging to different generations. Bequests, gifts, inheritances and financial support seem more frequent than predicted by the myopic or life cycle models. This observation leads to a new specification of the individuals' behaviour model, stemming from the seminal contributions of Becker (1974), Barro (1974) and Barro and Feldstein (1978).

### The intergenerational transfers model

The existence of transfers between generations reveals first of all that the time horizon of individuals extends beyond their lifetime. When planning their consumption expenditures, they take into account a large time period. They are indeed 'far-sighted'. Individuals derive utility not only from their own consumption but also from other individuals' consumption. Their lifetime budget constraint must then be modified to take into account bequests, gifts and inheritances both received and given.

In this new model of behaviour, consumption during retirement may be financed through transfers from working adults to the retired aged and not (only) through accumulation of assets, as in the simple life cycle model. The aged are taken charge of by their families because of the altruism of the younger generations. But the younger generations may well benefit from the altruism of their own children and receive some financial support when aged. If this is the case, there is a continuum of private transfers flowing from the young to the elderly. It is clear in this case that the kind of altruism we are dealing with appears somewhat special, since, after having been the generous initiator, one becomes, in turn, the beneficiary. We may call this reciprocal altruism to distinguish it from pure altruism where no later exchange takes place.

What we have just described is in fact a private social security scheme, where the young generations spontaneously transfer resources to the aged. In this perspective, it is important to stress the role played by the family. It is mainly within this structure that intergenerational transfers take place. The family can indeed function as a kind of private insurance company. Many risks may be covered by belonging to a family; this is notably the case with the risks related to old age (cf. Kotlikoff and Spivak, 1981).

### The intergenerational transfers hypothesis and social insurance schemes

If this model of altruistic behaviour prevails, it is difficult to understand the need for a social security scheme. Since consumption of the elderly is financed through operative private transfers, there is no need a priori for a system of public intergenerational transfers. Of course, if one and only one generation does not have the same preference as the preceding generations, for instance if one generation is fully myopic, the private chain letter mechanism comes to an end. There will be a generation that will have supported the aged but will not get any support in its turn. So for this model to really operate, it is necessary that all successive generations have roughly the same altruistic preferences.

Certain authors have also questioned these types of preferences. The existence of bequests can reflect not altruistic preferences, but rather a 'game' played by parent and child (cf. Bernheim *et al.*, 1985). Parents try to attract attention from their children that is remunerated in the form of non-pecuniary gifts or the prospect of bequest. There is a threat that children who do not pay attention to their parents may be disinherited. This 'game' is repeated until the parents die. According to this model, the children may or may not care for their parents, and the existence of a bequest reflects the positive outcome of this 'game'. If, for some reason, children do not continue to play this game, parents might well receive no attention when aged.

If we accept the altruistic intergenerational model of individuals' behaviour, the introduction of social security has no effect on wealth accumulation; its only effect can be on the level, or possibly the direction, of private transfers. If the government imposes transfers going much beyond what the households would have spontaneously done, the latter can react by private transfers in the opposite direction so as to compensate for the undesired transfer. If the public transfer is not large enough, the households simply complement it to reach the desired level once again.

### The intergenerational transfers hypothesis and the historical development of social security

To understand the creation of a social security scheme in a world where all individuals are altruistic and hence give and receive transfers, it is necessary to explore the potential difficulties that have prevented these transfers from operating.

It is interesting to note that the impact of wars, and especially of the First World War, has certainly been a major factor in disrupting the traditional transfers between generations. Many aged parents were not taken charge of by their children just before or after the Second World War because the latter had died twenty years before during the First World War at the age of 18 to 30 years. In the same perspective, the important migrations that took place both within and between countries in the first half of the twentieth century have strongly affected family structures and hence undermined the possibility of financing the elderly through private transfers. The creation of social security schemes operating on a pay-as-you-go basis would therefore force young generations to make transfers to aged generations because of the disruptions that have prevented the private transfer scheme from functioning. One could also argue that the increasing life expectancy and the growing propensity of the elderly to retire earlier entailed a growing intergenerational transfer that the younger generations were not so spontaneously willing to finance.

It should be noted that if the simple life cycle model were the actual model followed by individuals, social security would not be necessary but for the problems of the environment (uncertainty, capital market failures, etc.). If the intergenerational model was the actual model, social security would also be unnecessary were it not for the difficulties of operating private transfers (wars, uneven number of children, migrations, increasing financial burdens, etc.). The myopia hypothesis, the life cycle hypothesis and the intergenerational transfer hypothesis are helpful in understanding the reasons behind a compulsory social security scheme. But none of these hypotheses really explains why people retire. Nor do they explain why firms were active in implementing pension schemes. It therefore seems necessary to explore the labour market and how it functions.

## The labour market hypothesis

Retirement cannot be explained solely by the behaviour of individuals who allocate their time between work and leisure over their life cycle. If this were the case, individuals could choose periods for leisure other than the latter part of their lives. The hypothesis of an absolute need to retire for biological reasons can also be rejected since most people retire at an age when they can still work. This is even more true now than before, since life expectancy has risen and mean retirement age has declined (due especially to early retirement).

### The labour market hypothesis

The concept of retirement, and hence of social transfer schemes, must be analysed through a careful examination of labour markets. Social security and pension schemes play a very important role in the labour market both outside the firm (external labour market) and inside the firm (internal labour market).

Firms' behaviour concerning pensions and social security must be carefully examined. Our contention is that firms have a demand for such schemes. It is remarkable that in all industrialised countries, corporations have been actively implementing and extending old-age protection schemes. Therefore it should be of interest to try to understand the economic reasons underlying the behaviour of firms which lead to the increase of income transfers to retirees. To understand why firms are concerned by the well-being of retirees, a close look at this relationship is necessary.

Outside the firms, social security and pensions are considered as major factors of equilibrium of the labour market, since people who retire leave the labour force. There is usually a clause in the acceptance of social security and pension benefits which forbids a retiree from returning to the labour market. From its inception, social security has been a useful tool for reducing the aggregate rate of unemployment. Social security schemes and pension schemes therefore have an important role to perform in 'managing' the whole labour force. It is also true that old-age income transfers represent a way of acting on the level of global consumption expenditures and hence on macroeconomic activity.

But pension schemes also have some important microeconomic objectives. They play a role in the employer-employee relationship. First, a pension scheme is often created and expanded to attract the most productive workers from the labour force. Pension benefits are indeed an important feature of the compensation package taken into account by individuals in their choice of firm. A pension scheme is often tailored to needs so as to present a real advantage for employees and to incite job-seekers to apply to one or the other firm or sector. Pension schemes are a key part of the explicit and implicit contracts linking employers and employees. These contracts deal both with short-term and long-term aspects.

For numerous reasons, firms do not find a real advantage in 'spot labour markets', where contracts are signed for very short periods of time. There are transaction costs, training requirements, firm-specific skills, information costs, confidence problems and so on that explain why a firm is likely to prefer to make long-term contracts rather than short-term ones.

## The labour market hypothesis and old-age social insurance

Under these long-term contracts, firms agree to hire people over a long stretch of time, set some rules about the way wages will evolve in the future, and clearly indicate that, a priori, employees will remain hired, if they wish to, until some explicit age limit is reached. In these contracts, there are also some rules on career and promotion patterns, etc. The advantage for employees in being covered by such long-term contracts, with rather rigid clauses, is obvious. If we assume that employees are usually risk-averse, they seek to get a guaranteed job, with a guaranteed income. They also lose part of the wage they could get in accepting to be paid only on the basis of their productivity. If individuals were really risk-lovers, they would prefer short-term contracts. The advantage that firms find in such long-term contracts is to reduce the turnover. Such contracts help stabilise manpower.

It is more surprising to learn that pension schemes may allow an increase of productivity throughout the life cycle. The problem of having long-term contracts is that there is an uncertainty about the future productivity of workers. It has been shown that pension schemes are associated with an increasing income profile with age reflecting seniority rules. The income profile is thus steeper than the marginal productivity profile (cf. Lazear, 1982). At the beginning of the life cycle, wages are inferior to the marginal productivity of labour, but at the later working period of the life cycle, the reverse is true. In that case, workers, when young, are induced not to change firms at the beginning of their career. Moreover, by staying in the same firm, they accumulate pension rights. Workers are also induced to increase their productivity to get wage increases that have a multiplicative effect, since they increase pensions and social security entitlements.

But it is also necessary for the firm to be able to get rid of workers when they are too costly (high wages) and less productive (aged). In this case, social security and pension rights available at a certain age induce employees to leave the workforce (without major social problems). Pensions act as severance pay. Pension schemes appear therefore as an important feature of the complex contract, extending over a life cycle, between employers and employees, a contract which is beneficial to both parties. Pensions and social security benefits are not saving; they are not insurance benefits; rather they are deferred wages.

### The labour market hypothesis and the historical development of social insurance schemes

Why did the short-term labour contracts which prevailed until the implementation of social security and the extension of pensions disappear? Two reasons can be given. First, the high level of unemployment in the 1930s pushed the government to introduce social security as a device to reduce the tension on the labour market. Second, the new intensive methods of production introduced in the 1930s in Europe and in the US required a new long-term relationship between firms and their employees. Stability of manpower became necessary, because it takes time to train workers to carry out sophisticated techniques. It is worth noting that it is in the most advanced sectors of the economy (at that time) that pension funds were first created, and were the most generous.

## Conclusion

Four alternative economic explanations for the existence of social security and pensions are available. Three of them place importance on the individual's behaviour (myopic, life cycle, and intergenerational or far-sighted) and the characteristics of the environment (capital market imperfections, uncertainty, generation disruptions, etc.) and one of them considers the firm's behaviour to be more significant. Certain hypotheses appear more consistent with the existence and the historical development of social security and pensions, but none of these four explanations can be fully rejected. The nature of social security and pension schemes varies largely according to the explanation considered: is it an insurance against the risk of living to an advanced old age? Is it a forced saving scheme for myopic individuals? Is it a way of restoring intergenerational transfers that are prevented from operating? Is it a device to manage the workforce better? The existence of old-age social insurance schemes is still an open issue.

## References

Barro, R. J. (1974), 'Are government bonds net wealth?', *Journal of Political Economy*, LXXXVIII, pp. 1095–117.

Barro, R. J. and Feldstein, M. (1978), *The Impact of Social Security on Private Saving: Evidence from Private Time Series*, Washington, DC, American Enterprise Institute.

Becker, G. S. (1974), 'A theory of social interactions', *Journal of Political Economy*, LXXXVIII, pp. 1063-93.

Bernheim, B. D., Shleifer, A. and Summers, L. (1985), 'The strategic bequest motive', *Journal of Political Economy*, XCIII, pp. 1045-76.

Danziger, S., Haveman, R. and Plotnick, R. (1981), 'How income transfer programs affect work, savings and the income distribution: a critical review,' *Journal of Economic Literature*, XIX, pp. 975-1028 (September).

Feldstein, M. (1974), 'Social security, induced retirement and aggregate capital accumulation', *Journal of Political Economy*, LXXXVIII, pp. 905-26.

Hamermesch, D. (1985), 'Expectations, life expectancy, and economic behavior', *Quarterly Journal of Economics*, pp. 389-408.

Kessler, D. (1983), 'Les politiques sociales modifient-elles le comportement des individus? Le cas du système de retraite', *Revue d'Economie Politique*, XCIII, 3, pp. 328-44.

Kessler, D., Masson, A. and Strauss-Kahn, D. (1981), 'Social security and saving: a tentative survey', *Geneva Papers on Risk and Insurance*, 18, pp. 3-50.

Kotlikoff, L. and Spivak, A. (1981), 'The family as an incomplete annuities market', *Journal of Political Economy*, LXXXIX, pp. 706-32.

Lazear, E. P. (1982), 'Pensions as severance pay', Washington, DC, National Bureau of Economic Research, Working Paper no. 944 (July).

Modigliani, F. (1987), 'Measuring the contribution of inter-generational transfers to total wealth: conceptual issues and empirical findings', in D. Kessler and A. Masson (eds), *Modelling the Accumulation and Distribution of Wealth*, Oxford, Oxford University Press.

# Part II

## Paying for Retirement

# 6

# Pension Bargains: the Heyday of US Collectively Bargained Pension Arrangements

Steven Sass

Today's US private pension institution is very much the product of recent historical circumstance. It emerged quite suddenly, in the aftermath of New Deal reform, and has flourished in the intervening period of 'corporate-liberal' prosperity. Now that the economic and political structures created by the New Deal and corporate-liberal America are in decline, the pension institution can be expected to show signs of stress. Despite fifty years of increasing strength, those dependent on private pension benefits forty or more years in the future have reason to be concerned. To gauge the resilience of the institution, this paper analyses the rise and evolution of a key branch of the US system: the pension arrangements collectively bargained by unions and employers. Such programmes first emerged in the 1940s, and thereafter expanded swiftly. Since 1960 they have enrolled between 40 and 50 per cent of all participants in the US private pension institution and have exerted a major influence on general plan design. The scope and character of the larger pension structure rests, to a degree rarely appreciated, on the success of these union-negotiated schemes. Moreover plans are the programme with the weakest financial footing and the ones most heavily dependent on New Deal social institutions. They are, in other words, the most vulnerable part of the pension institution.

While this article argues that particular historical circumstances conditioned the rise of US collectively bargained pension arrangements, more permanent forces clearly underlay these institutions. In particular, twentieth-century US labour unions have consistently advocated old-age assistance programmes. This is the case even though they only established viable programmes on a widespread basis in the post-war period. Organised labour derives this affinity for pensions in two quite distinct ways. As shown by Freeman (1985), unionisation greatly strengthens the bargaining position of older, more sedentary workers. These employees are far more desirous of pensions than the younger marginal workers who define spot market contracts, and they use their influence in unions to shift compensation from cash to retirement benefits. Graebner (1980) describes labour's second path to pensions: the use of benefits to foster retirements. By so reducing the supply of labour, pension plans tend to boost wages or open up job opportunities for union members.

By the 1920s, several large and successful American unions established pension plans of their own. As described by Latimer (1932, pp. 8ff.), they generally grew out of the considerations described by Freeman and were designed to assure older workers of assistance should they become disabled by age. These unions were typically brotherhoods of skilled craftsmen who worked for many small firms over the course of a lifetime. Their employers had neither the resources nor the long-term employment relationships necessary to support ongoing pension and welfare programmes. Since the mid-nineteenth century, the stronger brotherhoods had thus taken on various insurance functions. Most union benefit funds originally provided just death and disability coverage. But as more of their members grew too old to work, pressure developed to provide some form of assistance – placement in an old age home, a lump sum grant, or a life annuity. Befitting their welfare function, the union plans paid meagre benefits and required applicants to demonstrate both poverty and the inability to continue to work (for a contrary view see Graebner, 1980, pp. 135–49).

Commentators such as Dearing (1954, pp. 30–2; see also Latimer, 1932, p. 126) argued that unions had 'extensive experience' with old age pension programmes prior to 1945. These writers based this assertion on the fact that 40 per cent of all union members in 1928 had been covered by some form of old age maintenance programme. This claim, however, cannot be sustained. At least half the workers so covered could only retire to a distant old age home or on the insufficient cash value of a life or disability insurance policy. Annuities were the fastest-growing form of union old age assistance throughout the 1920s, but only 20 per cent of the movement's membership participated in a bona fide labour pension plan in 1928. The railroad brotherhoods, with half of this covered population, merely offered voluntary individual annuities as supplements to corporate pension programmes. The remaining coverage was concentrated in just two groups: the printing trades (typographers and printing pressmen) and the building trades (bricklayers, masons, plasterers, electrical workers, and, in 1930, carpenters and joiners). Moreover, the labour movement was itself in decline. From a high point of 5 million members during the First World War, a vigorous employer offensive had reduced union membership to 3.4 million by 1930. Both the reach and the prospects of the labour pension movement were thus quite limited.

The actual union pension experience, as described by Latimer (1932, pp. 93ff.) and Dearing (1954, pp. 31–5), was also irregular. Testing for poverty, disability and organisational loyalty demanded far more bureaucratic efficiency than the unions could muster. Administration of the certification process thus devolved into the hands of local officials and opened the gates for widespread corruption. This decentralisation bloated claims against the plan, as local leaders had strong reasons to certify 'their' applicants for pensions and weak incentives to adhere strictly to plan requirements. While union pension liabilities grew all too quickly, plan assets were never adequate. These schemes were not developed on an actuarial basis, but proceeded in a quasi pay-as-you-go fashion. The membership set contribution levels at their annual conventions with an eye on current benefit disbursements. The typical union plan had but two to three years' current benefits put away at the end of the 1920s, and contributions were roughly 10 per cent of amounts needed to fund the programme properly. Nor were the assets secure. The plans explicitly allowed the sponsoring union to dip into the pension fund when faced with some 'emergency', and this happened quite frequently. Thus 40 per cent of the pressmen's pension fund was in the union treasury in 1928. Union officials also borrowed extensively from the pension fund for their personal business ventures. The pressmen's pension fund, for example, invested another 20 per cent of its assets in the president's playing card company.

The best that could be said for these early union pension schemes was that they were immature. But the Depression cut short the opportunity for further development. Benefit applications multiplied rapidly and absorbed all available resources. The unions responded by tightening eligibility requirements and raising contributions; they cut benefits, and finally terminated payments altogether. Of the thirteen plans sponsored by international unions in 1929, Goodman (1970, p. 31) found just five surviving in 1947.

Ironically, labour was to build a second pension system on a foundation laid in the Depression by Franklin Roosevelt's New Deal. The actual development of the new institution was not foreseen at the time and was hardly inevitable. Indeed, it needed the assistance of several fortuitous events during the crystallisation of post-New Deal employment relations in the late 1940s. And if labour had failed to win the pension at that particular historical moment, it probably would never have gained such significant benefits.

The Depression, which destroyed labour's original pension structure, brought compensation from the public sector. With social security, the New Deal established a public old age income assurance programme for many of the nation's wage and salary workers. Especially after the crucial 1939 amendments, the programme paralleled union schemes by emphasising the provision of basic benefits instead of assuring comparability between allowances and past contributions. Like the labour plans, social security was designed so that those already old could survive on a basic allowance. For the average worker, this would be a pension of roughly 30 per cent of active earnings. Because of the broad scope and resources of social security, workmen thenceforth looked to government, not to their unions, as the primary source of old age security. Any private plan would essentially be supplementary.

The Depression also brought the Wagner Act of 1935, which was to be the foundation for labour's second pension institution. The new statute transformed the basic framework of US labour relations by giving workers the right to form unions and bargain collectively. A revitalised labour leadership took the Wagner Act and launched the most sustained and long-lasting organising drive in American history. Union membership, which had fallen to a nadir of 2,973,000 in 1933 (11.3 per cent of employees in non-agricultural establishments), reached 10,489,000 in 1941 (28.7 per cent) and 14,796,000 by 1945 (36.6 per cent) (Peterson, 1945 p. 56; US BLS, 1980, p. 412, 1988, p. 43). The transition to collective bargaining, however, was far from smooth. Management bitterly resisted labour's great upsurge, and fought bitter battles to forestall union recognition. In labour's camp, the militant Congress of Industrial Organisations (CIO) broke away from the old American Federation of Labour (AFL) and fierce intra-union battles – especially between communist and non-communist CIO factions – further complicated the scene. Labour relations in the 1930s were thus marked by intense and often violent struggles. And as long as such fundamental issues remained open, nothing so mundane as old age pensions would receive much attention.

Because of its sensitivity to the new possibilities in collective bargaining, the CIO mainstream was to lead in establishing labour's post-New Deal pension programme. In terms of basic strategy, the AFL relied on a monopoly of craft skill; the communists looked to class consciousness and a future revolution; only the CIO made do with worker solidarity and the Wagner Act. But labour's new collective bargaining rights provided a sturdy platform from which to assert pension claims. Bargained plans were far stronger than the old stand-alone union programmes because they involved employer participation. Collective bargaining also framed a continuing employment relationship – the prerequisite and stimulus to employer-based pension schemes. The CIO was the first labour movement to recognise the promise of bargained plans, and pensions became a key item on its post-war agenda (CIO, 1946, pp. 14–17; see also AFL, 1944, p. 32).

Before much progress could be made in fashioning collectively bargained labour relations, America entered the Second World War. The government then imposed a thoroughgoing system of wage controls and brought the key negotiating issues under federal jurisdiction. This bargaining hiatus, and labour-management co-operation in the war effort, cooled passions all round and allowed unions to emerge from the conflict as an accepted institution. Post-war labour relations, although far less bloody than they had been in the 1930s, were nevertheless still rough and undefined. The parties were finally to strike their basic bargain in the period 1945–50, and it was then that pensions became an integral element in negotiated labour contracts.

Immediately following the war, the two parties were hardly prepared to agree on pensions or other innovative labour arrangements. In addition to the continuing tensions over collective bargaining and rifts within labour's camp, both business and labour expected a quick return to the Depression. Thus Harris (1982) found employers determined to hold down labour costs and maintain their 'right to manage' the productive process. Labour, on the other hand, used the new Keynesian economics to justify higher wages and expanded union job control as a means of fending off the downturn. The return to peacetime collective bargaining thus resulted in the disastrous strike wave of 1945–46 and a series of tentative one-year contracts. Work stoppages in 1946 alone absorbed over 100 million man-hours, triple the amount in any previous year, and one-year contracts remained the rule until the end of the decade (US BLS, 1980, p. 415).

The government saw little choice but to intervene. The Wagner Act had organised the nation's key labour markets as bilateral monopolies, where no automatic mechanism, based on rational calculation and marginal adjustment, promoted economic stability. The public interest, measured by the continuity as well as the efficiency of production, needed external intervention. Harry S. Truman, Franklin Roosevelt's heir, did what he could to right the New Deal's labour system. He seized or threatened to seize whole industries, he encouraged activism in his key labour agencies, and he established *ad hoc* fact-finding boards to help settle major labour disputes. An increasingly conservative nation meanwhile returned a Republican Congress in the 1946 elections. The new body lost little time in enacting the Taft-Hartley Act of 1947, an extensive pro-management revision of the Wagner Act. Each of these interventions was critical to the rise of labour's new pension arrangements, and each injected an element of public interest into the new design. And pensions became a device for bringing order to these unstable labour markets.

But critical to the emergence of the negotiated pension institution were two fortuitous circumstances which happened to be present during this jelling period of US labour-management relations. The first was prosperity. The war had set off a spiral of rising incomes and prices that undercut existing pension programmes, especially social security. The nation had just reached its consensus on public pensions, in 1939, when the war arrived. The conflict had generated a tremendous demand for labour, keeping large numbers of older workers productively employed. With the return of peace, the pay cheques stopped coming and the need for adequate old age income emerged anew. But with social security benefits defined in 1939 dollars, inflation and rising real incomes had eroded the value of the programme's allowances. According to Munnell (1982, p. 20) the average public pension replaced nearly 30 per cent of the average wage in 1940; that figure fell to 22 per cent in 1945 and 19 per cent by 1950. The elderly were little equipped to supplement these government allowances from their own resources as the Depression and then inflation had decimated their personal savings. With 50 per cent replacement commonly cited as the minimum acceptable retirement income, benefits in 1940 had hardly afforded a viable living. The inflation and rising living standards of the 1940s all but gutted social security as a reliable source of retirement income.

While government fell down in its new responsibility of providing basic old age pensions, federal labour law restricted management's ability and incentive to provide production workers with corporate benefits. Blue-collar employees now required special treatment, and it was unclear whether management could unilaterally install or reform a plan for their organised or organising workers. Moreover unions now stood between a company and its labour force and it would gain much of the credit should a firm establish or liberalise an existing corporate plan.

With the recession of working-class coverage in both government and corporate programmes, the unions emerged as the primary champion of labour's pension interests. The unions remained key defenders of the national social insurance programme, but the conservative climate of the times barred the easy restoration of social security replacement rates. Several CIO organisations therefore became active participants in the private pension arena.

The second fortuitous circumstance favouring the rise of labour's pension institution was the strength of the United Mine Workers and their particular interest in pensions. Led by the charismatic John L. Lewis, and enrolling 80 per cent of the nation's miners, the UMW dominated its industry as few other labour organisations did. Only the miners had been brazen enough to challenge the US government and strike during the Second World War; and only the government could seriously challenge their power in the immediate post-war period. Further separating the UMW from other labour organisations, as Reed (1955) points out, was its inordinate need for pension and welfare benefits. Mine workers' wages were ample in cash-poor Appalachia. But mining was a hazardous occupation with more than its share of injury, morbidity, disability and death. One could hardly expect aged miners to stay in the pits after a lifetime of exposure. Moreover coal mining was an industry benefiting, as it were, from rapidly rising labour productivity. Employment in the bituminous fields had dropped precipitously from a high of 700,000 in 1923 to 416,000 in the latter 1940s; it was to fall to 250,000 by 1955. For enough union-wage jobs to go around, the supply of labour would have to go down; the UMW therefore needed pensions to retire older workers.[1]

With both the means and the incentives to act, the UMW demanded an employer-financed, union-controlled pension and welfare fund in 1945. After the owners refused and the miners backed down, Lewis made the welfare fund the union's top negotiating priority in 1946. But that year the operators rejected all union demands. So the UMW went on strike effectively halting US coal production. As fuel shortages began choking American industry, Truman invoked the War Labor Disputes Act and seized the nation's coal mines. A week later, on 29 May, Secretary of the Interior J. A. Krug signed a contract providing an employer-paid $.05 per ton royalty to a jointly managed United Mineworkers Welfare and Retirement Fund. The plan's benefits and financial policies were left to the three trustees – the chairman from the UMW, one chosen by management (first government and then the private owners), and a neutral trustee selected by the other two. The parties immediately ran into trouble, failing to agree on a third trustee, on the retirement age and pension benefit, or on whether to fund the plan or to operate on a pay-as-you-go (paygo) basis.

Lewis called two strikes protesting the 'delays' and twice the courts ordered the men back to work and then fined Lewis and the union when they ignored the orders. Because of the turmoil, the first pension cheque was not mailed until September 1948. Payments were subsequently suspended in September 1949, and restored for good only in July 1950.[2]

The essential difference between the UMW plan and the classic union programme was that the new scheme was part of the collective bargaining contract. The plan took contributions directly from employers, who also assumed an administrative role in the plan. Unlike the traditional model, Lewis's scheme also fostered retirements by offering high pension benefits. The fund paid $100 per month and gave generous credit for past service. When added to a social security benefit of roughly $50, this represented a very attractive retirement allowance. In most other respects, Lewis had established a traditional labour pension scheme. Although the employers had argued for funding – and therefore less generous benefits – the UMW won a paygo policy that yielded the maximum current payments. Thus the miners' programme did not put aside funds to meet the benefit claims being accrued by active miners. Nor did the plan put away money to meet its initial 'past service' liability – its obligation to pay benefits based on service rendered prior to the plan's establishment. In 1955, Lewis (1955) estimated the deficit for current retirees alone at $1.25 billion – eight years' contributions to the fund. But it would be 'a crime of the highest order', he insisted, to deprive those now alive and in need merely to 'sequester and secrete these great sums of money' in a pension fund. Lewis justified a paygo policy on the stability of the industry and the UMW's position within it. It was unnecessary to build up an enormous reserve, he argued, 'when the fund is a going concern and has an annual revenue, and when any protection to that fund through experience can be brought about gradually with the distribution of the load over succeeding generations of men in the industry'.

As was the case with the early union paygo plans, pension costs increased steadily and pushed the programme off balance. As shown by Reed (1955, p. 1032), payments rose by 90 per cent, from $42 to $70 million, between 1951 and 1955. In response, the union negotiated royalty increases, to $.40 per ton by 1952. The plan trustees also tightened eligibility requirements in 1953 and in 1954 they discontinued disability and survivor annuities. Even expenditures on the medical programme, the great pride of the union, declined in 1954 and 1955 as pensions came to absorb nearly 60 per cent of all spending. As pensioners were given free medical benefits and were high users of such services, retirees actually consumed much more than 60 per cent of the UMW programme.

Despite the future difficulties in the mineworkers' programme, rival union leaders felt compelled to match Lewis and win pensions for their membership. 'Psychologically,' wrote Barbash (1967), 'it is likely that the miners' welfare fund was the single most influential force in the negotiated pension movement.' But no group of workers dominated an industry as the miners did theirs. And elsewhere management proved too hostile to accede to a pension and labour too weak to work its will. So it took several more years for blue-collar programmes to spread to other parts of the economy. Not until the end of the 1940s, when general economic conditions stabilised and relations ripened between labour and management, could the big CIO unions follow Lewis's example. Only then, and only with active government involvement, would management yield pensions.

The typical CIO situation is best illustrated by the experience of the United Auto Workers, which emerged as the union most influential in matters of plan design. The UAW faced far stiffer opposition that the UMW. It bargained with firms like General Motors, Ford and Chrysler, each far larger and stronger than the coal mine operators. These employers bargained separately with the UAW and exercised much greater control over their labour situation. The development of worker pensions in the automobile industry would thus require significant accommodation to corporate requirements. A UMW-style plan – a multi-employer paygo programme with a union-dominated pension fund – was hardly a reasonable expectation. In automobiles, as in other industries dominated by big business, blue-collar pensioning was to develop on a company-by-company basis.

To win pensions, the UAW first had to normalise the employment relationship. The big car manufacturing firms simply refused to enter into so costly, open-ended and long-term arrangements with the union unless the UAW controlled militant wildcat strikers and contract violators – in other words, until the UAW provided what was called 'company security'. Thus Ford wrote to the UAW that

> before we could entertain any thought of an Employee Retirement Plan we had to answer two basic questions. The first was the question of company security. If the company's ability to go on as a profitable progressive institution would be threatened, it was obvious that such a program could not be considered.
> On the other hand, if our employees were not encouraged to their best efforts and top efficiency by fair treatment, good working conditions, good wages, and a reasonable sense of security in their jobs, the ability of the company to succeed in competitive enterprises would be also placed in danger. (Selekman *et al.*, 1950, p. 303)

Disciplining militants was not so simple, as they had won many of the union's most dramatic successes and had developed a significant rank-and-file following. But as Lewis's aggressive strategy disrupted bargaining in coal, they also barred 'normalised' labour relations in car manufacturing.

Walter Reuther became president of the UAW in 1946, and according to Selekman *et al.* (*ibid.*, p. 289), the union then began the process of establishing 'long-term relationships of "normal" collective bargaining'. The agreements negotiated in 1946, continued Selekman *et al.* (*ibid.*), 'marked the transition to permanent continuing joint relationships, and spelled out mutual rights and obligations with explicit particularity.' And in their next contract negotiations, in 1947, Ford and the UAW actually announced tentative agreement on the first pension plan for US car workers. Although the UMW success had stimulated the car workers' interest, the Ford-UAW design was in the traditional corporate mould (*ibid.*, pp. 300–1). The plan was voluntary, demanded employee contributions, and paid very modest benefits.

External events, however, unravelled the 1947 Ford-UAW agreement. During the contract negotiations, Congress passed the National Labor Relations (Taft-Hartley) Act over President Truman's veto. The statute included stiff new 'company security' provisions, giving employers the right to sue unions and their officers for contract violations. Ford thus received more from Congress than it was to receive from the UAW, and it did so without yielding anything in return. The bargaining back in Detroit consequently began drifting, and after another two months of negotiations produced a surprising settlement. The parties agreed to two contracts – one with pensions and a modest raise, the other with more cash but no retirement benefits – and put the final choice to the rank-and-file. The union leadership campaigned vigorously for the pension plan, but as was reported in *Business Week* (27 September 1947, p.98), the membership voted for cash by a three-to-one margin.

When Ford and UAW negotiators returned to the bargaining table in 1948, they were further apart on pensions than ever. The chastened union leadership now insisted on a UMW-style programme. They demanded a non-contributory plan, funded by royalties on production, with the resulting assets managed by a joint labour-management board. But Ford, sharing in corporate America's growing assertiveness, now resisted bargaining over pensions at all. The company claimed that retirement programmes were discretionary instruments and would only be discussed at the bargaining table if the firm so chose. Inasmuch as Ford commented on the union proposal, it rejected it out of hand. Management insisted that workers contribute to any future plan and that the firm manage the disposition of all pension assets. There was little common ground between the two positions, and Selekman *et al.* (1950, pp. 310, 313, 318–22) found none developing during the negotiations. Although the UAW kept its plan on the table right up to the contract signing, the union settled for increased wages and insurance benefits, but no pensions.

While the two negotiating parties had hardened their positions, forces external to the bargaining process were becoming increasingly conducive to the establishment of labour pension programmes. The government set the stage in 1948, when the National Labor Relations Board declared, in the Inland Steel decision, that pensions 'lie within the statutory scope of collective bargaining'. After the Supreme Court upheld this position in 1949, management could no longer treat pensions as discretionary gratuities but had to bargain over the issue in good faith. In the economy, the post-war inflation suddenly came to a halt and the cost of living actually declined in 1949. This eased workers' demands for higher cash wages and increased their receptivity to pensioning. The public, which increasingly blamed unions for the rising prices, could be expected to resist another round of wage increases but barely to notice the cost of a pension programme. In union politics, CIO moderates were meanwhile gaining the upper hand over their left-wing rivals. Reuther, for example, only established his clear leadership in the UAW at the 1949 national convention. But by the end of the year he and like-minded CIO officials had begun purging their federation of communist influence. With mainstream unionism in the ascendancy, the prospects for increased cash wages now distant, the NLRB Inland Steel decision in place, and the value of social security benefits at their all-time low, pensions became the CIO's primary bargaining issue in the 1949 negotiations.[3]

But rather than digest pensions as inevitable in the evolution of bargained employment relations, Selekman *et al.* (1950, pp. 335, 556–77) found that the industrial system nearly choked on the issue. Pensions remained thorny, complex and expensive. Along with others, Kerr (1949, pp. 4,8) thought pensions simply too esoteric for the rough-and-tumble of collective bargaining. The influential American Institute of Certified Public Accountants (1948) had meanwhile issued a research bulletin alerting the business community to the magnitude of past service obligations. Thus US Steel claimed that the proposed United Steelworker plan involved an immediate $1 billion liability attributable to past service accruals in addition to heavy and ongoing annual 'normal' costs. Disputes over who should fund and who should invest pension assets also raised fundamental economic and political questions. Because of such differences over pensions, labour negotiations in automobile, steel, coal, and other basic industries began freezing up in the summer of 1949. Three days before the strike deadline in steel, on 12 July, President Truman intervened. He established a special Steel Industry Board (SIB) to conduct an investigation and recommend settlement terms, and he won a contract extension to give the SIB time to do its work.

The Steel Industry Board report (1949), issued on 10 September 1949, was the seminal document in the history of collectively bargained pension plans. Although put together in haste, and showing signs of it, the report commanded widespread support. US industrial relations were rapidly coming apart over the pension issue, with the coal miners about to strike to preserve their programme and the steel workers, car workers, and others threatening walk-outs to win plans of their own. The SIB recommendations seemed to be the country's last defence against another cycle of unrest and inflation and even critics could embrace its recommendations as the lesser of two evils.

The SIB tried to draw a compromise between management and labour in a way that explicitly served the public interest. It thus opposed union demands for inflationary wage increases but recommended new pension and welfare benefits, which it defined as essential employer obligations. As if defining a poor law for the industrial age, the SIB (1949, pp. 7–8) insisted that 'a social obligation rests upon industry to provide insurance against the economic hazards of modern industrial life, including retirement allowances, in adequate amount as supplementary to the amount of the security furnished by Government'. Should government not provide sufficient protection, continued the SIB, 'industry should step in to fill the gap.' It accepted the common definition of a basic pension – 30 per cent of pre-retirement income, or $100 per month. This figure represented the same proportion of income replaced by social security in 1940 and that the 1947 Ford-UAW agreement had targeted for the typical long-service employee. As government benefits had remained at their deflated, Depression era levels, and social security had been pitched to the average, less well-off worker, the SIB recommended that the companies 'fill the gap' between this $100 figure and a steel worker's social security allowance; in practical effect, the SIB placed half the burden of providing an 'adequate' pension on the private sector.

The SIB attempted to justify this extension of employers' social protection responsibility with the flawed and fiercely contested 'human depreciation' theory of pensions. It reasoned that 'human machines, like the inanimate machines, have a definite rate of depreciation', and blamed industrial work for this gradual loss in human productive power. It demanded, as compensation, pensions from the enterprises benefiting from that labour. This use of accounting analogies was far from precise, and it generated more heat than light. But the concept allowed the SIB to argue that 'insurance and pensions should be considered part of normal business costs to take care of temporary and permanent depreciation in the human "machine"'. Like depreciation expense, concluded the SIB, 'this obligation should be among the first charges on revenues.' Here it differed significantly from the typical views of both management and labour. The bargaining parties normally viewed pensions as a fringe benefit offered only by the most profitable firms. But the SIB insisted that pensions were a basic labour cost; employers had an obligation to pay, and workers had a right to receive their benefit.[4]

The United Steelworkers quickly accepted the entire SIB package. In so doing the union not only gave up its wage demands, which were little more than bargaining chips, but also a long-held position on how to 'integrate', or combine, employer pensions with social security. Labour had bitterly opposed integration methods that reduced the company pension by the retiree's entire social security benefit. Employers contributed just half of social security's revenues, they argued, so they could only claim credit, and reduce company pensions, by half of the government allowance. But the union accepted the SIB formulation to win a programme paying adequate pensions. As Reuther (1950) explained, this integration formula also aided the union campaign to raise social security benefits. Businesses accepting the full-integration design would be major beneficiaries of such an increase, and corporate influence could be expected to swing behind the liberalisation movement.[5]

US Steel claimed to accept the SIB proposal in general. But the steel company insisted, however, that the pension and welfare plans be voluntary and contributory. Clearly, management wanted to share the costs and risks of such programmes with labour. Enders Voorhees, steel company executive, also hoped 'to preserve an individual's right to spend or save as he sees fit', and argued that 'no one unwilling to contribute towards his own old age requirement has the moral right to demand that others make that provision for him' (SIB, 1949, p.10). The company hoped to avoid pension liabilities on those who chose not to participate in the plan. But more importantly, it thereby rejected the social responsibility assigned to it by the SIB. Unable to reach a compromise by the 30 September contract deadline, 500,000 steel workers went on strike to win pension benefits.

The breakthrough came not in steel, a mature industry with a large and expensive overhang of older workers, but in the much younger and more vigorously growing car industry. One day before the strike deadline in steel, on 29 September, Ford and the UAW signed a Memorandum of Agreement on Retirement and Health and Security Programs based on the SIB package. As detailed in Selekman *et al.* (1950, pp. 352–8), Ford agreed to pay pensions of $100 per month, reduced by social security benefits, to all eligible UAW retirees. The programme was non-contributory, granted full pension credit for past service, and, according to the agreement, would cost the company $.0875 an hour. The settlement naturally put great pressure on the steel firms, and on 31 November Bethlehem signed a labour agreement including a similar plan. The rest of the steel firms soon came to terms, establishing a pattern for other CIO industries. And by 1952, after the completion of the so-called 'fourth round' of post-war labour negotiations, pensions became a fixture in CIO contracts.

Company and union negotiators refined the plan design as pensioning spread throughout the CIO industries. Among the first issues to be settled was whether the agreement would define a contribution or a benefit. The Ford-UAW negotiators did both, specifying a benefit ($100 monthly, less social security), and a contribution ($.0875 an hour). But after Congress raised social security benefits in 1950, drastically reducing the defined company-sponsored benefits, it became clear that one of these conditions had to be relaxed. The firm saw that far smaller contributions were needed to support the new benefit level; the union recognised that the contractual contributions could fund far larger pensions. The issue was quickly resolved in favour of fixing benefits and allowing contributions to fluctuate. As explained by Hamilton and Bronson (1958), the unions were essentially interested in assuring adequate benefits and chose not to bear investment risks and responsibilities. In exchange for negotiated benefit levels, the CIO unions retired from the world of active pension fund management.

Advance funding was soon established as a second tenet of CIO plan design. The coal miners had opted for paygo and maximising current allowances for a given contribution. The steel workers contracted for specific pension benefits and allowed the companies to meet this liability in any manner they chose. But the UAW demanded a pension fund and its 1950 pact with General Motors even specified a maximum thirty-year amortisation of past service liabilities. That same year Chrysler Corporation, seeking to minimise its current pension outlays, insisted upon a paygo programme. But Reuther and the UAW insisted on the payment of normal costs plus a thirty-year amortisation of past service liabilities. The parties failed to reach a compromise, and the dispute precipitated a strike. The UAW won the battle, and funding thereafter became a CIO shibboleth. Plan assets were to be a primary source of participant security, a key assurance that pensions would be available to all down the road.

The sharp rise in social security benefits brought a third major adjustment in CIO pension design, the relaxation of full integration. The maximum government pension rose over time, from $46 in 1949 to $80 in 1950, $85 in 1952, and then $108.50 in 1954. Workers, report Hamilton and Bronson (1958, pp.299–303), found it hard to understand why a rise in social security benefits should cause their corporate pensions to decline and then vanish in 1954. Workers viewed the two schemes as independent, due largely to the contractual and equity elements built into the federal 'insurance' programme and to the fact that private pensions were secured in exchange for reduced cash wages. Led by the 1950 GM-UAW arrangement, subsequent designs thus dropped the full reduction for social security. Some plans called for 50 per cent integration – reducing corporate benefits by 50 per cent of the government amount. But most followed the GM programme – simply fixing an allowance over the course of the contract, implicitly taking social security into consideration.

By 1952 CIO single-employer plans had thus become largely standardised affairs. They were funded, non-contributory, defined benefit plans paying modest benefits and granting full credit for past service. In the larger context, the 'fourth round' of post-war contracts signalled a broader stability in US industrial relations. Confidence in the economy and the recession of labour radicalism had spawned a growing climate of mutual accommodation. As management and labour defined their new collectively bargained relationship, they reduced the uncertainty, ambiguity, and scope of opportunism that had plagued the American workplace. 'Fourth-round' contracts were thus multi-year pacts, breaking the previous pattern of annual renegotiation. The UAW agreements, for example, extended for a full five years. The rise of bargained pension plans in 1949 clearly benefited from this growing moderation. The stability of the 1950s, on the other hand, was to impede the development of such a significant new institution. Pensions thus slipped nimbly into the new set of bargained arrangements just as society's door slid shut on further structural change.

The CIO's success had legitimised pensions as part of the standard union contract. Although the pace of change in industrial relations slowed in the 1950s and the restoration of social security benefit levels assuaged the urgency of the old age income problem, the AFL was compelled to organise plans of its own. Despite the improvement in government benefits, they were hardly adequate replacements for good union wages. Older AFL members felt the need for supplementary allowances as much as their CIO brethren. The craft unions thus proceeded to establish multi-employer plans akin to the UMW programme in the mid-1950s. The successful AFL campaign, according to Skolnik (1976, pp.4–5; see also US BLS, 1962, pp. 1,4; Bartell and Simpson, 1968; and Ellwood, 1985, pp. 23–4), raised the number of workers in multi-employer arrangements from less than 1 million in 1950 to 3 million in 1960. The CIO and AFL plans together covered some 11 million workers in 1960, a bit less than half of all participants in the private pension institution. Total coverage since 1945 had leapt from 19 to 40 per cent of private non-agricultural employment, a jump essentially attributable to union initiatives.

After 1960, the character of bargained plans shifted to accommodate a new policy of early retirement. Many of the most powerful American unions found it increasingly difficult to find work for their members, and they turned to retirements to reduce the supply of labour. Between 1955 and 1960–64, according to the US Bureau of Labor Statistics (1980, p. 154), technical progress and the substitution of capital for high-wage union labour combined to reduce the number of production workers by 8 per cent in the key durable goods sector. Production worker employment fell 14 per cent in primary metals and 22 per cent in transportation equipment, both areas of particular union strength. In earlier years, labour's primary device for contracting the supply of labour was to shorten the length of the working week. But for reasons of technical efficiency, market control and worker preference, the working week had stabilised at forty hours. So as contracts came up for renegotiation in the 1960s, retirement beckoned as the most attractive device for clearing union labour markets.

Among the ways labour could gain retirements was to negotiate a mandatory age of separation or lower ages of compulsory, normal or early retirement. The normal retirement age remained 65 in all but one or two programmes, but union negotiators were able to adjust these other factors. Although older workers bitterly resented mandated retirement, and such a policy had previously entered negotiated plans primarily at the insistence of management, by 1965 compulsory retirement appeared in more bargained contracts and it arrived at younger ages. A Bankers Trust survey in 1960–65 of large corporate plans (1965, p.11) found compulsory retirement in 80 per cent of all bargained plans, up from 73 per cent in the late 1950s; and in those plans, the median age of mandated retirement had fallen from 68 to 65. Union negotiators were also able to increase the incidence of early retirement and liberalise its age and service requirements. Among multi-employer plans, Skolnik (1976, p.8) reports that 82 per cent included early retirement provisions in 1970 compared to just 23 per cent in 1960. While most CIO contracts already contained such provisions, the Bankers Trust (1965, p.13) found 89 per cent of the plans it surveyed in the early 1960s, versus 66 per cent in the late 1950s, allowed early retirement at the employee's election. And to induce such elections, the unions cut the actuarial reductions typically found in the earlier contracts – reductions reflecting the fewer years for accumulating investment income and the longer expected pay-out period for early retirees. In the late 1950s, just 16 per cent of the negotiated plans in the Bankers Trust survey paid early retirees more than the actuarial equivalent of their accrued plan benefits. And as social security benefits only commenced at age 65, or at age 62 with some reduction, reliance on a cut-back company pension was hardly attractive. By the early 1960s, however, 54 per cent of negotiated plans in the Bankers Trust survey paid early retirees more than the actuarial equivalent; and many also offered supplementary payments until the pensioner became eligible for full social security benefits.

Much to the chagrin of young workers and union leaders, the initiatives of the early 1960s failed to induce the desired workforce reductions. The unions had placed their greatest reliance on the new early retirement provisions, as most workers were already retiring at that age, and the various adjustments they had negotiated had little effect on retirement decisions. After several failures, most notably in the steel industry, the unions conducted series of investigations and discovered that pensions offered were simply too low to draw workers into retirement. For labour's programme to succeed, early retirement pensions would have to rise. Further reductions in the actuarial discount or increased pre-social security supplements would not suffice; basic plan benefits would have to rise.

The big CIO plans, reports Kryvicky (1981, pp.411–17), had replaced a steady 15 per cent of pre-retirement income from their inception until the early 1960s. When added to social security, total pension benefits had approximated 30 per cent of active earnings. But to stimulate early retirements, union negotiators in industries such as automobiles, steel and rubber pushed pension plan replacement rates to 30 per cent by the early 1970s. As social security allowances were also on the rise, workers in these basic industries could then retire on more than 50 per cent of pre-retirement pay. This rise in nominal replacement rates actually understates the real improvement in the retiree's economic status. Rising social security and income taxes, for example, absorbed ever greater portions of pre-retirement income; public and private pensions either escaped these levies or paid at lower rates. Retirees in the 1970s also owned more homes, household property, and financial instruments than their predecessors, and these assets provided significant streams of non-pension income. The unions, moreover, typically negotiated benefit increases for existing pensioners when raising allowances for new retirees. The entire pensioner population thus shared in benefit hikes resulting from inflation, plan liberalisation, or rising productivity. This expansion of retirement income, of which increased private pensions was a critical component, finally drew into retirement significant numbers of union workers.

With old age income at acceptable levels, liberalising the requirements for retirement was now to have a direct effect on labour supply. Union effort to reduce the active workforce thus took a major leap forward when in 1970 the UAW signed labour agreements allowing retirement after thirty years of service. Benefits in this plan were unreduced for retirements after age 62, reported Zink (1971), and they were only modestly discounted at earlier ages. The plan also paid supplementary benefits until employees became eligible for full social security pensions. The practical effect of the new arrangement was general retirement, on substantial allowances, between the ages of 58 and 62. Strong CIO unions in industries such as steel, copper, aluminium and containers, according to the Bankers Trust survey of the years 1970-75, also won 'thirty-and-out' in the early 1970s. The negotiated pension institution, originally focused on assuring minimal welfare benefits, thus became an instrument of labour market management.

Pension benefits in negotiated plans have not changed significantly since their expansion in the late 1960s. Nor is there much pressure for further improvement. Instead, the key question for the future is whether negotiated plans can continue providing the same level of benefit to the same proportion of the American workforce. And the answer, unfortunately, is probably no.

Limiting the continued strength and significance of the negotiated pension institution is the precipitous decline of unionism in the US economy. During the long period of pension development, in the 1950s and 1960s, union membership grew steadily, albeit slowly. According to the US Bureau of Labor Statistics (1988, p. 43, 1980, p.412) and the Bureau of the Census (1987, p. 424), unions represented 15,000,000 workers, 34.3 percent of US non-agricultural employment, in 1949, the year pensions became part of the standard negotiated contract. Membership rose to 19,381,000 by 1970, the year of 'thirty-and-out', and unions still spoke for 27.3 per cent of US employees. The number of organised workers stabilised in the 1970s – there were 20,246,000 organised workers in 1978 – but now they made up just 23.4 per cent of non-agricultural employment. Then in the 1980s, production worker employment in heavily organised US manufacturing industries fell before a wave of imported goods. Union membership slid 18 per cent in the seven years 1978–85, to stabilise at 16,595,000, but only 17 per cent of US employment. After such a decline in unionism, bargained pensions can hardly be expected to be as significant in the future as they were in the past.

As pointed out by Kryvicky (1981, pp. 408ff.), declining union membership exposed a second and more critical weakness in the negotiated pension institution – a significant funding deficiency. This was surprising, as unions had been vociferous champions of funding since the UAW-Chrysler strike of 1950. Labour nevertheless remained ambivalent when forced to choose between higher benefits and sounder finance. And as Treynor *et al.* (1976, pp. 39–58) point out, management, which had the basic funding responsibility in CIO programmes, had reasons of its own to underfund. So the financial management of negotiated plans systematically underestimated pension obligations and funding requirements. The actuaries calculated liabilities as though current dollar allowance would continue for all time. This was done even though subsequent contracts always raised benefits and the interest rate used to discount future pension obligations always incorporated expected inflation, the primary source of these increases. When pensions were raised in later negotiations, the actuaries merely increased the plan's existing past service liability and amortised, or stretched the repayment of these 'new' obligations over thirty years. A plan's initial past service liability, such as the huge sum assumed by Ford in 1949, was finite and was ultimately extinguished. But this continuous addition of fresh obligations, each amortised over a period much longer than the average employee's remaining active worklife, kept security forever ephemeral. With the arrival of early retirement and sharply higher replacement ratios, the reality of advance funding eroded still further: the thirty-year amortisation period remained unchanged even though fewer years of work now supported larger benefits over longer periods.

Kryvicky (1981, pp. 406–11, 419–20) graphically demonstrated the problem through a series of fifty-year simulations. According to Kryvicky's estimates, the negotiated plans of the 1950s could have expected expense as percentage of payroll to be constant and assets to stabilise at 45–60 per cent of total obligations. The critical 'advance funding ratio' (the asset/liability ratio calculated after meeting obligations to existing retirees) would eventually settle down in the 10–30 per cent range. But the new burdens of the 1960s – early retirement and higher benefits – increased pension expense while eroding the financial balance. Kryvicky estimated that contributions as a percentage of payroll would increase 20 to 90 per cent, depending on the actual reduction in the retirement age; the advance funding ratio would meanwhile settle at somewhere between –10 and 25 per cent. In other words, there would be few if any assets to cover obligations to active workers as annual contributions approximated liabilities for the year's cohort of new retirees. The plan would in effect be pursuing a 'terminal funding' policy, which is only slightly more sober than the straight pay-as-you-go of traditional union programmes. The equity accruing to the young and able, as in most social welfare schemes, had become cultural and political rather than economic.

The precipitous fall in union membership in the 1980s aggravated this weakness to the point of crisis. A shrunken workforce had to carry the fixed past service obligation, raising expense as a percentage of payroll. The lack of young workers, whose contributions exceeded the value of their benefit accruals, also eroded the plan's financial balance. Kryvicky (1981, pp. 423–4, 430) simulated a thirty-year 25 per cent workforce reduction – not altogether dissimilar from the 18 per cent membership decline from 1978 to 1985 – and found annual contributions rising to between 35 and 125 per cent above the 1950 baseline; thirty years after the workforce decline, the advance funding ratio falls to between –40 and 10 per cent. Assets are thus generally less than obligations to the retired; contributions, although enormous, are less than liabilities for new retirees. And unlike most other measures in Kryvicky's simulations, the advance funding ratio declines continuously, failing to converge to a stable level within the fifty-year time frame. Each year the plan grows more insolvent, becoming an accident waiting to happen.

In line with Kryvicky's projections, the 1980s were stressful times for negotiated pension plans. Their difficulties became painfully evident when the decade's economic pressures either induced or forced sponsors to terminate their pension schemes. Terminations triggered a settling-up process, making the insolvency apparent to all. They also precipitated the entry of the government's Pension Benefit Guarantee Corporation, established in 1974, which paid 'guaranteed' benefits and attached up to 30 per cent of the sponsor's net worth to finance this obligation. Large union plans, particularly those of the steel workers and secondarily those of the car workers, dominated the termination activity not only of the decade but of the entire post-war era. Including the huge LTV plans, which the government is attempting to 'restore' to the parent corporation, Ippolito (1988, Table 3.5) calculated that collectively bargained arrangements accounted for 95 per cent of the $4 billion in PBGC termination claims up till June 1986. As of 30 September 1987, terminated steel industry plans (largely although not entirely negotiated programmes) accounted for nearly 80 per cent of all claims ever filed against the PBGC and they were, on average, only 34 per cent funded on their date of termination.

One cannot comfortably predict the future of the negotiated pension institution. On the one hand, the foreign assault on US manufacturing appears to have abated, relieving the tremendous pressure it placed on the bargained plans. Union membership should rise, and their corporate employers should be able to avoid plan terminations. The government has also moved to shore up pension funding and is actively investigating further measures to improve plan balance sheets. But one cannot anticipate a simple revival in the bargained pension institution. The stepped-up contributions mandated by government to meet existing pension liabilities will absorb larger portions of labour compensation. And directing more of the surplus from the union's monopoly wage away from cash and current benefits will reduce the appeal of union employment to younger workers. More important, the financial climate of the 1980s has been unusually kind to pension plans and these favourable conditions cannot be expected to continue. Extra-ordinary increases in asset values in the 1980s caused pension funds to grow enormously, while persistently high interest rates heavily discounted future liabilities. Deft policy, a strong recovery in manufacturing, and continued good luck may allow the plans to escape in one piece. And barring a general economic crisis, the bargained pension institution should survive and pay benefits. But the most likely scenarios all call for a significant contraction in benefits and coverage.

The negotiated pension institution was the product of historical circumstances in the immediate post-war period. Initially a private welfare system serving modest and traditional social goals, the union plans were retooled in the 1960s to help clear the union labour markets. The high wages won through collective bargaining had stimulated a reduction in the quantity of labour demanded, and the unions adapted pensions in an expensive and ambitious programme of retirements. Old financial practices, never very conservative, became positively dangerous in the new regime. And with the decline in the heavily unionised industries, negotiated plans suffered sharp cutbacks and worse. The prominence of union programmes in the larger US private pension institution has as a result subsided, and the benchmark they provide for the rest of the universe has declined. The benefits provided to older union workers nevertheless maintain their claim on the compensation of everyone covered by the bargained agreement, and they are insured by a government agency. These claims have indeed become significant drags on the larger union and private pension institutions. Opportunities for younger union workers to gain comparable pensions are meanwhile less available. Unless the labour movement revives, expanding its reach while maintaining current benefit levels, this will be the case for the entire American population. As such a revival is highly unlikely, the larger private pension institution can be expected to make a smaller contribution to the future provision of American old age income.

## Acknowledgement

I would like to acknowledge the generous financial suppport of the Pension Research Council of the Wharton School of the University of Pennsylvania.

## Notes

1  Reed (1955, pp. 1027, 1019) found the UMW Welfare and Retirement Fund supporting 60,000 pensioners by 1955, nearly a quarter of the industry's active workforce and over a third of the workforce reduction over the previous decade.
2  Krug refused to go along with sole union management of the pension and welfare fund, as was typical in union schemes, and urged Congress to require, in Section 302 of the 1947 Taft-Hartley Act, joint union-management control over employer contributions to multi-employer welfare funds (Greenough and King, 1976, pp. 44, 65); the unions nevertheless tended to dominate their pension funds (see Finley, 1972, pp. 159–204 and James and James, 1965, pp. 213–317).
3  The NLRB took a 'forward' position in the Inland Steel decision, going far beyond the arguments made by either management or labour. The United Steelworkers complained that Inland Steel, by unilaterally reinstating compulsory retirement in 1946, violated a previously negotiated separation policy. Inland claimed that retirement policy was part of its pension plan, and thus beyond the purview of collective bargaining. Rather than narrowly uphold labour's position, the NLRB ruled that all 'emoluments of value, like pensions and insurance benefits' were 'wages', and that 'matters affecting tenure of employment, like the ... retirement rule' were 'conditions of employment'. Pension plans in their entirety therefore lay 'within the statutory scope of collective bargaining' (NLRB, 1948; see also Dearing, 1954, pp. 42–5; Joint Committee on Labor-Management Relations, 1949, pp. 94–5; Selekman et al., 1950, pp. 326, 340–6, 577–8).
4  The Steel Industry Board used the accounting concept of depreciation imprecisely, as depreciation is neither a measure of an asset's falling productivity nor a charge used to accumulate replacement costs. Rather, depreciation matches the expense of a durable asset with the value it delivers: it spreads an asset's cost over its useful life. There is a proper pension analogy to the accountant's depreciation. Viewing a worker as an economic entity – and the cost of that entity as the worker's income – an accounting approach could justify pensions as a form of lifetime income spreading. Labour's true cost is not just its income while at work, but its income over an entire lifetime. A depreciation approach would expense this cost – the lifetime income – over the worker's period of productive economic activity. The proper analogy to the accountant's 'depreciation' is thus accrual of benefit credits that spreads the cost of the old age annuity over the employee's active working lifetime. What remains unclear, however, is how depreciation theory justifies employer provision of pension benefits and employer responsibility for past service accruals. A retirement income programme could just as logically be funded and managed by the individual worker. US Steel's Enders Voorhees (SIB, 1949, p. 10) in fact argued that pensions ought to be an individual responsibility:

US Steel takes care of and replenishes its materials and machinery because it owns them ... Machines are not paid current wages which they can freely elect to spend or to save. US Steel does not own its employees; they are free men, each entitled to the respect of the other as such. US Steel 'cares for' – cooperates with – its employees by paying money to them representing the full value of services rendered, as judged by the public as customers.

The Steel Industry Board's assignment of pension responsibility to the employers is better seen as a statement of social welfare policy. In effect, the SIB adapted the morality of the Elizabethan poor law to modern industrial conditions: the ancient statute made propertied interests responsible for local welfare burdens; the SIB defined the firm, not the parish, as the relevant local economy. The spirit of depreciation accounting actually runs counter to such a welfare approach, as properly accruing and funding old age pension expense would eliminate future dependence. The depreciation approach lends itself to a programme of savings or insurance, not welfare.

5   In 1950 Congress did raise social security benefits dramatically, increasing the maximum allowance to $80 from $46. The proposed SIB corporate pension would thereby fall 63 per cent, from $54 to $20.

# References

American Federation of Labour (AFL), (1944), 'The Federation's postwar program', *American Federationist* (May), reprinted in E. W. Bakke and C. Kerr (eds) (1948), *Unions, Management, and the Public,* New York, Harcourt Brace.

American Institute of Certified Public Accountants (1948), *Pension Plans – Accounting for Annuity Costs Based on Past Service, Accounting Research Bulletin,* no. 36, New York, American Institute of Certified Public Accountants.

Bankers Trust (1965), *1965 Study of Industrial Retirement Plans,* New York, Bankers Trust.

Barbash, J. (1967), 'The structure and evolution of union interest in pensions', in US Joint Economic Committee, *Old Age Income Assurance,* Part IV: *Employment Aspects of Pension Plans,* 90th Cong., 1st Sess., Washington, DC, Government Printing Office.

Bartell, H. R., Jr and Simpson, E. T. (1968), *Pension Funds of Multiemployer Industrial Groups, Unions, and Nonprofit Organizations,* Occasional Paper no. 105, New York, National Bureau of Economic Research.

Bureau of the Census (1987), *Statistical Abstract of the United States,* Washington, DC, Government Printing Office.

Congress of Industrial Organisations (CIO) (1946), 'Resolutions', *CIO News* (25 November) reprinted in E. W. Bakke and C. Kerr (eds) (1948), *Unions, Management, and the Public,* New York, Harcourt Brace.

Dearing, C. (1954), *Industrial Pensions,* Washington, DC, Brookings Institution.

Ellwood, D. T. (1985), 'Pensions and the labor market: a starting point (the mouse can roar)', in D. A. Wise (ed.) (1985), *Pensions, Labor, and Individual Choice,* Chicago, National Bureau of Economic Research.

Finley, J. E. (1972), *The Corrupt Kingdom,* New York, Simon & Schuster.

Freeman, R. (1985), 'Unions, pension, and union pension funds', in D. A. Wise (ed.) (1985), *Pensions, Labor, and Individual Choice,* Chicago, National Bureau of Economic Research.

Goodman, E. K. (1970), *National Union Benefit Plans, 1947–1967,* Washington, DC, US Department of Labor, Labor-Management Services Administration, Office of Labor-Management Policy Development.

Graebner, W. (1980), *A History of Retirement,* New Haven, Connecticut, Yale University Press.

Greenough, W. C. and King, F. P. (1976), *Pension Plans and Public Policy,* New York, Columbia University Press.

Hamilton, J. A. and Bronson, D. C. (1958), *Pensions*, New York, McGraw-Hill.

Harris, H. J. (1982), *The Right To Manage: Industrial Relations Policies of American Business in the 1940s*, Madison, University of Wisconsin Press.

Ippolito, Richard A. (1988), 'The economics of pension insurance', *MS*, May.

James, R. C. and James, E. D. (1965), *Hoffa and the Teamsters*, Princeton, New Jersey, Van Nostrand.

Joint Committee on Labor-Management Relations (1949), *Report of the Joint Committee on Labor-Management Relations*, 80th Cong., 2nd Sess., Washington, DC, Government Printing Office.

Kerr, Clark (1949), 'Social and economic implications of private pension plans', *The Commercial and Financial Chronicle*, I, December, in Reprint no. 16, University of California Institute of Industrial Relations, Berkeley.

Kryvicky, R. C. (1981), 'The funding of negotiated pension plans', *Transactions of the Society of Actuaries*, XXXIII, pp. 405–72.

Latimer, M. W. (1932), *Trade Union Pension Systems and Other Superannuation and Permanent and Total Disability Benefits in the United States and Canada*, New York, Industrial Relations Counselors.

Lewis, J. L. (1955), Statement to US Congress, Senate, Committee on Labor and Public Welfare, Welfare and Pension Plans Investigation, Hearings Before a Subcommittee of the Committee on Labor and Public Welfare, 84th Cong., 1st Sess., Washington, DC, Government Printing Office.

Munnell, A. (1982), *The Economics of Private Pensions*, Washington, DC, Brookings Institution.

National Labor Relations Board (NLRB), (1948), Inland Steel Company v. United Steelworkers of America (CIO), 77 NLRB 4 (1948).

Peterson, F. (1945), *American Labor Unions: What They Are and How They Work*, New York, Harper & Brothers.

Reed, L. S. (1955), Report submitted to US Congress, Senate, Committee on Labor and Public Welfare, Welfare and Pension Plans Investigation, Hearings Before a Subcommittee of the Committee on Labor and Public Welfare, 84th Cong., 1st Sess., Washington, DC, Government Printing Office.

Reuther, W. (1950), Testimony, Social Security Revision, Hearings before the Senate Finance Committee, 81st Cong., 2nd Sess., Part 3, Washington, DC, Government Printing Office.

Selekman, B. M., Selekman, S. K. and Fuller, S. H. (1950), *Problems in Labor Relations*, New York, McGraw-Hill.

Skolnik, A. M. (1976), 'Private pension plans, 1950–74', *Social Security Bulletin*, XXXIX, 6, pp. 4–5.

Steel Industry Board (1949), *Report to the President of the United States on the Labor Dispute in the Basic Steel Industry*, Washington, DC, Government Printing Office.

Treynor, J., Regan, P. and Priest, W. (1976), *The Financial Reality of Pension Funding Under ERISA*, Homewood, Illinois, Dow Jones-Irwin.

US Bureau of Labor Statistics (1962), *Multiemployer Pension Plans under Collective Bargaining*, Bulletin no. 1360 (Spring 1960), Washington, DC, US BLS.

US Bureau of Labor Statistics (1980), *1980 Handbook of Labor Statistics*, Washington, DC, US BLS.

US Bureau of Labor Statistics (1988), *Employment and Earnings*, Washington, DC, US BLS (September).

Zink, V. (1971), '1970 General Motors settlement', offprint of address given to American Pension Conference, New York (21 January).

# 7

# Public Pensions as Intergenerational Transfers in the United States

## W. Andrew Achenbaum

'We were formed to promote stewardship in the name of younger and future generations,' declared Paul Hewitt, a member of the US baby boom cohort who served as first executive director of a new citizens' lobby, Americans for Generational Equity (AGE). 'Our social insurance programs don't seem safe.... In every area of public policy we've borrowed from our grandchildren' (S. Kaplan, 1987, p. 13). Established during the second Reagan administration, AGE has been calling for economic justice for young adults and proposing cuts in the nation's social security system. Many academics and defenders of the status quo have voiced alarm over the rhetoric. According to *Ties That Bind*, a report of the Gerontological Society of America, the generational equity debate is 'a cynical and purposively divisive strategy put forth to justify and build political support for attacks on policies and reductions in programs that benefit all age groups' (Kingson *et al.*, 1986, pp. 13–14). If so, it has hit a raw nerve. Richard Lamm, former governor of Colorado and AGE board member, sees merit in late-life euthanasia to counterbalance the excesses of the 'prodigal father'. Ethicist Daniel Callihan, a member of AGE's advisory board, advocates using chronological age as a clear, simple criterion for the (negative) allocation of health care resources. The case he makes in his book *Setting Limits* (1987) was featured in *Time*, the op-ed page (page written by readers) of the *New York Times*, and on television. AGE has been asked to share statistical data, conference reports and its expertise as debators and their coaches in 20,000 American high schools debate whether 'the federal government should implement a comprehensive program to guarantee retirement security for all US citizens over the age of 65' (Fawcett, 1988). But has AGE foisted an extraneous issue on to the US policy agenda? Or, will the issue of intergenerational justice become the basis for a power struggle in a rapidly ageing society?

Framing public choices in terms of competition and conflict between generations is not new (Esler, 1984). The potential fight between the kids and the canes reverberates especially throughout the American experience. 'For America in her infancy to adopt the maxims of the Old World,' warned Noah Webster in his popular spelling book, 'would be to stamp the wrinkles of old age upon the bloom of youth' (Kaestle, 1983, p. 6). Having overthrown the British crown, leaders of the young republic had no desire to subject themselves to the tyranny of their elders. Thomas Jefferson, author of the US Declaration of Independence, wrote to James Madison in 1789:

> The *earth belongs in usufruct to the living*.... No man can, by *natural right*, oblige the lands he occupied, or the persons who succeed him in that occupation, to the payment of debts contracted by him. For if he could, he might during his life, eat up the usufruct of the lands for generations to come; and then the lands would belong to the dead, and not to the living.... The conclusion then, is, that neither the representatives of a nation, nor the whole nation itself assembled, can validly engage debts beyond what they may pay in their own time, that is to say, within thirty-four years of the date of the engagement. (Koch and Peden, 1944, pp. 488–90).

Thirty years later, at age 76, Jefferson observed, 'Each generation is as independent of the one preceding, as that was of all which had gone before. It has, then, like them, a right to choose for itself the form of government it believes most promotive of its own happiness' (*ibid.*, p. 675; Maier, 1980).

The notion that Americans could repudiate their elders as they looked forward became a central cultural tenet. 'Not only does democracy make every man forget his ancestors, but it hides his descendants and separates his contemporaries from him,' Alexis de Tocqueville contended in 1836. 'It throws him back forever upon himself alone, and threatens in the end to confine him entirely within the solitude of his own heart' (p. 194). D. H. Lawrence detected the same pattern in his *Studies in Classic American Literature* (1923, p. 54): 'There is a gradual sloughing of the old skin, towards a new youth. It is the myth of America.' In the wake of the tumultuous 1960s, commentators saw the battle lines being drawn for the current generational skirmish. Philip Slater (1970, p. 61) observes that 'the young are challenging the fundamental premises on which their elders have based their lives, and they are attacking at all of the weakest points'. Christopher Lasch, stressing that the young feared growing old in a *Culture of Narcissism* (1978), goes on to put some of the blame on the aged: 'Because the older generation no longer thinks of itself as living in the next, of achieving a vicarious immortality in posterity, it does not give way gracefully to the young' (p. 213).

Those who join AGE in decrying present generational inequities point to three novel features in the American condition that warrant consideration. The first is the magnitude of population ageing: 'By having fewer children and living longer than any Americans in history, the baby boomers will become the first cohort of senior citizens unable to draw on the economic output and financial support of a much larger number of younger Americans,' argues Philip Longman in *Born to Pay* (1987, p. 3). The second is economic: instead of saving limited resources and investing in youth, the nation is consuming too much and saddling its children with debt (Davis and van den Oever, 1981; Hewitt and Howe, 1988). Above all the generational equity debate rests on a political dilemma. 'It is fair to assume that the United States has become the first society in history in which a person is more likely to be poor if young rather than old,' contends Senator Daniel Patrick Moynihan (1987, p. 112). 'Wide disparities in the main benefit programs serving children and the elderly contributed to this dramatic change in the composition of poverty.' Are these propositions equally valid?

Talk about the 'graying' of America has become so commonplace that commentators frequently overlook two points that might temper dire rhetoric. On the one hand, except for some racial and ethnic variations, trends in the United States do not differ markedly from those that obtain in other advanced industrial societies (Siegel and Taeuber, 1986; US Senate, 1988). There are proportionately more older people in Japan and many western European countries than in the United States; solutions abroad to common challenges may prove instructive. On the other hand, because the impact of declines in fertility is greater than advances in adult longevity, the 'overall dependency ratio' in the US is not expected to exceed levels attained in 1964 for the next sixty-five years. And should more older people (especially women) be inclined to seek part-time employment, then pressures on public retirement pensions will be lessened (Moody, 1988). Such factors should not lead to complacency about the demographic imperatives behind political reform but neither do they appear to demand immediate action.

Alarm over the state of the US economy is, however, cause for action, but not because Medicare (the elderly's hospital insurance programme) may be spiralling towards bankruptcy or because the aged are getting more out of the American system than they have contributed. As a result of changes in the tax code and increases in defence spending enacted during the Reagan administration, a budget deficit that had taken nearly two centuries to accrue doubled in eight years (Sawhill, 1988). Furthermore, the penchant for automatically adjusting public policy expenditures for inflation – which currently affects 30 per cent of the federal budget directly and another 20 per cent indirectly – constrains congressional options in reducing the deficit or changing priorities (R. K. Weaver, 1988; Ippolito, 1981).

Because government programmes have considerable impact on the US political economy, the generational equity debate not surprisingly focuses on public policy making. At a time when the average US married couple has more parents than children, it is striking that total federal outlays on child-orientated programmes (Aid to Families with Dependent Children (AFDC), Head Start, food stamps, child health and nutrition, and aid to education) was roughly a sixth of total spending for the elderly in 1984 (Preston, 1984). Between 1970 and 1984, the average expenditure per social security recipient increased 54 per cent in constant-dollar terms while the average AFDC expenditure declined 34 per cent. No wonder that social security, which is the country's largest and costliest domestic programme, has been attacked by Americans for Generational Equity.

A major challenge of US social security policy making has become to defuse the charge of unfairness associated with age-based entitlements by convincing people of all ages that it remains in everyone's best interest to minimise old-age dependency. The case for public pensions as intergenerational transfers has always depended on persuading workers that they will benefit in due course from helping senior citizens now. Such a proposition has never been terribly convincing philosophically, given the North American way of policy making. But until recently, trends in US history had enabled social security advocates to muster a solid argument on pragmatic grounds. The following discussion focuses on US attempts to provide public support for the aged from the 1930s to the present. Particular attention is given to the ways in which Americans have grappled – and failed to deal – with generational issues in developing their public policy.

## Tensions in the original Social Security Act

Relieving older Americans from financial straits was a primary – but not the only – objective of the original Social Security Act. The Great Depression had exposed the weakness and inadequacies of existing means of preventing and coping with dependency. Those means varied enormously from state to state. By 1933, twenty-one states and Alaska and Hawaii operated old-age relief programmes; seven other jurisdictions made coverage optional at the county level. Roughly half the states adopted age 65 as the minimum age for receiving a pension; the other half selected 70; in North Dakota, a potential beneficiary had to be at least 68. Most states imposed residency requirements and set income and/or property limits; New York required that recipients be wholly incapable of supporting themselves. Three jurisdictions established no 'means test'. The typical Maryland senior citizen on relief received a monthly pension worth $29.90, nearly five times greater than that paid in Indiana; the average nationwide in 1933 was $19.25 (US Bureau of Labor Statistics, 1932; Lubove, 1968; C. L. Weaver, 1982).

At least three different utopian schemes advanced between 1933 and 1935 promised older people far greater assistance than was available from the state or private charity. Upton Sinclair wanted to grant pensions worth $50 to all Californians who had resided in the state for at least three years. Senator Huey P. Long's 'Share Our Wealth' Society promised $30 a month to all citizens over 60 with annual incomes of less than $1,000 and property valued at not more than $10,000. Dr Frances E. Townsend rallied millions of frustrated older Americans behind her proposal that all persons over 60 be given $200 monthly, on the conditions that they not be gainfully employed and that they spend their pensions within thirty days. The allowances were to be financed from the proceeds of a new nationwide tax on transactions (Putnam, 1970; Neuberger and Loe, 1936; Committee on Old-Age Security, 1936). Providing a flat grant at a level deemed 'adequate' to permit an older person to live comfortably had wide appeal.

The Committee on Economic Security (CES), assigned the task of formulating an income maintenance measure for President Franklin D.

Roosevelt, was clearly mindful of the appeal of the Townsend Plan and other panaceas. Although the architects of social security presumed that public assistance would always be an integral part of any plan to prevent old-age indigency and promote the elderly's well-being, they did not expect it to be the cornerstone:

> An effective old-age security program for this country involves not a choice between assistance and insurance but a combination of the two.... Regular benefits are unquestionably to be preferred to assistance grants.... Assistance, moreover, in fairness to the legitimate demands of other needy groups, must limit all grants to a minimum standard. Insurance benefits, on the other hand, can be ample for a comfortable existence, bearing some relation to customary wage standards. (US Committee on Economic Security, 1937, pp. 189–90)

Congress reworked the bill drafted by the Committee on Economic Security in ways that reinforced the reciprocal relationship between welfare and insurance. A proposal to offer government-administered voluntary annuities was dropped. Under Title I of the original Social Security Act, Congress initially appropriated $49,750,000 'for the purpose of enabling each State to furnish financial assistance, as far as practicable under the conditions in such State, to aged needy individuals'. Under an old age insurance scheme (Title II), plans called for raising funds for an Old-Age Reserve Account by imposing an annual 0.5 per cent tax on an employee's covered wages (up to $3,000) and collecting the same amount from his or her employer. After 1 January 1942, people over 65 who had contributed a sufficient amount would be able to collect a monthly pension (worth up to $85) based on those prior contributions. As the Senate Finance Committee noted, this approach at once 'represents a minimum of what the American people have a right to expect' and would 'go far toward realizing "the ambition of the individual to obtain for him and his a proper security"'(US Senate, 74th Congress, 1935a, p. 28; Douglas, 1936; Brown, 1969).

Title I did not ensure that old-age assistance be either uniform or equitable throughout the nation. The CES bill had stipulated that states provide 'subsistence compatible with decency and health' in order to establish minimum national standards for helping needy older Americans. In the course of congressional hearings, however, several corporate executives, senators and the president of the US Chamber of Commerce denounced the phrase as an infringement on a state's sovereignty and complained about the difficulties in defining and implementing 'decency' (US Social Security Board, 1935; US Senate, 74th Congress, 1935b). As a result, the maximum amount of personal and real property, income and child support an aged person could possess and still qualify for relief varied greatly.

Besides inequities in state eligibility requirements, elderly Americans who were equally poor were not treated equally under Title I. The average Mississippian receiving old-age assistance was given $3.92 a month in 1936; the average pension in California was $31.36. Even taking into account differences in the cost of living, such variance in the average level of support was truly astounding. Furthermore, since federal aid under Title I was an inducement to states to disburse pensions to the elderly on a matching basis, the operation of Title I could be 'equitable' without being 'adequate'. Thus, citizens in Arizona, Georgia, Kansas, North and South Carolina, Tennessee and Virginia received no aid from Washington as late as 1937, because legislators in their states had not yet established a relief programme; older people in Nevada were denied federal assistance, because the state's pension law remained optional at the county level.

Nor were all workers able to reduce the likelihood of old-age dependency through the nation's new system of social insurance. At least 9.4 million wage earners (including farmers, domestic servants and government employees) were not required initially to contribute to the programme. And since the law did not mandate that 'employers' make contributions for their own later years, it was not certain how many people would actually participate in the programme: economists at the time estimated that 7 or 8 million workers were intermittently or simultaneously 'employers' and 'employees' (US House of Representatives, 74th Congress, 1935; Douglas, 1936; Woytinsky, 1936).

Older people, moreover, could not rely solely on Title II benefits. Suppose a worker who was 60 years old in 1937 (when social security contributions would first be collected) satisfied the requirements that he or she have five years of covered employment for receiving benefits (initially scheduled to be distributed in 1942). If that employee had earned on the average $600 each year during this period, he or she could have expected a pension worth $15 a month. Had that worker earned five times that amount, the pension would still have been only $25 a month (C. L. Weaver, 1982). To put these dollar amounts into perspective, the average *weekly* earnings for production workers – the very category of people to be covered by social security at the outset – were $23.82. By 1942 the figure had risen to $36.68 (US Department of Commerce, 1975). Social security obviously did not replace all earnings; intergenerational transfers would hardly enrich the old. Still, it was designed to provide a floor for retirement income.

With the passage of the Social Security Act in 1935, an important initiative had been undertaken to relieve older people in desperate straits and to help younger workers make provisions to prevent old-age dependency. Once this cornerstone was in place, policy makers hoped that a more balanced programme between insurance and assistance would evolve. While we shall limit our analysis to the evolution and impact of Titles I and II, it should be noted that the 1935 Social Security Act also addressed the needs of citizens who were not 'old'. Under Titles III and IX Congress guaranteed funds for a public-private unemployment scheme. Nearly $25 million was allocated as 'aid to dependent children' under Title IV; relief for the blind was provided under Title X. The other titles authorised grants to states for maternal and child welfare, vocational rehabilitation, and to the Public Health Service. Rather than promise *trans-generational* protection from cradle to grave as the Beveridge Report would recommend, the creators of US social security used 'age' as a surrogate for identifying segments of the population vulnerable to various social risks

(Achenbaum, 1986a). Such a tack, as we shall see, fostered cohort-centric perspectives concerning the impact of social security on workers and pensioners.

## The significance of the 1939 amendments

In its initial public relations campaign, the Social Security Board tried to convince Americans that social insurance was not the alien institution which its unfamiliar terminology and new-fangled identification cards made it appear. Social security 'makes extensive use of the principles of insurance which have been accepted by the American people to such a degree that there is more insurance in the United States than all other countries combined' (Witte, 1962, p. 11). Far from dampening an individual's responsibility to save and to make provisions for his or her family, social security enabled employees in a way consistent with 'the fundamentals of our capitalistic and individualistic economy'. Workers earned 'a right' to future benefits – not a 'dole' – that would bear a relationship to the amount that had been deducted from their wages over the years (Cates, 1983; Davis, 1979).

And yet the analogy could be overdrawn. Purchasing private insurance was a voluntary decision; contributing to social security was required of all covered under the system. Commercial insurance companies tried to anticipate and cater to the needs of the *individual* buyer in order to make profits. Social insurance, in contrast, was moulded by *society's* need to reduce the cost of unemployment or old-age dependency, hazards borne by the public when citizens could not take care of themselves. Reinhold Hohaus, vice-president and actuary of the Metropolitan Life Insurance Company, claimed in 1938 that guaranteeing a 'precise' relationship between contributions and benefits, which was critical to his business, should be secondary to the goal of assuring 'social adequacy' under social insurance (Hohaus, 1960). Hohaus well understood that most Americans did not understand the difference between commercial insurance and social insurance. He was willing to capitalise on the fuzziness to enable the latter concept to take root. Social security would more fully achieve the primary objectives of social insurance, in Hohaus's view, if benefits (particularly for the initial recipients) were liberalised and coverage extended as far as practicable.

Hohaus's critique of Title II's goals and functions received a hearing before the first old-age pension was ever paid. An economic downturn, President Roosevelt's evolving political agenda, the continuing strength of the Townsend movement and a larger than anticipated reserve fund impelled a fresh look at the social security system. Social security officials feared that if the old-age assistance programme were greatly expanded to mollify public demand, Congress might be reluctant to liberalise the contributory pension programme in the future. The social security leadership presumed that the 'stigma' associated with any means-tested relief would constrain popular support for any old-age assistance programme, and that in the long run, the public would recognise the advantages of *preventing* the incidence of dependency in later years afforded by old-age insurance.

The 1939 amendments to the Social Security Act placed greater emphasis on the 'social adequacy' aspects of social insurance than had appeared in the initial version. More people, including employees of banks and loan associations and seamen, were covered by the programme. The first monthly benefits became payable two years earlier than scheduled. Probably the most significant change was that Congress established monthly benefits for the survivors and dependants of retired workers. By introducing a whole new set of eligibility criteria and payment schedules for elderly wives, elderly widows, widows with children, dependent children, surviving children and, under certain circumstances, the needy parents of workers who had died, policy makers underscored through social legislation the importance of maintaining the family's integrity. Rather than raise taxes to cover the costs of increased coverage, Congress opted for a 'pay-as-you-go' system of financing.

'Safeguarding the family against economic hazards is one of the major purposes of modern social legislation,' observed John McCormack in the House debate. 'Old-age legislation, contributory and noncontributory, unemployment compensation, mothers' aid, and general relief by several States and their political subdivisions, aid to the blind and incapacitated, all have an important bearing on preserving the family life' (*Congressional Record*, 1939, p. 6964). Social Security Administration data sustains the point. Nearly a quarter of the old-age insurance beneficiaries in 1940 were 'survivors' under 18. And yet, under the 1939 amendments, protection was still related to the amount a wage earner had contributed to the system. Nor had federally supervised old-age insurance become a universal right: pensions would be paid only to those 'dependants' and survivors who qualified for support because of their relationship to a worker who satisfied the system's eligibility criteria.

Thus the 1939 amendments to the Social Security Act put considerations of adequacy and concern for equity into dynamic equilibrium. More than had been the case at the outset, social insurance was designed to provide (through the prudent management of a limited amount of funds) a minimal level of support for a worker and his or her family. As revised, Title II was not primarily a welfare package, but it no longer so closely resembled a private insurance annuity. Therein lie both the grounds for the system's subsequent development and a major reason why social insurance's purposes have been so often misunderstood and misrepresented in the United States.

Thoughtful commentators were concerned that the enactment and maturation of a governmental social insurance programme in the United States would pit the immediate claims of the old against the legitimate interests of the young. Were intergenerational transfers from workers to pensioners a sustainable arrangement, they wondered, in an uncertain economy? In forecasting a 'nation of elders in the making', social scientists and journalists in the 1930s speculated that addressing the financial needs of older Americans might disrupt national production, consumption and inheritance patterns, and thereby threaten the stability of the country's economic and political institutions (Thompson and Whelpton, 1930; Dallach, 1933; Chen, 1939; Linton 1942). Social security's architects themselves expressed reservations about the wisdom of seeming to give the aged preferential treatment. 'The only result' of changes in financing public pensions that were adopted in 1939, an internal memorandum confided, 'may be that the present younger workers are taxed for the increased benefits to the older people without any assurance whatsoever that they will get similar benefits when they are old' (Witte, 1939).

## Staying the course, 1940–63

Talk of the generational implications of social security came to little, however. The evolution of the system was spearheaded by those who wanted to go further in promoting 'social adequacy' by expanding the scope and impact of social insurance (Altmeyer, 1942). Yet during the war Congress was disinclined to expand the Title II programme. Consequently, twice as many people in 1949 were receiving old-age assistance as were drawing Old Age and Survivors Insurance (OASI) (Title II) benefits; the average Old Age Assistance (OAA) (Title I) benefit was $42 a month, compared to the average Title II retirement cheque of $25 – a figure that was only 10 per cent greater than it had been in 1939. Such statistics were disturbing to those who felt that 'from the standpoint of freedom, democratic values, and economic incentives', social insurance was preferable to relief. 'The goal of a progressive social security program should be to reduce the need for assistance to the smallest extent possible' (Ball, 1947, p. 343; Hilliard, 1946; Altmeyer, 1968).

Under the 1950 amendments, nearly 8 million employees (including agricultural workers and domestic servants) were brought into the system, and voluntary coverage was extended to another 2.5 million workers. New beneficiary categories and reduced eligibility requirements afforded more people a higher level of 'basic' protection than ever before. Average benefits for current recipients were increased 77.5 per cent – a boost that exceeded the rise in prices since 1937 by 1.5 per cent, though it represented only two-thirds of the increase in wage levels (*Annual Report of the Federal Security Administration: 1951*, 1952). The expansion of old-age insurance continued during the Eisenhower administration. Amendments enacted in 1954, 1956, and 1958 increased and liberalised benefits, extended compulsory coverage, and introduced new programmes, such as disability insurance. Conservatives' resistance to programme expansion was overwhelmed by the legitimacy the federal old-age insurance programme had gained during its first quarter-century of operation.

More and more Americans perceived social security to be indispensable to their future welfare. About 222,000 Americans received Title II benefits in December 1940; two decades later, the figure exceeded 14.8 million (*Social Security Bulletin*, 1978). Furthermore, a reciprocal relationship between old-age assistance and insurance seemed to be emerging – just as social security policy makers had anticipated. In February 1951, the number of persons receiving old-age insurance pensions for the first time exceeded the number receiving Title I benefits; six months later, more money was distributed to Americans through Title II than through Title I. Officials used such evidence to foster the belief that public assistance for the aged would continue to diminish in the years ahead (Cohen, 1952; Steiner, 1974).

The proportion of the workforce paying social security's taxes grew. The total number of contributors expanded at a faster rate than the current number of beneficiaries. As income rose in a booming economy, the system collected more and more revenue, making it possible to raise benefit levels as wage levels increased without making a noticeable dent in taxpayers' take-home pay. Hence policy makers were able to promote 'social adequacy' as they capitalised on prosperity – all the while honouring a definition of equity that had long demanded that benefits bear some relationship to contributions. Particularly in the 1950s, Americans affirmed their belief that poverty would continue to wither away if government provided financial incentives to encourage people to work. The public and private sectors assumed complementary, not adversary, positions: efforts to care for those in need should not be abandoned, but no initiative should threaten the pre-eminent value placed on ensuring a fair return – and, ideally, a handsome profit – on investments of time and energy. Such preferences and assumptions were imbued with a middle-class vision of reality, wherein American capitalism would continue to flourish with few imperfections or inequities in its power to allocate jobs and to create economic rewards (Free and Cantril, 1967; Patterson, 1981).

While the increasing availability and generosity of social security benefits certainly reduced the incidence of poverty among older Americans, it had not eliminated the risk. A sizeable proportion of the elderly were in desperate straits. The Social Security Administration reported that 35.2 per cent of all men and women over 65 had inadequate incomes in 1959. James Morgan and his associates at the University of Michigan estimated that whereas 28 per cent of all American families were potential welfare recipients, 48 per cent of all households headed by an aged person in 1959 were in this predicament. This paradox of poverty amidst prosperity was soon to move the nation.

## Americans build a 'Great Society'

In the depths of the Great Depression, preserving the democratic policy, reviving the economy and delivering immediate financial relief to needy Americans were the major items on the policy agenda. In contrast, those who advised John F. Kennedy and Lyndon B. Johnson believed that America's blessings would continue indefinitely. With an expanding economy and rising productivity, policy makers were confident that all citizens could look forward to a better standard of living (Orshansky, 1965b). Significant progress in helping the poor would require a more progressive distribution of incomes, but few anticipated that a *radical* shift would be necessary. In its 1964 report, the Council of Economic Advisers estimated that approximately $11 billion would guarantee all poor families at least $3,000 in income a year. That figure represented less than one-fifth of the then current defence budget and less than 2 per cent of the Gross National Product (US President, 1964; Dunne, 1964; Brauer, 1982). Money and commitment would make all good things possible.

To peg the true cost of waging a war on poverty, policy makers needed an instrument to gauge the full dimensions of need in America. The index of poverty adopted by federal officials to define the policy problem was originally developed by Mollie Orshansky, an economist in the Social Security Admini-stration. Orshansky's standard attempted to calculate the amount of money required to enable people to eat a minimal yet balanced diet and still have enough dollars left over to pay for all other essentials of living. From the start, critics questioned the validity of the measure. All Orshansky's figures were predicated on the assumption that an average family of four could maintain an adequate daily diet for 70 cents per person and would need only $1.40 for all other vital items, including housing, medical care, clothing and transportation. 'The standard itself is admittedly arbitrary, but not unreasonable,' she contended. Almost half of all Americans who lived alone or with non-relatives were 'poor', according to Orshansky (1965a, 1976). So were 14 per cent of all of the nation's families; the incidence of poverty among households headed by women and blacks far exceeded the national average. Furthermore, 40 per cent of all men and nearly 65 per cent of all women over 65 who lived alone in 1963 had an income below 'the economy level'.

'Whatever definition of poverty is used, a significant proportion of the Nation's poor are aged and a large proportion of the aged are poor,' claimed Wilbur J. Cohen (1966), the first employee of the Social Security Administration who had risen to become Assistant Secretary of Health, Education and Welfare. 'Only through improvements in their economic status can we make progress toward our national goal of reducing and eventually eliminating poverty.' To remedy the situation, Cohen recommended a 'decent income in retirement' through higher social security benefits, better private pension plans and greater opportunities to save, 'the best health care that modern medical science can provide', adequate housing, a complete and accessible range of community and social services, and greater opportunities for the elderly to choose the sort of 'meaningful' lifestyle they wanted to pursue. Cohen's agenda was consistent with the 1965 Older Americans Act. So were improved benefits under Titles I and II and their analogues, the new Medicare and Medicaid programmes, which made hospital care and medical assistance accessible to the age group in the poorest health (Achenbaum, 1983). Promises to ameliorate the quality of late life represent an important shift in public policy priorities in the 1960s. No one, however, was suggesting that the elderly were benefiting at the expense of the young or middle-aged.

Even the most fervid Great Society dreamer knew that the equity issue (in a financial rather than a generational sense) remained dear to middle-class America. Special efforts were made to demonstrate the advantages of social insurance throughout an average person's life course. Ida C. Merriam, an assistant commissioner of social security, traced the protection and benefits that the 2,270,000 Americans born in 1935 had received through the first thirty-three years of their lives. She found that 140,000 members of this 'social-security generation' had received or were receiving benefits, mostly because they were the children of retired or deceased workers insured under the programme (though 8,000 were currently entitled to benefits due to their own childhood disability). Merriam was also able to calculate the number of people deriving support from social security who were potentially or actually dependent on this age cohort. She noted that 750,000 of the parents of the group under consideration were receiving Title II benefits in 1968, thereby relieving the 33-year-olds with children of their own to support of much of their financial responsibility to their mothers and fathers. And because 13,000 workers in the social security generation had become eligible for Old Age and Survivors Disability Insurance (OASDI) or Old Age and Survivors Disability and Hospital Insurance (OASDHI) benefits before they died or became disabled, 57,000 of their survivors or dependants were receiving pensions. Indeed, 16,000 women born in 1935 were already entitled to widow's benefits, and another 7,000 got benefits because their husbands were disabled (Merriam, 1968). Even at this stage in their lives, Merriam concluded, young adults had benefited greatly from the expansion and liberalisation of social security: they had gained a measure of financial security on the basis of their 'stake' in the system long before they attained old age.

Furthermore, the concern for equity enshrined in the social insurance programme also spared many older Americans the curse of dependency. 'Had it not been for OASDHI benefits,' Social Security Administration researchers found, 'two to three times as many beneficiary couples would have been classified as poor in 1967 – more than half of all the beneficiary couples – instead of one fifth,' (Bixby *et al.*, 1975, p. 138). Independent experts confirmed that the intergenerational transfer system significantly reduced the extent of old-age poverty in America. Benefit increases enacted since 1958 had made social security an important tool in efforts to reduce financial insufficiency. In absolute dollars, social security provided larger transfers to the elderly poor than did unemployment insurance, public assistance, public housing, veterans' benefits, or the government's health programmes (Moon, 1977; Plotnick and Skidmore, 1975; Schulz, 1980).

By the mid-1960s, it seemed economically feasible and politically shrewd for Washington to take advantage of social security's popularity in evincing its concern about reducing poverty *while* providing benefits to those who probably would not have to depend on public assistance. 'Social insurance as a way of providing economic security is an important social invention,' declared Social

Security Commissioner Robert M. Ball (1965, p. 20). 'Perhaps a third to a half of the poverty that exists in the United States could be prevented by the improvement and broader application of the social insurance program.' Three decades of experience had shown that social insurance could prevent and/or reduce poverty through income redistribution. Now that more than 90 per cent of the workforce was covered under the programme, and nearly every older person was entitled to some benefits, Ball and the liberal-orientated Social Security Administration leadership thought this arrangement could serve as the basis for a 'socially adequate' standard of living in later years.

This restatement of the goals and operations of social insurance must be placed in historical perspective. Other initiatives, such as those taken by the Office of Economic Opportunity, attracted far greater attention and generated more controversy. The Bureau of Labor Statistics, moreover, had devised a poverty index which counted greater numbers of needy Americans than did Orshansky's measure. But, as the nation's commitment to building a Great Society faltered amidst growing engagement in Vietnam, race riots and rising tensions at home, social security's gradual and incremental approach ironically made it the most appropriate vehicle for implementing bold innovations that would have been rejected had they required new bureaucratic structures and large amounts of revenue in order to be implemented. Indeed, the next step in social security policy development should be interpreted as a compromise tactic in the context of a politically volatile and ideologically charged atmosphere at the national level.

Progress had been made in reducing the extent of dependency in all regions of the country, but the soaring costs of waging a war against poverty gave Americans ample reason to consider alternative approaches. Consider the remarkable growth of the Aid to Families with Dependent Children (AFDC) programme, which began modestly as Title IV of the 1935 Social Security Act. In an average month in 1960, roughly 3 million people were receiving benefits under AFDC at a total cost of about $1 billion. By the end of the 1960s, the cost of supporting more than 6.7 million AFDC recipients reached $3.5 billion. Nearly 90 per cent of the potential pool of poor people were making claims to AFDC; growing awareness of their rights in the black community, recent court rulings, simpler bureaucratic procedures and higher benefits fuelled demand (Ross and Sawhill, 1975; Piven and Cloward, 1971; Hoffman and Marmor, 1976). Some experts thought the growing caseloads were indicative of more ominous developments. Conservatives seized on incidents of fraud and carped about the 'malingerers' and 'cheaters' who were abusing the system. 'There is no humanity or charity in destroying self-reliance, dignity, and self-respect,' Ronald Reagan proclaimed in his 1967 inaugural address as governor of California. Liberals worried that increased federal support might be accelerating the rise in the number of black families headed by women, or worse, accentuating a 'tangle of pathology' and violence among poor people. Public opinion polls revealed middle-class respondents's growing frustration with the system. The American way of welfare, in short, was increasingly seen as a 'mess'.

To remedy the situation, President Richard M. Nixon unveiled his Family Assistance Plan (1969), under which every unemployed family of four would receive at least $1,600 from the federal government. The plan, attacked from all quarters, languished in congressional committees (Moynihan, 1973; Burke and Burke, 1974; Piven and Cloward, 1977). Some wanted a negative-income tax programme, citing experiments in New Jersey and Pennsylvania that indicated that guaranteed income plans did not inevitably foster disincentives to work. Fiscal conservatives praised Reagan's welfare reforms in California, which tightened eligibility criteria, forced fathers and other responsible relatives to take financial responsibility for dependent children, and required welfare recipients to work as much as possible (Levine and Lyon, 1975; Anderson, 1978). None of these ideas, however, gained the support and momentum necessary to win congressional passage and presidential approval.

Instead, the stalemate was broken by adopting a plan advanced by the Social Security Administration. Policy makers recommended that the existing federal-state programme of providing assistance to the aged, blind and disabled be replaced by a Supplemental Security Income (SSI) programme. Such a step, they argued, would guarantee a uniform if 'minimal' level of support across the nation for those who had long been deemed 'deserving' of public assistance. Congress assented and in the process increased widower(er)s' Title II benefits from 82.5 per cent to 100 per cent of deceased workers' benefit, approved a 20 per cent across-the-board increase in social security benefits, and stipulated that benefits would be automatically indexed after 1975.

By the end of 1972, social security seemed to have aspired to the best of all possible worlds. By balancing the goals of individual equity and social adequacy, policy makers felt that they had reached a dynamic equilibrium that could serve as the basis for eventually enabling Americans of all ages to maintain (and in many cases, enhance) their self-reliance without sinking into dependency. There was little concern over the possibility that promoting adequacy through equity – and vice versa – might require difficult trade-offs. Few noted how difficult it would be to achieve these aims simultaneously through a single (albeit complex) set of regulations. Far from worrying about the spectre of generational inequities, policy makers wanted to build on popular confidence in a demonstrably effective programme. Law makers and citizens could not – or would not – grapple with the extent to which poverty in the United States resulted from class-, race-, and gender-based inequalities. Addressing certain risks and age-specific dependencies under the social insurance umbrella appeared the best tack to take.

## The crisis in US social security

The Supplemental Security Income programme has been fairly successful in meeting its objective of reducing the incidence of old-age poverty. Guaranteeing at its inception an income floor higher than existed in twenty-six of the nation's poorer states, SSI's combined minimum and supplemental benefits ranged from 90 per cent to 170 per cent of the poverty line for couples (Stein, 1980; Schieber, 1978; Lynn, 1977). Nearly 3 million more Americans were able to qualify for federal aid than had been the case under state-administered programmes. Nevertheless, there is surprisingly little co-ordination among various anti-poverty measures. A change in benefit rates or eligibility criteria in any categorical programme benefiting the poor sometimes had the paradoxical effect of reducing the attractiveness of the SSI programme for the aged (Estes, 1979; Nelson, 1982; Neugarten, 1983). An increase in social security benefits could simultaneously give SSI beneficiaries more money but also make them ineligible for federal in-kind benefits such as Medicaid and food stamps.

Other problems surrounding social security suggest that the 1970s may mark a critical turning point in the programme's history. Congress made a serious technical error in the 1972 amendments to the Social Security Act by adopting a double-indexed formula that overadjusted Title II benefits against the deleterious effect of inflation on retirement income (R. S. Kaplan, 1977). Although the formula for calculating benefits was subsequently corrected, this embarrassing – and expensive – error presaged a new phase of criticism against the system itself. Conservatives noted with dismay that the 'replacement ratio' for workers retiring at age 65 with average earnings under social security rose from 31 per cent to 44 per cent between 1952 and 1981. They increased during the same period from 46 per cent to 62 per cent for low-income workers. Providing such generous levels of support, critics feared, jeopardised the system's solvency.

Actually, the degree to which social security benefit levels can be shown to have (over)expanded depends on the policy-relevant historical baseline adopted. Benefit levels in the early 1980s were not much above what had been anticipated under the 1939 legislation; on the other hand, there had been 'significant' expansion beyond that intended in the 1950 legislation (Myers, 1982a and b). Furthermore, comparing the old-age pension for a US male worker with average earnings with those of employees in a dozen western advanced-industrial nations indicates that the American replacement rate fell into the 'intermediate' range. Individuals fare somewhat worse than their European counterparts, but benefits for couples were higher (Horlick, 1970; Fox, 1982). But during a period of rampant inflation when social security outlays greatly surpassed revenues, such comparisons hardly assuaged fears.

Policy makers gingerly debated economic options for putting social security on a sounder financial basis. Was the programme simply reducing the risk of old-age dependency? Or, was it trying to guarantee middle-class wage earners more than a fair return on their prior contributions upon retirement? Some suggested that new benefits be measured in terms of the prevailing standard of living. Others wanted a uniform replacement ratio. Still others advocated limiting future retirement benefits to the level enjoyed by current recipients

(Campbell, 1977; Robertson, 1978). Benefits, of course, would vary enormously depending on whether an individual's equity were strictly preserved, or people in different situations but with similar earnings records were treated equally, or if benefits were allocated among recipients with different levels of lifetime earnings according to a formula that took account of vertical equity. No consensus on such thorny issues was reached.

Meanwhile, media reports that social security was on the brink of bankruptcy shook public confidence. Older Americans feared that a major source of their economic security might be curtailed. More and more young people doubted that social security would be as good a financial deal for them as it was for their grandparents and p rents. Amid the controversy over the programme's future, analyses of US government spending between 1969 and 1980 revealed that appropriations for direct benefits for the aged had risen from 20 per cent to more than 40 per cent of the total federal budget. Many appropriations for the elderly were regarded as 'uncontrollable items' bound to become even more expensive with the ageing of the population (Samuelson, 1978; Hudson, 1978; US Senate, 1981). Blaming the elderly simultaneously focused and distorted issues:

> One clear consequence of the emergence of the aged as scapegoat is that intergenerational conflict is being engendered.... The crisis in Social Security has provided a rare political opportunity for substantially reforming the public mechanisms of support for older persons, which we are able to control far better than market mechanisms. Yet, because of the emergence of the aged as scapegoat, the moment is not being seized. (Binstock, 1983, p. 141)

The system's rapidly deteriorating short-term financial situation, however, did encourage action. The 1982 Social Security Trustees' report indicated that there would not be adequate funds to pay old-age benefits within eighteen months.

To avert a crisis, Congress and the President in 1983 endorsed proposals made by the National Commission on Social Security Reform (Light, 1985; *Report of the NCSSR*, 1983). The package included mandatory coverage of new federal employees and workers in non-profit organisations, a phased increase in the 'normal' retirement age, taxation of benefits paid to the wealthiest recipients, and a six-month delay in cost-of-living adjustments. 'The changes in this legislation will allow social security to age as gracefully as all of us hope to do ourselves,' President Reagan predicted, 'without becoming an overwhelming burden on generations still to come.' To fail to pay obeisance to future generations is dangerous politically; for a public official to pretend to know what burdens have been spared is presumptuous.

The 1983 amendments succeeded in defusing social security's immediate financial crisis. Trust funds appear solvent for the next half-century. Actuaries do not expect a shortfall in Medicare funds for a decade. Because social security provides more than half the income of two-thirds of all beneficiaries, the system has played a significant role in reducing poverty among the aged – to 13 per cent, about the same as for the population as a whole. Yet all is not well. Late in 1985, the Reagan administration admitted that its manipulation of social security funds could cost the system \$1.1 billion by 1990. The huge surpluses that are accruing to pay for the baby boomers' retirement — an amount that will exceed several trillion dollars by the turn of the century – pose a different threat. Liberals will wish to use the funds to improve the nation's health care system or increase existing entitlements; conservatives will want to apply the sums to reduce via fancy book-keeping the staggering deficit – or to justify cutting current benefits (Achenbaum, 1986b). The times demand candour about Americans' present and future stake in the system.

## Future choices

The potential for generational conflict in the United States over perceived inequities in the public pension system is genuine. Tensions between young and old, as we have seen, are deeply embedded in the American grain. Since the 1938 Advisory Council, social security policy reports have tried to minimise friction by affirming that 'we should not commit future generations to a burden larger than we should want to bear ourselves' (Brown, 1977). For if current and projected Title II entitlements even *seem* unduly generous, support for social insurance becomes commensurately precarious. The present-day belief that one age group benefits at the expense of another clearly hampers rational consideration of the nation's welfare priorities and resources *en bloc*.

Yet it must be emphasised that a persuasive case has not been made, on theoretical or empirical grounds, to sustain the proposition that 'age' is the most salient predictor of inequality in the US. American researchers have not advanced much beyond Karl Mannheim in stipulating the criteria for demarcating the chronological and sociological boundaries of a generation or for disentangling the effects of age, period, or cohort in analysing relations between age groups. Thus Paul Light's examination (1988) of the 'baby boomers', those born in the US between 1946 and 1964, emphasises their considerable demographic heterogeneity, lack of economic unity and disengagement from politics. Similarly, few analysts deny that the increasing number of poor children in an affluent nation has calamitous implications amidst societal ageing. But it is not self-evident that more public dollars would be automatically available for the young if federal expenditures for the old were reduced. Advocates for defence, agriculture and urban renewal make competing claims. Washington, in any case, is not the sole source of support. State-level expenditures for children are already equal to federal allocations. Neither state nor federal data reveal the extent to which intra-family transfers are stimulated or constrained by governmental outlays. The family is the major societal support for children, just as it remains for older people. No wonder anecdotes and assertions about the importance of age in explaining differences in well-being across the life course have counted for more than good theory or hard data thus far.

Nor has it been demonstrated that any unfairness in generational transfers historically results from an age-based power struggle vested in the rights (or masked in the rites) of age. With more than 36 million members, the American Association of Retired Persons (AARP) is the largest voluntary organisation in the United States except for the US branch of the Roman Catholic Church. Despite its wealth and savvy leadership, AARP can rarely mobilise its membership around any specific policy issue. The assets, interests and needs of the elderly population are simply too diverse to rally them as a monolithic, single-minded political force. There is, in fact, no evidence that those who advocate the rights of the elderly take a position on social insurance at odds with the views expressed by groups advancing the interests of children or young people (Hudson and Strate, 1985). All age groups say that they are willing to support the old. If anything, the elderly are the least supportive of social security increases and slightly more supportive than average of transfers to low-income families with children (Ponza *et al.*, 1988). Middle-aged Americans, moreover, do not usually organise along age-specific lines. Their role in mediating among the concerns and demands of various age groups is paramount (Foner, 1984). Thus it is not surprising that it was middle-aged workers, not older people, who were mainly responsible for the passage of social security and whose support remains so vital.

Readjusting the balance between adequacy and equity under social security, in other words, is not just an issue between the ages. Two major segments of the population – minorities and women – have argued that they are unfairly penalised because their needs, expectations and lifestyles diverge from those of the average white male worker who is the prototypical social security contributor and beneficiary. These groups, for instance, were heavily concentrated in agriculture and domestic service jobs, occupations not covered under the system until 1950. As a result, black men and women of all races 'lost' earnings credits and benefits they would have gained had they been employed in other sectors (Levitan *et al.*, 1975; Burkhauser and Holden, 1982). In 1980, nearly three-fifths of all white males but only one-third of all black males were employed in the four highest-paid occupational categories. According to the Bureau of Labor Statistics, most women remain clustered in twenty out of 420 occupations, mainly as clericals, domestics, nurses, teachers and service workers (Stallard *et al.*, 1983; Williams, 1983). Because women and minorities have traditionally earned less than white men, their average social security benefits are smaller. That fact is hardly shocking, but it is ironic, since at age 65 members of both groups can expect on the average to live longer than white males. If Americans truly mean to reduce old-age poverty, there are employment and welfare issues to be redressed that affect key groups within the ageing population. The most efficacious strategy would adopt needs-based rather than age-based criteria.

'The policy criteria of solidarity have never been a strong suit in the US political system,' argues Hugh Heclo (1988), a student of European and American welfare systems. 'Whatever policy might stipulate, the generations will owe something to each other only if they believe they do.' Features of the American political system – interest group liberalism, bureaucratic inertia, voter apathy, as well as checks and balances in the federal polity – do confound efforts to clarify issues. Nonetheless it is still possible to break out of the institutional gridlock that seems to arise from viewing distributional issues as a zero-sum game. The elderly themselves may prove to be catalysts for change. Within twenty years a third of the US population will be between the ages of 50 and 75. Recent studies of cohort-specific political behaviour and attitudes, moreover, indicate that there is enormous potential for change in adult populations heretofore unrecognised (Jennings and Niemi, 1981; Pifer and Bronte, 1986). Two points should be kept in mind.

First, the US public pension system is not – and should not be – viewed as the only way to provide for the vicissitudes of late life. Policy makers and the public alike too often discuss social security's scope and financing as if they operated in a vacuum. Yet as Stephen Sass's article (this volume) makes clear, the history of US private pensions has been intimately connected to the evolution of programmes in the public sector. Social security, along with private savings and employer pensions (which range from the cafeteria-like options provided by multinational corporations to the plans designed for self-employed individuals), represent the country's three-pronged strategy for ensuring a decent means of support in late life (Upp, 1980).

Analysts must take account of the roles that other institutions in American life – the family, the church and synagogue, voluntary groups, private organisations – play in contemporary society. These mediating institutions facilitate Americans' individual and collective efforts to maintain a measure of security against the risks of modern times. They do so in part by affording an extraordinary range of options that thereby promote divergent choices. What we need is better appreciation of how the support and networks offered by these private institutions complement the income transfers provided by public and private pensions.

Second, a historical perspective is required to leaven what too often has been a static policy discussion. The US generational equity debate surprisingly neglects differences in experiences and opportunities that are bound to exist among separate birth cohorts who live(d) in real time. Public pension policies change as programmes mature. So far the absolute worth and current range of US social insurance benefits have not been cut back by the whims and desires of those in power. The social security crisis defused by the crafting of the 1983 amendments, however, suggests that the era of enthusiastic expansion of intergenerational transfers in the US may have passed. A rising generation's expectations will not inexorably become automatic entitlements. Programme expansion more than ever before requires transgenerational political action. To rally such support, Americans should stress that *old-age* programmes must ultimately be subsumed into a comprehensive US policy designed, as the US Constitution puts it, 'to promote the general welfare' from womb to tomb. But this universalist strategy requires acknowledging that the ways that rights and obligations are distributed across historical cohorts at a given moment in a given place are not the same as the abstract bonds that exist across age groups.

Discussion of the allocation of resources between young and old cannot be limited to a particular instant in a country's experience. A fairer comparison requires examining cohorts' cumulative experiences in their proper historical context. Hence talking with envy or anger about a 'lucky' generation simply ignores the perduring truth that historical circumstances have a way of providing a distinctive set of opportunities and problems for members of each cohort over this individual and collective life course. Public policy cannot homogenise historical vectors but it need not sanction injustice based on age, class, gender, poverty or race. It makes more sense for Americans to join other advanced industrial nations in establishing the minimal standards of decency every citizen deserves regardless of age, and then to build on that precedent in its distinctive manner of incremental public policy making. Old-age entitlements lie at the interstices of America's welfare and employment policies, whether it is made explicit or not. European policy makers, in contrast, should not fall into the trap of accepting AGE-like notions of generational equity that invite trade-offs between groups that are 'dependent' in divergent ways. Instead of worrying about the extent of intergenerational justice between workers and pensioners, a more constructive task would be to reaffirm the transgenerational inter-dependence of shared needs and dynamic opportunities that binds the working population with non-working groups.

# References

Achenbaum, W. A. (1983), *Shades of Gray*, Boston, Little, Brown & Co.

Achenbaum, W. A. (1986a), 'Social security's three R's', in N. Pugash *et al.* (eds), *Social Security at Fifty*, Albuquerque, University of New Mexico Press.

Achenbaum, W. A. (1986b), *Social Security*, New York, Cambridge University Press.

Altmeyer, A. J. (1942), 'The desireability of expanding the social insurance program now', *Social Security Bulletin*, V, pp. 3–8 (November).

Altmeyer, A. J. (1968), *The Formative Years of Social Security*, Madison, University of Wisconsin Press.

Anderson, M. (1978), *Welfare*, Stanford, California, Hoover Institution Press.

*Annual Report of the Federal Security Administration: 1951* (1952), Washington, DC, Government Printing Office.

Ball, R. M. (1947), 'Social insurance and the right to assistance', *Social Service Review*, XXI, pp. 338–45 (September).

Ball, R. M. (1965), 'Is poverty necessary?', *Social Security Bulletin*, XXVIII, pp. 16–21 (August).

Binstock, R. H. (1983), 'The aged as scapegoat', *The Gerontologist*, XXIII, pp. 136–43 (April).

Bixby, L. E. *et al.* (1975), *Demographic and Economic Characteristics of the Aged*, Washington, DC, Government Printing Office.

Brauer, C. M. (1982), 'Kennedy, Johnson, and the war on poverty', *Journal of American History*, LXIX, pp. 98–119 (June).

Brown, J. D. (1969), *The Genesis of Social Security in America*, Princeton, New Jersey, Princeton University, Industrial Relations Section.

Brown, J. D. (1977), *Essays on Social Security*, Princeton, New Jersey, Princeton University, Industrial Relations Section.

Burke, V. J. and Burke, V. (1974), *Nixon's Good Deed*, New York, Columbia University Press.

Burkhauser, R. V. and Holden, K. D. (eds) (1982), *A Challenge to Social Security*, New York, Academic Press.

Callihan, D. (1987), *Setting Limits*, New York, Simon and Schuster.

Campbell, R. R. (1977), *Social Security*, Stanford, California, Hoover Institution Press.

Cates, Jerry R. (1983), *Insuring Inequality: Administrative Leadership in Social Security, 1935-54*, Ann Arbor, University of Michigan Press.

Chen, A. S. Y. (1939), 'Social significance of old age', *Sociology and Social Research*, XXIII, pp. 519-29 (July-August).

Cohen, W. J. (1952), 'Income maintenance for the aged', *Annals of the American Academy of Political and Social Science*, CCLXXIX, pp. 153-60 (Spring).

Cohen, W. J. (1966), 'Improving the status of the aged', *Social Security Bulletin*, XXIX, pp. 3-10 (December).

Committee on Old-Age Security (1936), *The Townsend Crusade*, New York, Twentieth Century Fund.

*Congressional Quarterly* (1983), 'Social security plan wins final Hill approval', XXXIII, pp. 131-32 (26 March).

*Congressional Record* (1939), Hearings on Social Security Amendments (10 June).

Dallach, M. L. (1933), 'Old age, American style', *New Outlook*, CLXII, p. 50 (October).

Davis, K. S. (1979), 'The birth of social security', *American Heritage*, XXX, pp. 49-51 (April/May).

Davis, K. and van den Oever, P. (1981), 'Age relations and public policy in advanced industrial societies', *Population and Development Review*, VII, pp. 3-16 (March).

de Tocqueville, A. (1836), *Democracy in America*, ed. R. D. Heffner (1956), New York, Mentor.

Douglas, P. H. (1936), *Social Security in the United States*, New York, McGraw-Hill.

Dunne, G. H., SJ (ed.) (1964), *Poverty in Plenty*, New York, P. J. Kenedy & Sons.

Esler, A. (1984), *The Generation Gap in Society and History*, Monticello, Illinois, Vance Bibliographies.

Estes, C. (1979), *The Aging Enterprise*, San Francisco, Jossey-Bass.

Fawcett, D. (1988), 'Aging resolution is topic of 1988-89 high school debate competition', *The Generational Journal*, I, p. 60 (April).

Foner, N. (1984), *Ages in Conflict*, New York, Columbia University Press.

Fox, A. (1982), 'Earnings replacement rates and total income', *Social Security Bulletin*, XLV, pp. 3-23 (October).

Free, L. A. and Cantril, H. (1967), *Political Beliefs of Americans*, New Brunswick, New Jersey, Rutgers University Press.

Heclo, H. (1988), 'Generational politics', in J. L. Palmer, T. Smeeding and B. B. Torrey (eds), *The Vulnerable*, Washington, DC, Urban Institute.

Hewitt, P. S. and Howe, N. (1988), 'Generational equity and the future of generational politics', *The Generational Journal*, I, pp. 8-11 (April).

Hilliard, R. M. (1946), 'Public institutions in our social insurance structure', *Social Service Review*, XX, pp. 492-3 (December).

Hoffman, W. and Marmor, T. (1976), 'The politics of public assistance reform: an essay review', *Social Service Review*, L, pp. 11-22 (March).

Hohaus, R. (1960), 'Equity, adequacy and related factors in social security', in W. Haber and W. J. Cohen (eds), *Social Security: Programs, Problems, and Policies*, Homewood, Illinois, Richard D. Irwin (article first published 1938).

Horlick, M. (1970), 'The earnings replacement rate of old-age benefits: an international comparison', *Social Security Bulletin*, XXXIII, pp. 3-16 (March).

Hudson, R. B. (1978), 'The "graying" of the federal budget and its consequences for old-age policy', *The Gerontologist*, XVIII, pp. 428–40 (December).

Hudson, R. B. and Strate, J. (1985), 'Aging and political systems', in R. H. Binstock and E. Shanas (eds), *Handbook of Aging and the Social Sciences*, 2nd edn, New York, Van Nostrand Reinhold.

Ippolito, D. (1981), *Congressional Spending*, Ithaca, New York, Cornell University Press.

Jennings, M. K. and Niemi, R. O. (1981), *Generations and Politics*, Princeton, New Jersey, Princeton University Press.

Kaestle, C. (1983), *Pillars of the Republic*, New York, Hill & Wang.

Kaplan, R. S. (1977), *Indexing Social Security*, Washington, DC, American Enterprise Institute.

Kaplan, S. (1987), 'The new generation gap', *Common Cause Magazine*, XIII, pp. 13–15 (March).

Kingson, E. R., Hirshorn, B. A. and Cornman, J. M. (1986), *Ties That Bind*, Washington, DC, Seven Locks Press.

Koch, A. and Peden, W. (1944), *The Life and Selected Writings of Thomas Jefferson*, New York, Modern Library.

Lasch, C. (1978), *The Culture of Narcissism*, New York, W. W. Norton.

Lawrence, D. H. (1923), *Studies in Classic American Literature*, New York, Viking.

Levine, R. A. and Lyon, D. W. (1975), 'Studies in public welfare', *Journal of Human Resources*, X, pp. 445–66 (Fall).

Levitan, S. A., Johnston, W. B. and Taggart, R. (1975), *Still a Dream*, Cambridge, Mass., Harvard University Press.

Light, P. C. (1985), *Artful Work*, New York, Random House.

Light, P. C. (1988), *Baby Boomers*, New York, W. W. Norton.

Linton, R. (1942), 'Age and sex categories', *American Sociological Review*, VII, pp. 592–601 (August).

Longman, P. (1987), *Born to Pay*, Boston, Houghton Mifflin.

Lubove, R. (1968), *The Struggle for Social Security*, Cambridge, Mass., Harvard University Press.

Lynn, L. E., Jr (1977), 'Poverty developments in the income maintenance system', in Robert Haveman (ed.), *A Decade of Federal Antipoverty Programs*, New York, Academic Press.

Maier, P. (1980), *The Old Revolutionaries*, New York, A. A. Knopf.

Merriam, I. C. (1968), 'Young adults and social security', *Social Security Bulletin*, XXXI, pp. 3–12 (August).

Moody, H. R. (1988), *Abundance of Life*, New York, Columbia University Press.

Moon, M. (1977), *The Measurement of Economic Welfare*, New York, Academic Press.

Moynihan, D. P. (1973), *The Politics of a Guaranteed Income*, New York, Random House.

Moynihan, D. P. (1987), *Family and Nation*, New York, Harcourt, Brace, Jovanovich.

Myers, R. J. (1982a), 'Money's worth comparison for social security benefits', Washington, DC, National Commission on Social Security Reform, Memorandum 45.

Myers, R. J. (1982b), 'Relative changes in social security benefit levels', Washington, DC, National Commission on Social Security Reform, Memorandum 33.

Nelson, G. (1982), 'Social class and public policy for the elderly', *Social Services Review*, LVI, pp. 85–107 (January).

Neuberger, R. L. and Loe, K. (1936), *An Army of the Aged*, Caldwell, Idaho, Caxton Printers.

Neugarten, B. L. (ed.) (1983), *Age or Need?*, Beverly Hills, Sage Publications.

Orshansky, M. (1965a), 'Who's who among the poor: a demographic view of poverty', *Social Security Bulletin*, XXVIII, pp. 3–9 (July).

Orshansky, M. (1965b), 'Counting the poor: another look at the poverty profile', *Social Security Bulletin*, XXVIII, pp. 3–25 (January).

Orshansky, M. (1976), 'Study of the measure of poverty', *Social Security Bulletin*, XXXIX, pp. 34–7 (September).

Patterson, J. T. (1981), *America's Struggle Against Poverty*, Cambridge, Mass., Harvard University Press.

Pifer, A. and Bronte, L. (eds) (1986), *Our Aging Society*, New York, W. W. Norton.

Piven, F. F. and Cloward, R. A. (1971), *Regulating the Poor*, New York, Vintage Press.

Piven, F. F. and Cloward, R. A. (1977), *Poor People's Movements*, New York, Pantheon.

Plotnick, R. D. and Skidmore, F. (1975), *Progress Against Poverty*, New York, Academic Press.

Ponza, M., Duncan, G. J., Corcoran, M. and Groskind, F. (1988), 'The guns of autumn?', *Public Opinion Quarterly*, forthcoming.

Preston, S. H. (1984), 'Children and the elderly in the US', *Scientific American*, CCLVI, pp. 44–9 (December).

Putnam, J. K. (1970), *Old-Age Politics in California*, Stanford, California, Stanford University Press.

*Report of the National Commission on Social Security Reform* (1983), Washington, DC, Government Printing Office.

Robertson, A. H. (1978), *Social Security*, New York, William M. Mercer.

Ross, H. L. and Sawhill, I. V. (1975), *Time of Transition*, Washington, DC, Urban Institute.

Samuelson, R. J. (1978), 'Busting the budget: the graying of America', *National Journal*, pp. 256–60 (18 February).

Sawhill, I. V. (ed.) (1988), *Challenge to Leadership*, Washington, DC, Urban Institute.

Schieber, S. J. (1978), 'First year impact of SSI on economic status of 1973 adult assistance populations', *Social Security Bulletin*, XLI, pp. 18–46 (February).

Schulz, J. (1980), *The Economics of Aging*, Belmont, California, Wadsworth Publishing.

Siegel, J. S. and Taeuber, C. M. (1986), 'Demographic dimensions of an aging population', in A. Pifer and L. Bronte (eds), *Our Aging Society*, New York, W. W. Norton.

Slater, P. E. (1970), *The Pursuit of Loneliness*, Boston, Beacon Press.

*Social Security Bulletin* (1978), *Annual Supplement*, Washington, DC, Government Printing Office.

Stallard, K., Ehrenreich, B. and Sklar, H. (1983), *Poverty in the American Dream*, New York, Institute for New Communications.

Stein, B. (1980), *Social Security and Pensions in Transition*, New York, Free Press.

Steiner, G. J. (1974), 'Reform follows reality', in E. Ginzburg and R. M. Solow (eds), *The Great Society*, New York, Basic Books.

Thompson, W. S. and Whelpton, P. K. (1930), 'A nation of elders in the making', *American Mercury*, XIX, pp. 392–5 (April).

Upp, M. (1980), 'Relative importance of various income sources for the aged, 1980', *Social Security Bulletin*, XLVI, pp. 3–10 (January).

US Bureau of Labor Statistics (1932), *Public Old-Age Pensions and Insurance in the United States and Foreign Countries*, Washington, DC, Government Printing Office.

US Committee on Economic Security (1937), *Social Security in America*, Washington, DC, Government Printing Office.

US Department of Commerce (1975), *Historical Statistics of the United States, Colonial Times to 1970*, Washington, DC, Government Printing Office.

US House of Representatives, 74th Congress, 1st sess. (1935), *The Economic Security Act: Hearings on H. R. 4120*.

US President (1964), 'The problem of poverty in America' (1964), *Economic Report of the President*, Washington, DC, Government Printing Office.

US Senate, 74th Congress, 1st sess. (1935a), *Report of the Senate Finance Committee on the Social Security Bill*.

US Senate, 74th Congress, 1st sess. (1935b), *The Economic Security Act: Hearings on S. 1130*.

US Senate, Special Committee on Aging (1981), *Developments in Aging: 1980*, Washington, DC, Government Printing Office.

US Senate, Special Committee on Aging (1988), *Developments in Aging: 1987*, Washington, DC, Government Printing Office.

US Social Security Board (1935), *Social Security Bill, Summary of Provisions, Comparison of Text of Original Bill, and Ways and Means Redraft, Compilation of Proposed Amendments, etc., for Committee on Finance*, Washington, DC, Government Printing Office.

Weaver, C. L. (1982), *The Crisis in Social Security*, Durham, North Carolina, Duke Press Policy Studies.

Weaver, R. K. (1988), *Automatic Government*, Washington, DC, Brookings Institution.

Williams, J. D. (1983), *The State of Black America*, New York, National Urban League.

Witte, E. (1939), Memorandum to W. J. Cohen, National Archives, Record Group 47, 095.

Witte, E. (1962), 'Social security: a wild dream or practical plan?', in R. J. Lampman (ed.), *Social Security Perspectives: Essays by Edwin E. Witte*, Madison, University of Wisconsin Press (article written in 1939).

Woytinsky, W. S. (1936), *Labor in the United States: Basic Statistics for Social Security*, Washington, DC, Social Science Research Council.

# 8

# Labour Force Participation and Social Pension Systems

## Winfried Schmähl

## Introduction

Structural changes in demography, economy and society create enormous long-term challenges for pensions systems in industrialised countries. This is a highly complex subject, especially taking into account the institutional framework. This is partly because of the high degree of interdependence between fields and institutions of economic and social development and policy, a factor often not considered adequately in analysis or political debate about possibilities for future development. So, for instance, demographic changes greatly influence social security through changes in the labour market. Social security regulations influence labour market conditions (labour demand and supply) as well as demography (mortality, immigration, perhaps even fertility). And if conditions for receiving pension benefits are changed – increasing retirement ages is only one of the possibilities being discussed in many countries – the financing of pension schemes and labour market conditions both depend on the behavioural responses of employers and employees, while on the other hand the labour market situation determines to a large degree the responses themselves. And the way in which people's changing employment behaviour affects the pension scheme depends on the specific institutional rules of the system – how benefits are calculated, how financing is organised, etc. Therefore we must consider institutional arrangements when analysing the effects of changing conditions on social security, as well as the effects of political decisions about social security.

In this article I will demonstrate the need for an integrated view as well as considering institutional factors in analysing and preparing political decisions, using the example of possible effects of changing labour force participation, in particular of women and the elderly, on social pension schemes. Two types of such schemes are considered: an earnings-related system and a flat-rate scheme. The analysis, however, is mainly focused on an earnings-related scheme, using West Germany's statutory pension system for wage- and salary-earners as an example. This is by far the most widespread old-age pension scheme in

Germany. Germany is interesting because of its remarkably low fertility rate and the considerable consequences for the future age structure of the population, and because its pension scheme was founded as far back as 1889 (as part of Bismarck's social security reform) and has had a great influence internationally.

In November 1988 the Federal Minister of Labour and Social Affairs published the first draft of a law on pension reform (BMA, 1988), which would adjust this system to changing conditions while defending the main elements of the statutory pension scheme (in particular earnings-relatedness, the insurance concepts of reciprocity and equivalence, and financing pensions mostly by earnings-related contributions, paid equally by employees and employers, and only in part by federal grant). During the lively public debate on the need and possibilities of reforming the existing statutory pension scheme in Germany, a central topic, beside demographic ageing, was the future development of labour force participation. One example of this is the proposal made by the Minister (BMA, 1988) to increase retirement ages step by step and to introduce the possibility of partial retirement into the statutory pension scheme. Another is the discussion on the expected effects of increasing labour force participation by women on the financing of the pension scheme, leading some researchers, as well as politicians, to the conclusion that problems of future financing of pensions are exaggerated, in particular if taking into account only the effects of demographic ageing.

The questions discussed in this article are relevant not only for Germany but also for many other countries. They include some of the complex interactions of labour force participation, employment behaviour, earnings development over the life cycle and statutory pension schemes. One of the central questions is: will changing employment behaviour increase or reduce the problems of pension financing? I will show that there is no easy answer to this question, because many different effects have to be taken into account. A fully comprehensive discussion of the possible effects is outside the scope of this article. For instance, whether a higher labour force participation by women influences the fertility rate, or vice versa, is not considered. Demographic development is taken here to be an exogenous factor. However, there are many direct interdependencies between labour force participation and social security. A selection of topics is necessary. My starting point is the effect of an ageing population in an earnings-related statutory pension scheme and the main alternatives for coping with these problems. The social insurance system for wage- and salary-earners in West Germany is then used as an example for a more detailed analysis. Next, some changes in employment behaviour and some possible consequences of the changing age structure of the population on overall labour force participation are pointed out. Then some information on earnings development over the life cycle for German male and female workers is given, based on longitudinal data. In the penultimate section the effects of these changes on the financing of the German system are discussed from a longitudinal and cross-sectional perspective, as well as some future tasks for pension policy arising from these effects.

Finally, a comparison is made with the consequences of such changing conditions on a flat-rate tax-financed pension system.

## Ageing of the population and some consequences for pension financing – a global view

In looking at the future development of the 'financing burden' of a pension system, the following well-known (simplified) equation for a balanced budget is useful (see also the Appendix):

$$c = \frac{NP}{NW} \times \frac{PA}{WA} \times (1 - z)$$

$$\frac{NP}{NW} = PR = \text{pensioner ratio} \tag{1}$$

$$\frac{PA}{WA} = APL = \text{average gross pension level}$$

where
c = earnings-related contribution rate necessary in the statutory system to balance the budget
NP = number of pensioners
NW = number of wage- and salary-earners
PA = average (gross) pension payment
WA = average (gross) earnings
z = ratio of federal grant (subsidy) in financing pension expenditure.

For West Germany several model projections are published, either based on demographic development only or integrating possible future economic changes too. We shall not discuss assumptions or model projections here, but shall mention some results. A very simple calculation is based on the assumption of APL as well as z being constant over time and making PR depend on the growth rate of the (old-)age dependency ratio (ADR). For instance:

$$ADR = \frac{\text{number of persons age 60 and older}}{\text{number of persons in the earnings span, e.g. aged 20–60}} \tag{2}$$

The development of ADR depends above all on fertility and mortality assumptions (and, if we include foreigners, immigration). Most actual projection figures by the Federal Statistical Office (BMI, 1987) are based on three variants, which are summarised in Table 8.1. The effect on c for the German statutory

**Table 8.1** *Demographic development and age structure, West Germany, 1985-2030*

| Year | Projection | | | | | | | |
|------|------|------|------|------|------|------|------|------|
| | I | | II | | III | | I + C | |
| | a | b | a | b | a | b | a | b |
| 1985 | 56.6 | 38.5 | 56.6 | 38.5 | 56.6 | 38.5 | 61.0 | 36.1 |
| 2010 | 51.5 | 51.1 | 50.0 | 51.5 | 53.8 | 50.9 | 57.8 | 48.5 |
| 2030 | 42.6 | 81.2 | 39.7 | 87.6 | 47.5 | 72.7 | 48.4 | 80.6 |

*Notes*

a = absolute number of people (in millions)

b = age dependency ratio (in %) $\dfrac{\text{60 years and older}}{\text{20 years up to 60 years}}$

*Differing assumptions*

I    = net reproduction rate constant (0.6)
II   = net reproduction rate decreasing by 16% up to 1995, then constant
III  = net reproduction rate increasing by 23% up to 1997, then constant
I-III   German population only
C   = net immigration 55,000 persons p.a. up to 2009, then net immigration 0

*Source:* BMI (1987).

social old-age and disability insurance system for wage- and salary-earners (GRV) is shown in Figure 8.1, together with the results of a complex simulation (made by the Swiss Prognos-Institut) taking into account changing economic variables, using two scenarios which give an idea of the upper and lower limits of possible development (Eckerle *et al.*, 1987). The development of c is similar to that of the purely demographically based calculation. This can be interpreted to mean that demographic change seems to be the dominating factor in the future development of the financial needs of the pension system (at least in the long run). More than a doubling of c will be necessary if APL does not change and z does not increase.

The discussion of possible measures is concentrated in Germany, as in most other countries, on the key variables of the budget equation (1) (see Figure 8.2), lowering PR, especially by increasing the 'retirement age', reducing APL by changing the pension formula, in particular by the adjustment procedure, and increasing z (financed by changes in the expenditure structure of public budgets or by increasing taxes).

However, it is not the task of this article to discuss politically induced changes within the system (for this see Schmähl, 1988b), but rather the effects of changing employment behaviour. Here effects on PR as well as APL have to be considered; the latter are often neglected. How the pension system (and APL in particular) is affected depends especially on the pension formula for calculating and adjusting pensions and on the financing system.

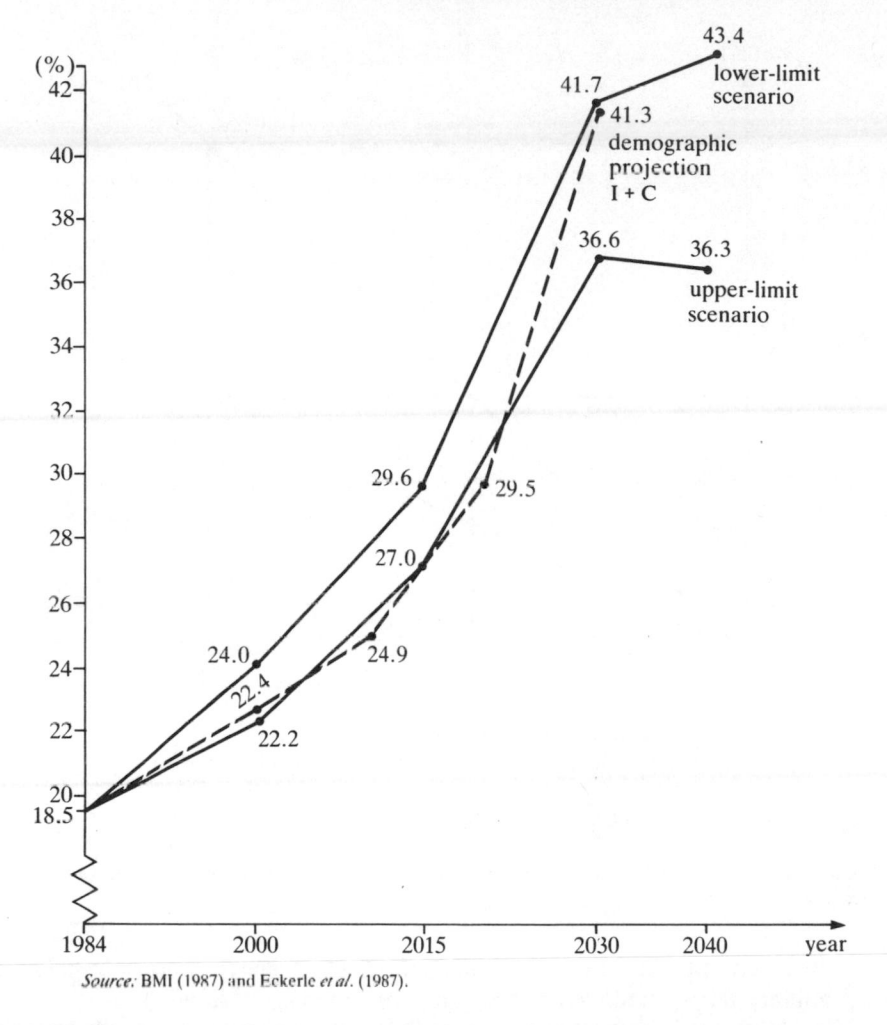

**Figure 8.1** *Necessary contribution rates in the statutory social insurance system (GRV), West Germany, 1985–2030*

## Main elements of the earnings-related pension scheme for wage- and salary-earners in West Germany

In this central West German pension scheme all four factors of the existing pension formula are relevant to our discussion.

Initial pension calculation depends on:

(1) the number of years of coverage, including years with contribution payments based on covered gainful employment as well as years without gainful employment, e.g. during unemployment (only for the time in which benefits

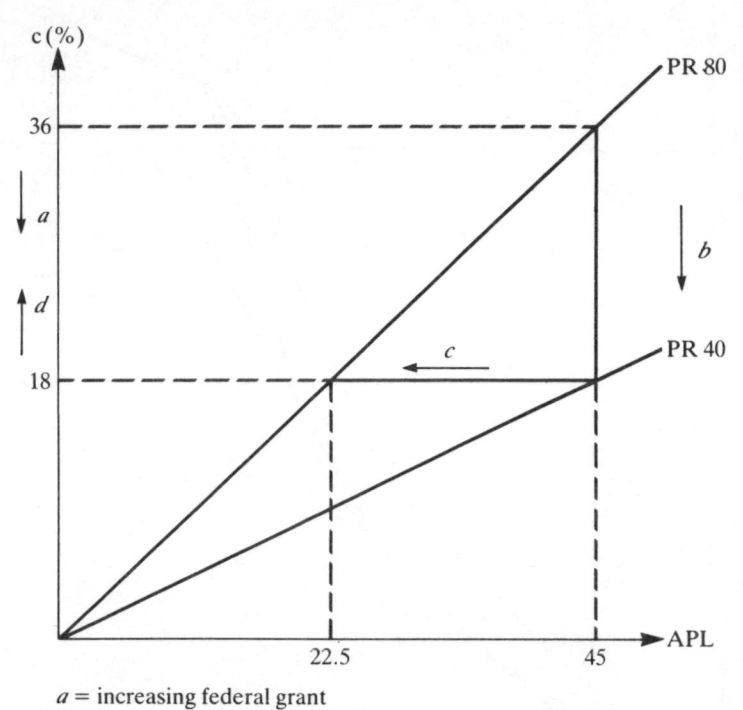

*a* = increasing federal grant
*b* = increasing average retirement age
*c* = changing the pension formula (and reducing average gross
     pension level (APL))
*d* = increasing the contribution rate (c)

**Figure 8.2** *Possibilities for balancing the social insurance budget in times of a rising pensioner ratio (PR)*

are received from the unemployment insurance agency), education, sickness, military service and childcaring (only for one year up to now);

(2) the (percentage of the) personal (individual) earnings base, which depends on the average relative gross earnings position of the pensioner during his years of gainful employment;

(3) a constant factor of 1.5 per cent in the case of old-age pensions for each year of coverage;

(4) the general earnings base (in DM). This amount is adjusted every year by the growth rate of average gross earnings of the last year. (For a detailed analysis in English of the German pension formula and some of its economic effects, see Schmähl, 1986a.)

Pension calculation is not based on last earnings, as in the special pension system for civil servants in Germany and Austria, nor on earnings during, say, the last ten or twenty years of employment or on the best years, as in many countries.

The 'normal' retirement age is officially 65 (only five years of coverage are required). However, women can retire at 60 (after fifteen years of coverage) and men at 63 (thirty-five years of coverage). Unemployed older workers and handicapped people can retire at 60, under certain conditions. Only the reduced number of years of insurance lowers the pension payment in the case of earlier retirement.[1]

Besides pensions for the insured person, widow(er)'s pensions exist, calculated in principle as 60 per cent of the pension of the late spouse. Whether the full amount is paid, however, depends on other income of the widow(er), especially on own pensions and earnings. If these exceed a certain amount then only a reduced amount is paid. This can be important in any discussion of the effects of social security on employment behaviour as well as on the development of total expenditure.[2,3]

Pensions are adjusted by the growth rate of average gross earnings during the previous year. This is also the factor for increasing the general earnings base. All pension payments are therefore based on an identical general earnings base independent of the year of their first calculation. However, a political decision is made annually on the adjustment rate by means of a special adjustment law. During the last few years there have been some *ad hoc* reductions of the adjustment rate compared to the increase in gross earnings, aiming at an adjustment of pensions in accordance with the increase in average net earnings. It can be expected that the adjustment formula will be changed by law from 1992 onwards

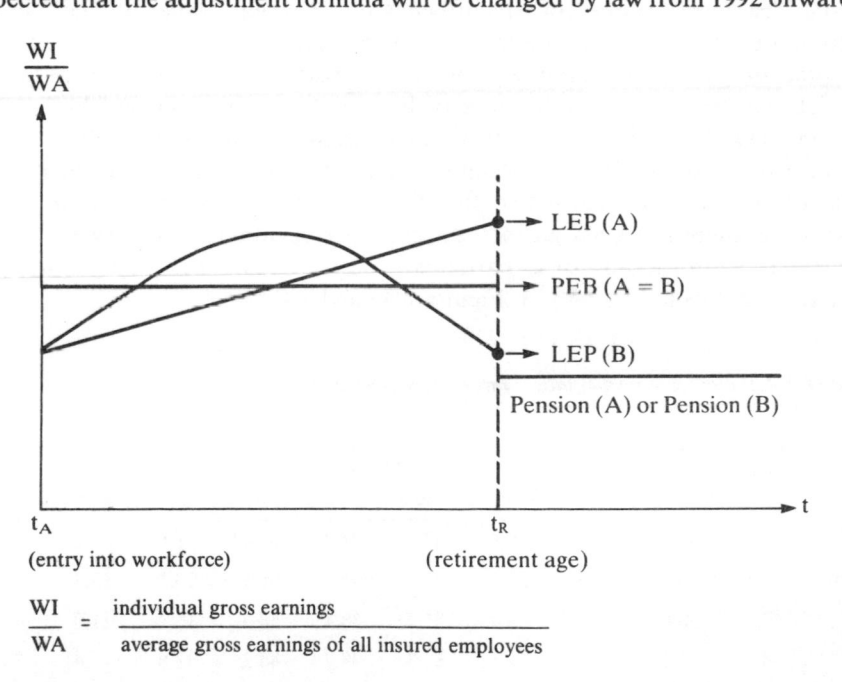

$$\frac{WI}{WA} = \frac{\text{individual gross earnings}}{\text{average gross earnings of all insured employees}}$$

**Figure 8.3** *Relative earnings curves with equal personal earnings base (PEB) and equal pension but different last earnings position (LEP)*

from average gross earnings to net earnings increase. There is a broad political consensus in West Germany to introduce such a net adjustment formula (which will also determine the increase of the general earnings base for initial pension calculation).

The number of years of coverage, earnings development over the whole time of coverage and the development of average earnings of all wage- and salary-earners are dominating factors for individual pensions as well as for total expenditure. One of the interesting questions is: how do changes in employment behaviour influence individual as well as average earnings and the pensioner ratio as well as the average pension level? Before discussing these factors the influence of earnings development on the (earnings) replacement rate of pensions must be pointed out. Let us assume two earners with the same number of earning years (here, years of coverage) and an equal personal earnings base (i.e. relative earnings position) (see Figure 8.3). Therefore their pensions are identical too. However, the age-earnings profiles over the life cycle differ. Therefore the (gross) replacement rate is also different; it depends on the ratio of average relative earnings over all years of coverage to last earnings.[4]

## Some changes in employment behaviour

A significant change in employment behaviour in recent years is the later entry into and earlier exit from employment. The phase of gainful employment has become shorter, both absolutely and in comparison to the retirement phase (which has become longer because of both earlier retirement and higher life expectancy). This can be seen from cross-sectional, age-specific labour force participation rates (LFPR), especially for men (see Table 8.2). For women this is true for the youngest and the two oldest age groups, but in the age groups 20–24 and 55–59 there has been an increase since the beginning of the 1970s. Some information on labour force participation of German men and women by different age groups is given in Figures 8.4a and 8.4b.

Table 8.2 *Labour force participation rates, West Germany*

| Year | Age group | | | | | | | | | |
|------|-----------|-------|-------|-------|-------|-------|-------|-------|-----|-------|
| | 15–19 | | 20–24 | | 55–59 | | 60–64 | | 65+ | |
| | Men | Women | Men | Women | Men | Women | Men | Women | Men | Women |
| 1960 | 86.8 | 84.5 | 91.2 | 74.6 | 87.7 | 31.2 | 67.4 | 18.6 | 20.6 | 7.4 |
| 1970 | 65.5 | 63.1 | 86.3 | 68.7 | 87.8 | 35.7 | 69.5 | 20.2 | 18.3 | 6.1 |
| 1975 | 57.2 | 50.6 | 79.9 | 68.4 | 85.7 | 38.4 | 58.3 | 16.4 | 11.0 | 4.4 |
| 1980 | 48.5 | 41.4 | 82.0 | 71.1 | 82.3 | 38.7 | 44.2 | 13.0 | 7.4 | 3.0 |
| 1985 | 47.9 | 41.9 | 80.1 | 73.8 | 79.1 | 37.7 | 33.0 | 10.9 | 5.4 | 2.1 |

*Source:* Data taken from Mikrozensus.

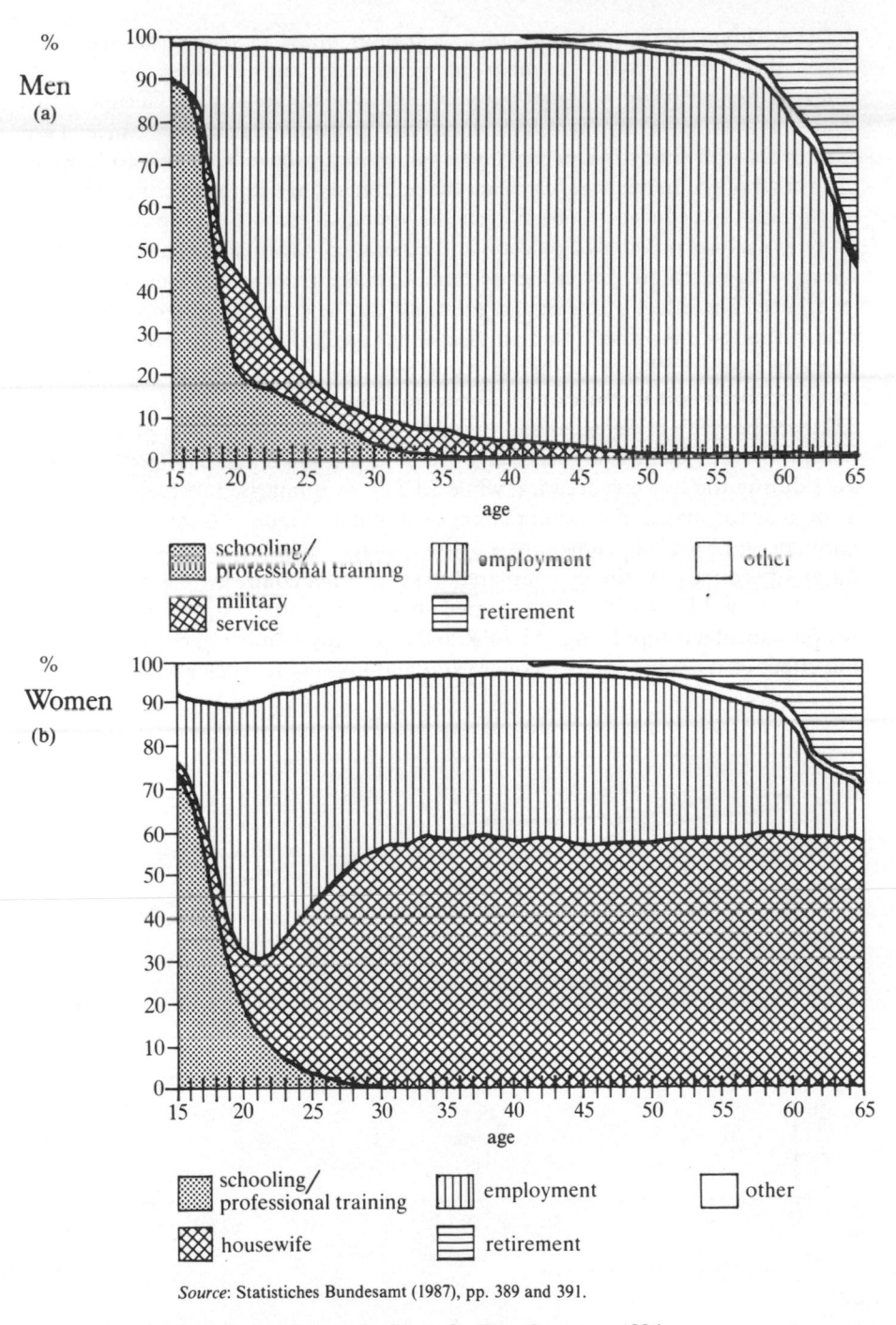

%
Men
(a)

| | | |
|---|---|---|
| schooling/professional training | employment | other |
| military service | retirement | |

%
Women
(b)

| | | |
|---|---|---|
| schooling/professional training | employment | other |
| housewife | retirement | |

*Source*: Statistiches Bundesamt (1987), pp. 389 and 391.

**Figure 8.4a and b** *Activities during the life cycle, West Germany, 1984*

Other things being equal, a shorter earnings phase increases the pensioner ratio; there is a higher number of pensioners and a lower number of contributors, therefore a higher contribution rate is necessary. In Germany this tendency has been strongly influenced by pension legislation. Since 1973 employees with thirty-five or more years of coverage have been able to retire at 63 instead of 65. In the next few years the retirement age for handicapped people was gradually reduced to 60. Within the system there is a strong incentive to retire as early as possible (if pension and other income are high enough) because the only 'price' to pay for earlier retirement is the reduced number of years of insurance. The effect of the new regulations can be seen from Figures 8.5a and 8.5b, although it is difficult to disentangle the various factors influencing LFPR. The effect on LFPR for women is much less than for men because since 1957 they have been able to retire at 60. The hypothesis that social security regulations influence people's preferences and opinions about when to retire is plausible.

Employment behaviour, especially of married women, has changed considerably during the last few decades, while LFPR for unmarried women are nearly as high as for men and have not changed so much. Figure 8.6 shows LFPR for German and Swedish women, based on cross-sectional information (LFPR for different groups over time). Compared to some other countries (e.g. Sweden and the USA) the LFPR of German women are relatively low. For this reason many people expect a future rising of LFPR and a growing number of employees, with the effect of reducing the pensioner ratio and making it much easier to finance

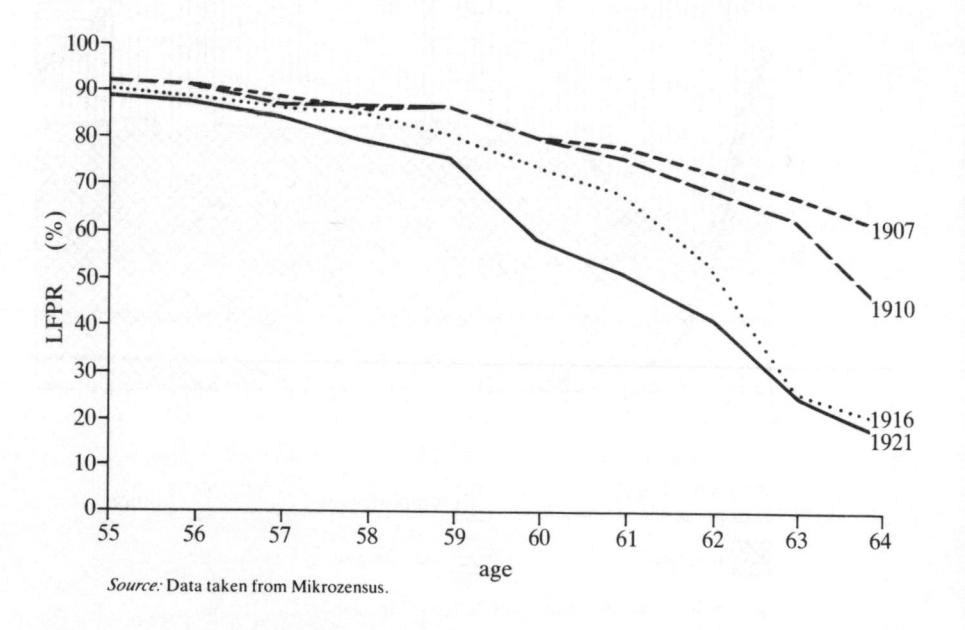

*Source:* Data taken from Mikrozensus.

**Figure 8.5a** *Labour force participation rates of male cohorts, West Germany*

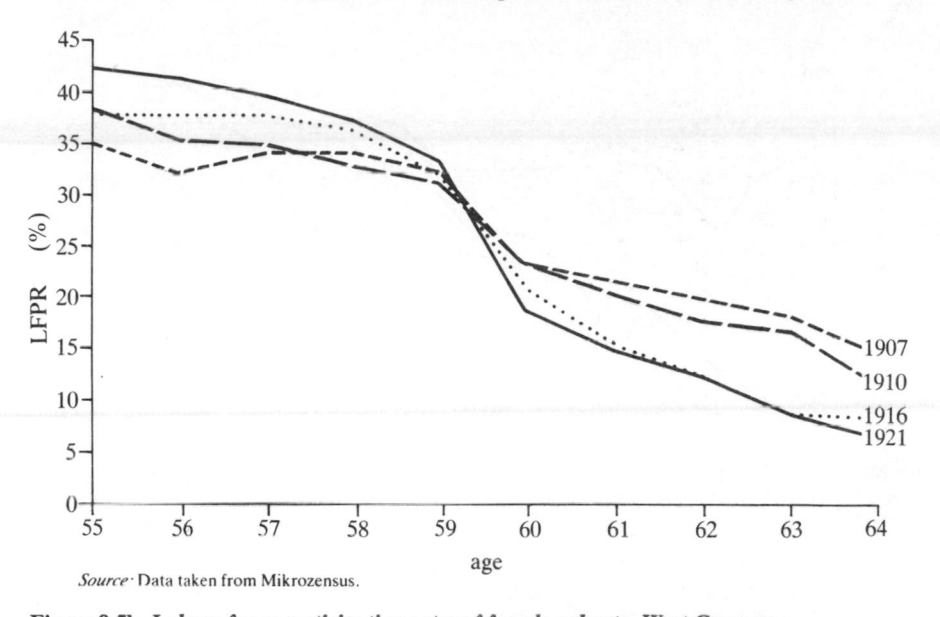

*Source·* Data taken from Mikrozensus.

**Figure 8.5b** *Labour force participation rates of female cohorts, West Germany*

pensions than a simple analysis of the effect of demographic ageing on pension financing would suggest.

Cohort- and age-specific LFPR have to be considered here too. For the cohorts in Figure 8.7 LFPR are in most cases higher for the younger cohorts. Even allowing for the limited reliability of retrospective answers, on which the data in Figure 8.7 are based, the tendency is quite clear. Differences in age-specific LFPR according to the number of children and the number of cases in each subgroup are relevant when calculating overall LFPR, because it is a weighted average of LFPR of the subgroups. Structural changes between the different groups have to be considered as well as the changing age structure of the population. However, adequate data are often lacking.

The effect of ageing, under the assumption of constant, age-specific LFPR for Germany, shows only little change for the next fifty years. Based on age-specific LFPR for 1984 and the demographic projection variant I (BMI, 1987), total LFPR (for ages 15–65) change for men from 0.82 in 1984 to 0.80 in 2030 (minimum 0.79, maximum 0.83), for women from 0.52 in 1984 to 0.49 in 2030 (varying between 0.48 and 0.53). Other things being equal, demographic ageing will reduce LFPR for both men and women slightly.

More interesting is whether cohort-specific development of LFPR will show the same tendency as in the past, especially the increasing age-specific LFPR of married women. How strong is the effect on the number of contributors? Can it compensate for the increasing number of pensioners so that the pensioner ratio will remain constant or increase considerably less than demographic projections

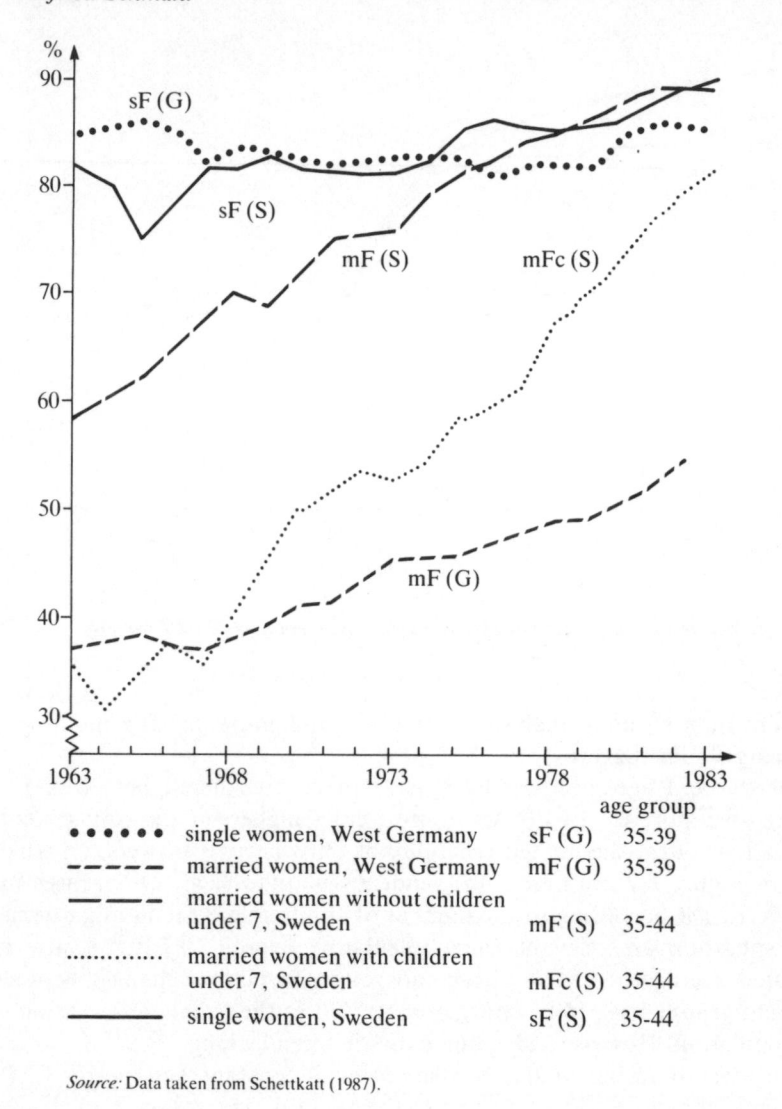

**Figure 8.6** *Labour force participation rates for different groups of women, West Germany and Sweden*

anticipate? The other question concerns LFPR in the higher age groups near retirement age. Will they remain constant, further decrease or increase? What effects can be expected from political activities and changing labour market conditions, as well as from changes in industrial structure, technology, and their consequences for labour demand, both numerically and in relation to particular skills? Will rising LFPR for women make it unnecessary to increase retirement ages? Up to now no comprehensive simulations have been done for West

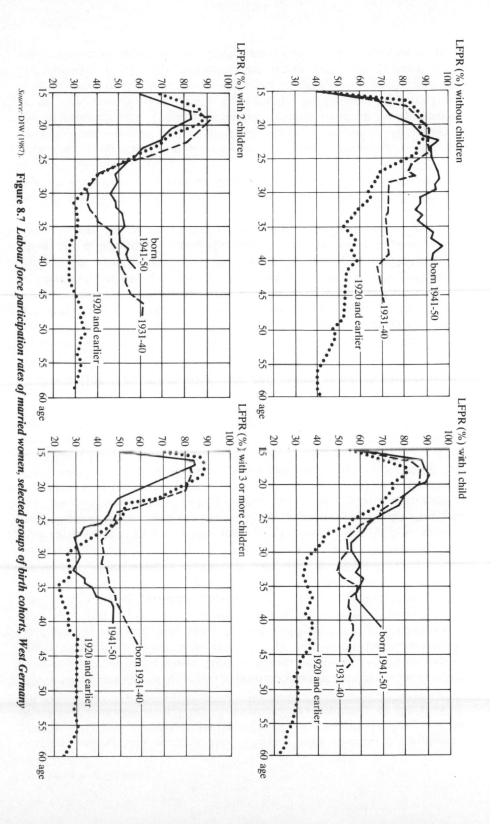

LFPR (%) without children

LFPR (%) with 1 child

LFPR (%) with 2 children

LFPR (%) with 3 or more children

*Source:* DIW (1987).

**Figure 8.7** *Labour force participation rates of married women, selected groups of birth cohorts, West Germany*

Germany taking into account the different cohort-specific developments, possible structural changes in the number of the different subgroups of the population (considering different behavioural assumptions), or the possible influence of political measures.

However, simply 'counting heads', as is often done when looking at the development of LFPR, is not enough. Hours worked are also important for labour supply, earnings, contribution payments and pension claims. Part-time work in Germany has increased remarkably. More than 90 per cent of part-time workers are women and 83 per cent of all part-time working women are married (June 1984). The ratio of part-time working women to all employed women has increased steadily from about 9 per cent in 1960 to 24 per cent in 1970 and 32 per cent in 1985 (Brinkmann *et al.*, 1986, p. 362). Most part-time working women are between 30 and 55 years old. It will be interesting to see whether part-time work for men will increase in the future too. Part-time work for both spouses makes it easier to combine work and family life, especially for women. Part-time work for men could probably be extended in general if phased retirement is introduced into the statutory pension scheme (as now proposed in Germany, BMA, 1988) or by negotiations of unions and employers' organisations. The possibilities for this, as well as the many effects on labour market, labour demand and supply, health and income cannot be discussed here (see Schmähl, 1988a, 1989 and further references given there).

## Cross-sectional earnings structure and earnings development over the life cycle

It is not only LFPR and the ratio of full-time to part-time employment that determine the necessary contribution rate, but also earnings gained from employment. A cross-sectional snapshot view of 1984 gives an idea of the earnings structure between full-time and part-time employment as well as between men and women. Figure 8.8 is restricted to people with year-round employment. The frequency distributions for the three groups included show remarkable differences in earnings between the sexes (which arise from a multitude of factors, among them differences in qualifications between cohorts).[5] The lower level of part-time earnings is not surprising compared to the level of earnings of full-time employed women. Figure 8.8 also explains why the earnings structure in total as well as average earnings of all employed persons are strongly determined by male earners.

Cross-sectional information alone can be misleading in discussing future development. Cohort-specific and longitudinal, life-cycle-orientated information is also of great interest. The cross-sectional earnings structure for age groups depends on, among other factors, demographic development (age structure), often neglected in distributional analysis, and cohort-specific age-earnings profiles (see, e.g., Welch, 1979; Stapleton and Young, 1984). The U-shape of the well-known cross-sectional age-earnings profile for different age groups seems

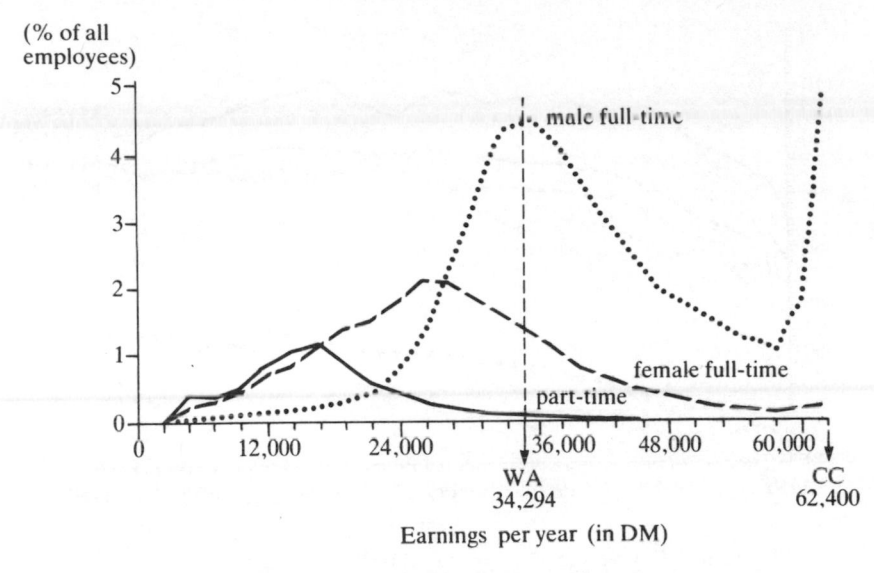

(% of all employees)

WA = average earnings    CC = contribution ceiling

Source. Author's calculation based on Employee Statistics
(Beschäftigtenstatistik), Becker (1987), p. 377.

**Figure 8.8** *Frequency distribution of earnings, year-round, full-time and part-time employees, West Germany, 1984*

not to give a true picture of the development of individual earnings during the life cycle, at least not for German male and female employees (see Schmähl, 1983, 1986b). This can be seen from earnings profiles taken from social security earnings records. For birth cohorts of male workers, after a steep increase in the first part of the working career a more or less constant relative earnings position (REP), compared to all wage- and salary-earners in a certain year, could be found; see Figure 8.9.[6]

For women the cohort profiles during the years after the Second World War show a more or less steady increase of the relative earnings position (REP). However, in this data set full-time and part-time employment cannot be separated. Earnings development over the life cycle is relevant not only for changes in cross-sectional earnings structure and average yearly earnings, but also, as pointed out above, for pension claims and the pension replacement rate.

## Some consequences of changing labour force participation for the earnings-related German pension scheme

In this section I will point out several effects of structural changes mentioned above for the German statutory pension system. As shown in Figure 8.10, the

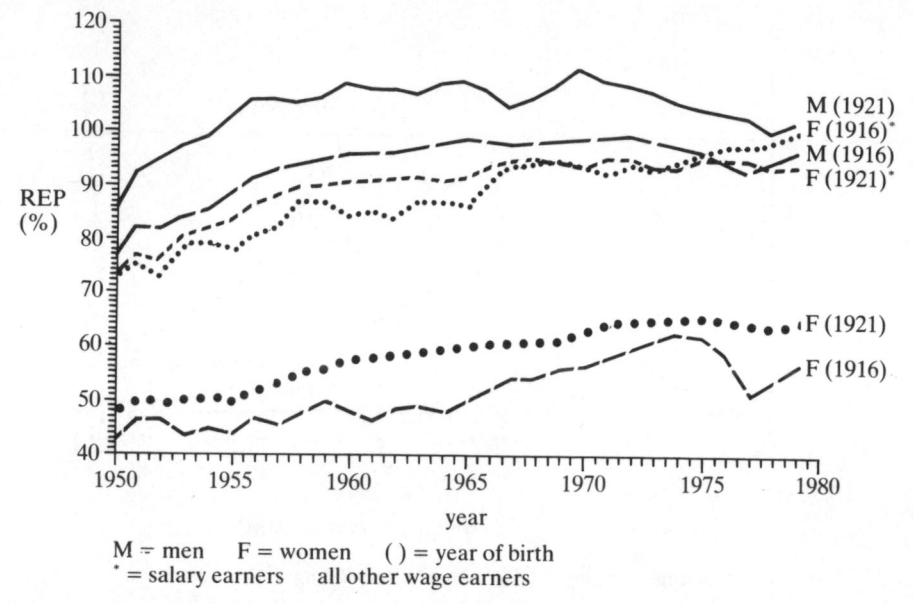

Source: Data taken from social security earnings records: author's calculations.

**Figure 8.9** *Cohort- and sex-specific age-earnings profiles, West Germany, 1950–79*

effects of the labour force participation rate on the pensioner ratio, and together with changing working time, as well as of earnings on the (average) pension level, have to be considered, the two ratios determining the necessary contribution rate (see Equation 1). In the first instance such a differentiated analysis may seem rather technical. But without going into detail, we must note that no adequate results of the many different effects can be obtained. In the German debate at least, some of the quick answers given in scientific and political discussions on future pension financing neglect important factors. It is a task of future research to give an overall quantitative view of the different effects, integrated in a comprehensive simulation model, to analyse their quantitative impact. Only some important elements of such simulation procedures, as well as some tentative results, can be explored here.

### Effects on the pensioner ratio (PR)

Other things being equal higher LFPR increase the number of contributors (NW) and, in the first round, lower PR (see Equation 1). Therefore, (the increase of) the contribution rate is reduced. However, contributors later become pensioners, and so PR rises again. Only if there is a continuous increase of LFPR could PR be reduced permanently. But LFPR cannot increase infinitely. Therefore the time path of LFPR as well as the age structure of the persons working are also important. If, for instance, LFPR for women at age 40 or more

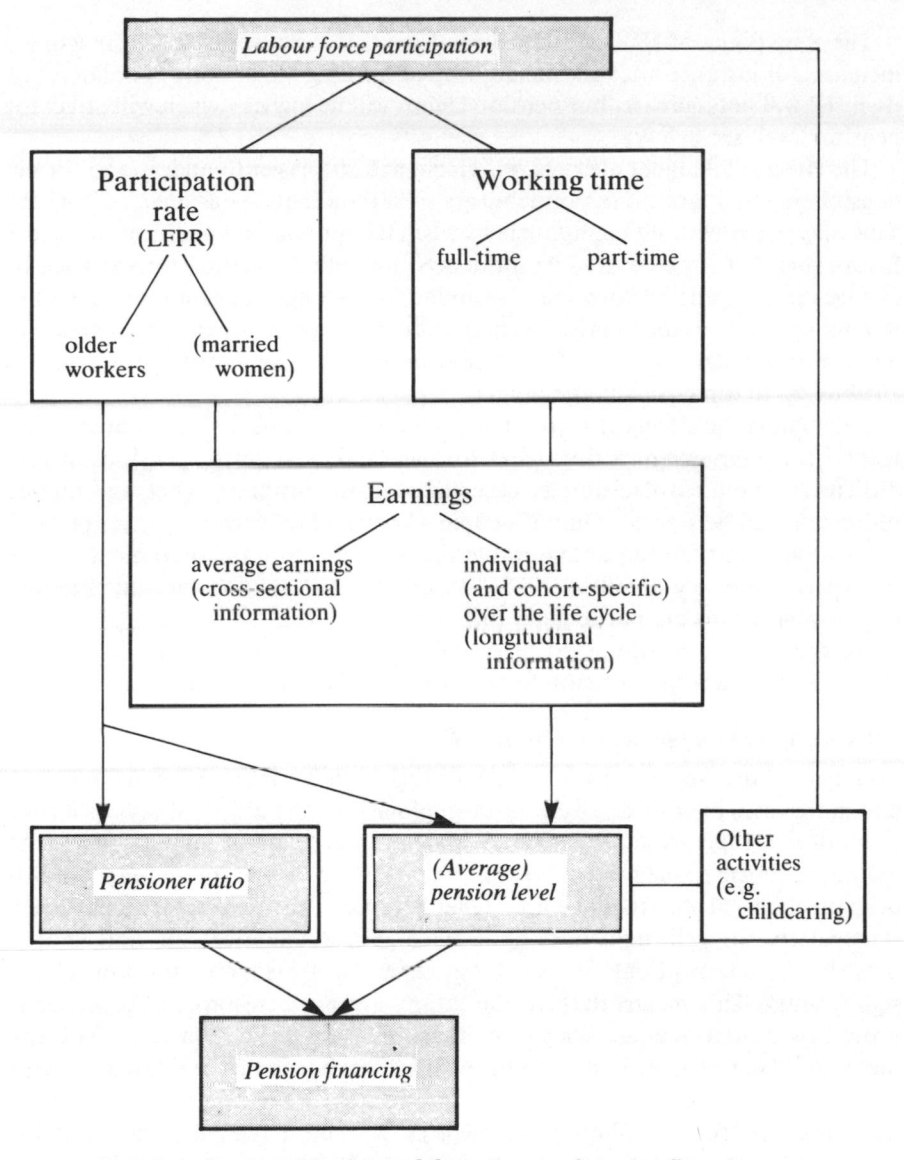

**Figure 8.10** *Labour force participation and determinants of pension financing*

are increasing in year t, then the number of pensioners (NP) will increase in about t+20. To calculate the effect of LFPR on PR it is therefore necessary to know:

(1) in which age group there will be an increase;
(2) how many persons are in this group;
(3) whether the change is temporary or lasting.

The time paths of NW and NP are relevant. If, however, LFPR for women increase, for instance after an interruption of working life because of childcaring, then NP will not increase, but pension claims will be higher (which will affect the pension level; see below).

The effects of a higher average retirement age[7] are easier to understand. Fewer pensioners (NP) and more contributors (NW) lower the pensioner ratio (PR). This may occur without changing laws when labour market conditions are more favourable, but it could also be influenced by political action, for instance by changes in the pension formula. Assuming the average pension level (APL) to remain unchanged, then in the German statutory pension scheme the increase of average retirement age by one year reduces the necessary contribution rate in 2030 by up to three percentage points.[8,9]

Calculating the effects of introducing possibilities for partial or gradual retirement, i.e. to combine part-time work for the elderly and partial pensions, is very difficult. A political decision is necessary on, for instance, what age phased retirement can be started. Only if people who would otherwise fully retire work for a while part-time can a favourable financial effect on the retirement system be expected (see, e.g., Müller, 1988). Assumptions about behavioural reactions to new regulations are particularly difficult.[10]

All this cannot be discussed or calculated without considering the possible effects on the (average) pension level, further complicating the matter.

### Effects on the average pension level (APL)

Younger cohorts seem to have on the average higher relative earnings positions and more years of coverage by gainful employment than older cohorts. But total years of coverage are not very much higher; fewer years of military service by younger cohorts is one reason for this. Table 8.3 shows that for younger cohorts pension claims at a certain age are higher because of the two factors mentioned. Particularly for full-time working women, better qualifications and shorter periods of interruptions in working career will increase pension claims significantly. This means that, in the future, average pensions will continue to grow faster than average wages, so that the average pension level will also increase.[11] On the other hand, the following effect has to be considered: if either own actual earnings or pension from own insurance are above the exemption limit relevant for calculating widow(er)'s pension payments, then pension expenditure will increase at a lower rate (as will average pension). Increasing female labour force activity and higher female earnings can, on the other hand, reduce the accumulation of own pension claims because of their possible negative effect on the employment of women. Up to now it has not been clear what will be the net effect, or the effect of widow's pensions alone, in the future.

But there are other factors besides the effect of more female employment and more part-time work on average earnings development. Increasing part-time work, as well as lower earnings of women compared to men, reduces the growth rate of average earnings.[12] This is relevant for the personal as well as for the

**Table 8.3** *Pension claims for different cohorts and their components, social insurance pension system (GRV), West Germany*

| Cohort | Men | | | Women | | |
|---|---|---|---|---|---|---|
| | 1921–25 | 1931–35 | 1941–45 | 1921–25 | 1931–35 | 1941–45 |
| Age group | Months of coverage | | | | | |
| 30–34 | 179.61 | 189.41 | 193.67 | 112.62 | 110.46 | 120.72 |
| 40–44 | 272.80 | 294.11 | – | 163.48 | 167.10 | – |
| 50–54 | 368.41 | – | – | 224.65 | – | – |
| | Percentage of personal earnings base | | | | | |
| 30–34 | 106.60 | 107.88 | 109.37 | 67.60 | 72.51 | 80.09 |
| 40–44 | 110.72 | 112.03 | – | 68.70 | 70.30 | – |
| 50–54 | 112.12 | – | – | 68.70 | – | – |
| | Pension claim per month in DM | | | | | |
| 30–34 | 454.4 | 485.0 | 502.8 | 180.7 | 190.1 | 229.5 |
| 40 44 | 717.0 | 788.0 | – | 266.6 | 278.8 | – |
| 50–54 | 988.0 | – | – | 366.3 | – | – |
| Number | 168 | 276 | 307 | 243 | 232 | 257 |

*Source:* Von Rosenbladt *et al.* (1987), pp. 351–6.

general earnings base and therefore for pension claims and pension adjustment. The *relative* earnings position of those employed full-time will rise but the *absolute* amount is lowered, via a reduced general earnings base. The net effect is unclear.

The effect on total pension claims and future pension payments depends on the time path of pension claims and the age structure of the pensioners of the future. Individual pension claims will tend to rise. When in the future these persons become pensioners and the group of those who then have to finance these pension payments includes (relatively) more part-time workers compared to those of pensionable age, then future financing problems are likely to become more serious because of the relatively higher claims of the older cohorts. However, the absolute amount of future pension payments is determined by the future development of average earnings. Here also the net effect is not clear in advance.

Another effect is easier to estimate: if the growth rate of average earnings is reduced, then also pension adjustment is reduced, long before people with the new employment pattern become pensioners. A lower pension adjustment rate means, other things being equal, fewer pension payments to be financed.[13]

The effects of an ageing population and changing cohort size on age-earnings profiles must also be mentioned. In an ageing labour force with relatively higher earnings for older workers, average earnings will increase. For a given development of the age structure, the age-earnings profile of the relevant subgroups of the population (e.g. men, women) and structural changes between these groups determine the quantitative effect. Among other questions, we have to ask whether the age-earnings profiles are stable over time, particularly when cohort sizes change.

One last aspect must be considered in connection with increasing part-time employment. Will pension claims be high enough to receive a pension above the poverty line if there are long periods of part-time work during individuals' working lives? If not, additional social assistance could be necessary. Even if earnings from part-time work are high enough to finance a decent standard of living, are they also high enough for the period of old age and of receiving a pension in an earnings-related scheme like Germany's? This system was constructed in a period when marriage and full-time employment of the husband were the norm, as well as a low divorce rate and a high rate of remarriage among divorcees and widow(er)s. The answer to this question depends partly on the development of family and household structure. Do employees with long part-time working periods live together with a partner and have a household income well above the poverty line, not only during the active years but during the retirement phase too? If there is a high degree of instability in relationship of partners the danger of insufficient income as they grow older is higher. Particularly for women, this may be an 'incentive' to work more.

All this taken together shows that simple answers are not possible and that the complex interactions between demographic development, labour market conditions and social security must be considered. And it is not enough to look at some general aspects of the social security system; a careful investigation of institutional rules is necessary. Structural changes obviously imply more challenges for the German system than can be seen from the development of the contribution rate necessary to balance the social security budget, which is often used as the main indicator for future financing problems.

As has become obvious, the German system is very complicated, which makes the analysis of effects, either structural or of measures implemented, so difficult. Is the situation different in countries without earnings-related schemes, such as Germany's, but with flat-rate schemes?

## Consequences for a tax-financed flat-rate pension scheme

In this last section I shall only discuss effects in a flat-rate tax-financed system (financed out of the general budget), not, for instance, in a system financed by earmarked minimum contributions (as discussed, among other reform proposals, in Germany during the last few years). Assuming, for the sake of simplicity, a flat-rate pension (FP) financed only by income tax, several remarkable differences compared to the earnings-related scheme discussed above can be mentioned. We start with the budget equation:

$$t = \frac{NP}{NT} \times \frac{FP}{YA} \qquad (3)$$

where
t   = income tax rate
NP = number of pensioners
NT = number of taxpayers
FP = flat-rate pension
YA = average (taxable) income.

A higher ratio of old people also increases the pensioner ratio (here defined as NP/NT), but less than in the earnings-related scheme, because the number of pensioners (NP) is included in the group of all taxpayers (NT). This can be illustrated by the simple example shown in Table 8.4.

Consequences for the FP/YA ratio are not so obvious. A higher number of pensioners receiving FP reduces YA, because of FP being less than YA. However, not only FP but also the total income of pensioners is relevant for the development of YA.[14] FP development does not depend on individual employment behaviour and earnings. Higher LFPR and higher individual earnings may increase average income. If the relevant adjustment rate for FP is the growth rate of YA, then the pension level remains constant over time.

The retirement age is also relevant for the financing of this system. A higher retirement age means fewer pensioners and fewer pension payments. The income tax base will be higher for a longer time. These effects are similar to those of the earnings-related scheme and lower the financing burden. Because NP is included in NT, the effect on tax revenue does not only depend on the average income of pensioners compared to other taxpayers, but also on the kind of taxation of (different types of) retirement income, if special conditions exist.

Summing up, the effects of changing labour force participation and employment behaviour on the financing situation of a flat-rate system seem to be less complicated than for an earnings-related system. This does not mean that structural changes do not influence the financing situation. Although effects in this kind of system are fairly straightforward, this should not be taken too readily as an argument in favour of such a system. Such a conclusion would be based on

Table 8.4 *Effects of an increasing number of pensioners on the pensioner ratio in an earnings-related scheme and a flat-rate scheme*

| Case | Number of people employed (NW) | Number of pensioners (NP) | Sum (NT) |
|------|-------------------------------|---------------------------|----------|
| (1) | 100 | 50 | 150 |
| (2) | 75 | 75 | 150 |
| Earnings-related pension scheme | NP/NW  (1) = 0.5     (2) = 1.0 increase of pensioner ratio = 100% | | |
| Flat-rate pension scheme | NP/NT  (1) = 0.33    (2) = 0.5 increase of pensioner ratio = 51.5% | | |

much too limited a view. Many additional aspects must be considered when comparing different systems. In the present context, effects on incentives to work are only one important factor (see, e.g., Schmähl, 1988c and references given there). Last but not least, in most countries with a flat-rate pension system additional (mostly earnings-related) public systems exist. The interdependency of the systems and their combined effects must therefore be considered, a task that is far beyond the scope of this article.

## Some concluding remarks

What can be learned from the above analysis, both in general and for the German debate in particular? As far as the future development of the German statutory pension scheme is concerned, my conclusion is that at least in the long run demographic development is the dominating factor influencing its financing situation, other things being equal and above all if the structure of the system remains unchanged. Higher employment and in particular higher female labour force participation cannot be expected to solve financing problems. To cope with the challenges of structural changes, above all in demography, political activities remain necessary. Realistically these must comprise a combination of measures (see Schmähl, 1988b), a strategy most political parties in Germany agree upon. This instrument mix must aim to reduce the rate of expenditure increase as well as to distribute the additional burden in a politically and economically reasonable way, seen by the population as a fair solution. As far as the reduction of demographically induced pension costs is concerned (see Schmähl, 1987), an increase in the retirement age is of central importance. Higher employment of younger women (which in practice means above all of married women) does not obviate the need for a higher retirement age.

The examples used in this article clearly demonstrate the need to take into account institutional arrangements, because they determine to a large degree the impact of structural changes on social security systems as well as on variables and factors influenced by social security systems, such as the income situation of employees and pensioners. We must consider not only the effects of statutory systems, but also their interaction with supplementary schemes, above all with occupational pension systems, as well as with taxes and transfer payments in general (see Schmähl, 1986c). Such an integrated view is easier to demand than to realise politically. Research has to point out the need for such integrated approaches not only to pension systems but also, very clearly, to decisions concerning retirement ages where, among other things, the labour market, social security systems, health and income are affected. And such questions must not only be discussed from a cross-sectional perspective but must also take account of longitudinal aspects; the impact of structural changes, as well as political measures, on social security must be viewed from a life-cycle perspective and cohort-specific developments must be considered. There are difficult tasks ahead in research as well as politics.

# Appendix

*Variables determining the necessary contribution rate (c) for balancing the budget of an earnings-related pension scheme*

(1) $C_t + FG_t = P_t$
  where
  $C_t$ = sum of contribution payments in t
  $FG_t$ × federal grant in t
  $P_t$ = pension expenditure in t
(2) $FG_t = z_t \times P_t$
  where $0 < z_t < 1$
(3) $C_t = P_t - z_t P_t$
    $= P_t (1 - z_t)$
(4) $C_t = c_t \times NW_t \times WA_t$
(5) $P_t = NP_t \times PA_t$
(6) $c_t \times NW_t \times WA_t = NP_t \times PA_t \times (1 - z_t)$
(7) $c_t = \dfrac{NP_t}{NW_t} \times \dfrac{PA_t}{WA_t} \times (1 - z_t)$

where

c = earnings-related contribution rate necessary in the statutory system to balance the budget
NP = number of pensioners
NW = number of wage- and salary-earners
PA = average (gross) pension payment
WA = average (gross) earnings
z = ratio of federal grant (subsidy) in financing pension expenditure.

# Notes

1 The average retirement age for men and women is below 60 because of invalidity pensions. Looking at old-age pensions alone, in 1986 31.1 per cent of men and 53.4 per cent of women retired at 65, the rest between 60 and 64.

2 An important question is how much the factor of earning (own) money is influencing the labour force participation of married women. If a recently published study based on cross-sectional data for West Germany (Merz, 1987) is correct, the income motive seems to be of minor importance for employment behaviour of married women; in this case hardly any noticeable effect could be expected from the actual form of widow(er)'s pension calculation.

3 For persons (or households) with total income below a certain amount, means-tested social assistance is paid (based on household income and household structure). The (gross) income of the elderly is determined additionally by occupational pensions in the private and public sector, other transfer payments (e.g. rent subsidy) or income from employment or assets. None of these are discussed here, nor is the special pension scheme for civil servants.

4 Taking a progressive income tax and tax-splitting for couples into account, then the net replacement rate even of people with identical gross replacement rates can differ when they have different absolute earnings in their last year of employment or different family status.

5 All information on relative frequency is calculated on the basis of the total number of covered employees. Nearly 45 per cent of them are year-round male full-time earners, 22 per cent female full-time, 7 per cent part-time year-round. For male earners the effect of the contribution ceiling is obvious (1984 = 62,400 DM p.a.).

6 REP is defined in accordance with the calculation of the personal earnings base in the pension formula, i.e. cohort-specific (gross) earnings in t compared to average gross earnings of all insured employees in year t. Behind this high stability of cohort-specific REP there is, however, a high degree of individual earnings mobility. This is shown for the first time for Germany in Schmähl and Fachinger (1989).

7 A clear distinction between the average retirement age and the legal age of retirement is necessary. The first points to the effect of behavioural responses to retirement ages, retirement conditions, etc. It is the weighted average of individual retirement ages. It cannot be expected that by changing the conditions within the pension system, e.g. increasing the 'normal retirement age' by one year, the average retirement age will increase by one year too.

8 This result depends on the assumption that no other measures to influence pension benefits are taken. If, for example, the adjustment rate is lowered (perhaps using average net wages instead of gross wages), then the sum of pension payments is reduced and increasing the retirement age has a smaller effect on the necessary contribution rate. In calculating the financing consequences of measures one always has to look at the whole set of instruments under consideration. For an overview of measures discussed in Germany to reform the pension system see Schmähl (1988b).

9 Another question is how to influence retirement behaviour. One way could be a gradual lowering of the constant factor in the pension formula, so that additional years of coverage are needed to get the same pension as before. The individual costs of retiring earlier will increase. Legislation has been introduced in the USA to influence the retirement age in this way. Another instrument is the introduction of actuarially fair reductions into the pension formula. In the long run, the costs of retiring earlier will be imposed on the retirees. The effects of all these measures depend on many circumstances, not only on the labour market and health conditions but also on other factors influencing the income of workers/retirees by tax-transfer policy and occupational pension schemes. When labour market conditions are unfavourable, obviously the worker often has no free choice as to when to retire. The decision may be effectively made by his firm.

10 A broad-based discussion on problems of redefining the process of retirement in Germany, in an international perspective, can be found in Schmähl (1988a, 1989).

11 Here it is assumed that the development of average wages determines pension adjustment, as is the case in Germany.

12 In addition the effect of growing part-time employment on total employment has to be discussed. Opinions differ on the employment effects of different types of working time reductions, but these cannot be discussed here.

13 Lower average earnings have however an additional effect, relevant to the development of contribution revenue. Because the growth rate of average earnings determines the general earnings base, this also lowers (relatively) the upper ceiling for contribution payments, because it is linked to the general earnings base (being 200 per cent of it). Therefore higher earnings are relatively less burdened by contributions. This reduces contribution revenue.

14 As long as the average income of pensioners is lower than the average income of other income recipients, and other things being equal, YA is reduced.

# References

Becker, B. (1987), 'Sozialversicherungspflichtig Beschäftigte nach Beschäftigungsdauer und Bruttoarbeitsentgelt: Ergebnis der Beschäftigtenstatistik 1984', *Wirtschaft und Statistik*, pp. 371–81.

BMA (Bundesminister für Arbeit und Sozialordnung (1988), 'Diskussions und Referentenentwurf eines Rentenreformgesetzes 1992', Bonn (mimeo).

BMI (Bundesminister des Inneren) (1987), 'Modellrechnungen zur Bevölkerungsentwicklung in der Bundesrepublik Deutschland – aktualisierte Fassung', ed. Bundesminister des Inneren, Bonn (mimeo).

Brinkmann, C., Kohler, H. and Regher, L. (1986), 'Teilsarbeit und Arbeitsvolumen', in *Mitteslungen aus der Arbeitsmarkt- und Berufsforschung*, pp. 362–5.

DIW (1987), *DIW-Wochenbericht*, 29.

Eckerle, K., Barth, H. J., Hofer, P. and Schilling, P. I. (1987), *Gesamtwirtschaftliche Entwicklungen und gesetzliche Rentenversicherung vor dem Hintergrund einer schrumpfenden Bevölkerung*, Basle, Prognos.

Merz, J. (1987), 'Das Arbeitsangebot verheirateter Frauen in der Bundesrepublik Deutschland', in H. -J. Krupp and U. Hanefeld (eds), *Lebenslagen im Wandel: Analysen 1987*, Frankfurt-am-Main, Campus.

Müller, H.-W. (1988), 'Finanzielle Aspekte einer Einführung von Teilrenten', *Deutsche Rentenversicherung*, pp. 378–400.

Schettkat, R. (1987), *Erwerbsbeteiligung und Politik: Theoretische und empirische Analysen von Determinanten und Dynamik des Arbeitsangebots in Schweden und der Bundesrepublik Deutschland*, Berlin, Sigma.

Schmähl, W. (1983), 'Income analysis based on longitudinal data from social security earnings records: the relative earnings position (age-earnings profile) and the individual replacement rate of German workers', in A. B. Atkinson and F. A. Cowell (eds), *Panel Data on Incomes*, London, London School of Economics, International Centre for Economics and Related Disciplines.

Schmähl, W. (1986a), *Economic Problems of Social Retirement*, Maastricht, Presses Interuniversitaires Européennes.

Schmähl, W. (1986b), 'Lohnentwicklung im Lebensverlauf', *Allgemeines Statistisches Archiv*, LXX, pp. 180–203.

Schmähl, W. (1986c), 'Public and private pensions for various population groups in the Federal Republic of Germany: past experience and tasks for the future', *International Social Security Review*, XXIX, pp. 258–276.

Schmähl, W. (1987), 'Social policies for reducing demographically induced costs in social security', *European Journal of Population*, III, pp. 439–57.

Schmähl, W. (ed.) (1988a), *Verkürzung oder Verlängerung der Erwerbsphase?*, Tübingen, Mohr.

Schmähl, W. (1988b), *Beiträge zur Reform der Rentenversicherung*, Tübingen, Mohr.

Schmähl, W. (1988c), 'Übergang zu Staatsbürger-Grundrenten: Ein Beitrag zur Deregulierung in der Alterssicherung?', in T. Thiemeyer (ed.), *Regulierung und Deregulierung im Bereich der Sozialpolitik*, Berlin, Duncker & Humblot.

Schmähl, W. (ed.) (1989), *Redefining the Process of Retirement in an International Perspective*, Heidelberg, Springer.

Schmähl, W. and Fachinger, U. (1989), 'Über Richtung und Ausmass der Lohnmobilität: Eine Kohortenanalyse für Arbeiter in der Bundesrepublik Deutschland von 1960 bis 1970', in K. Gerlach and O. Hübler (eds), *Effizienzlohntheorie, Individualeinkommen und Arbeitsplatzwechsel*, Frankfurtam-Main, Campus.

Stapleton, D. and Young, D. (1984), 'The effect of demographic change on the distribution of wages, 1967–1990', *Journal of Human Resources*, XIX, pp. 175–201.

Statistisches Bundesamt (1987), *Datenreport 1987*, Bonn, Bundeszentrale für politische Bildung.

Von Rosenbladt, B., Kiel, W. and Milenović, J. (1987), *Zukünftige Rentnergenerationen: Anwartschaften in der Alterssicherung der Geburtsjahrgänge 1920–1955*, Bonn, Bundesminister für Arbeit und Sozialordnung.

Welch, F. (1979), 'Effects of cohort size on earnings: the baby boom babies' financial bust', *Journal of Political Economy*, LXXXVII, pp. 65–74.

# Part III

## Restructuring the Life Course

# 9

# The Trend Towards Early Labour Force Withdrawal and the Reorganisation of the Life Course: A Cross-national Analysis

Anne-Marie Guillemard

For the last fifteen years labour force participation rates for persons aged 55 to 64 years old have been rapidly decreasing in most developed industrial societies. This trend first engulfed the 60–64-year-old age group and now embraces 55–59-year-olds. Significant changes have taken place in the pathways and calendar of definitive withdrawal from the labour force. In this article I shall use international comparisons of how people leave the labour market in order to shed light on the social implications of this massive trend, which is marking out new boundaries between work and retirement.

## The theoretical framework of sociological inquiry into labour force withdrawal

Two main objectives have guided this inquiry into this trend: first, to analyse how the life course and the welfare state are being reorganised; and second, to interpret the institutional arrangements regulating definitive labour force withdrawals as social constructions both of age categories, in particular of old age, and of the relationship between the life course and work.

The changes in definitive labour force withdrawal provide special evidence for examining the inter-relations between the reorganisation of the life course (how various socially defined ages are assigned the functions of work, education and leisure) and the reorganisation of social policies (notably how the internal boundaries between various welfare subsystems are being modified). Given the first objective, this sociological research has focused on the presumptive significance of these changes, particularly as embodied in the institutions providing coverage following definitive withdrawal, and the presumed meaning of what is considered to be a trend that is undermining our societies' model of the life course.

Should the changes now affecting the end of 'working life' be interpreted simply as following from an enlarged application of the life course model that has been slowly developed during the industrialisation of our societies? In this threefold model, there is, successively, a time for education, a time for work and, finally, a time of rest. If this interpretation holds, the phenomenon of early withdrawal from the labour force, like that of the late entry of young people into the labour market, merely amounts to concentrating the time spent working on an ever-narrower group of adults. Accordingly, a person's life still takes shape around his working life; and the major social determinant is still employment, the problem of jobs. Therefore, the chronological thresholds separating the three phases, though variable, are still set by the first entrance into and the last exit from the labour force. It follows that the meaning of work and, therefore, of its counterpart, retirement, have not been altered.

Another interpretation is possible. The changes under way can be taken to be signs that the threefold model of the life course is being deinstitutionalised. This interpretation has guided the hypotheses underlying this research. The boundaries between economic activity and 'inactivity' seem to be shifting as a result less of simply applying the retirement logic to younger age groups (with, as a consequence, early withdrawal) than of relinking the welfare system and the life course (with, as a consequence, the eventual overthrow of the threefold model).

As for the second objective, the institutional arrangements ensuring the transition out of the labour force can be taken to be the means of defining the relationship between age and employment. They give a meaning to growing old, to ageing, to acquiring an 'inactive' economic status. The rules governing these arrangements and the eligibility requirements under them provide evidence of how the transition towards economic inactivity is being socially redefined.

**Working hypotheses**

At first glance, one might suppose that the present rapid lowering of the age for definitive labour force withdrawal results from the acceleration of an age-old trend that started when pension systems were set up and has continued as coverage has been expanded. Accordingly, the date for admission into the third phase of life has simply advanced without any other change of importance. It is necessary to show why this interpretation does not fit the facts. A comparative analysis of several countries leads to another interpretation, one that sees these changes as a trend, and this trend as a radical transformation of the end of the life course, as the milestones are torn up that used to chronologically mark ages, give direction to career paths and point out the limits wherein individuals could draw up their plans. The meaning of this trend has to do not with reinforcing the threefold model of the life course but with 'dechronologising' and deinstitutionalising it. After presenting the data that prove that the labour force participation rates of 55–64-year-olds have dropped considerably, the institutional arrangements used to handle labour force withdrawal in the countries under study will be compared. In general, definitive withdrawal corresponds to entry into a (public or private) welfare subsystem. The most common of these sub-systems will be described, and their eligibility requirements will be examined so as to clarify the principles governing how work and non-work are being redistributed in the later years of life. Examining these principles leads, in conclusion, to an analysis of how the life course is being socially reorganised.

Of course, a fundamental question comes to mind: how are old-age insurance funds and pension systems involved in this trend? If they have lost the power to regulate definitive withdrawal from the labour force, then may not both our conception of retirement and the underlying idea of a contract between generations be coming up for reassessment? Is a new conception arising of what is just in exchanges from one generation to another?

## Early withdrawal: a major trend in developed industrial societies

The OECD's data on labour force participation rates during the past fifteen years for persons from 55 to 64 years old reveal a general, massive, downward trend. From 1975 to 1985, the rates for men fell, as Figure 9.1 shows: from 75 to 50 per cent in France, from 80 per cent to 53 per cent in the Netherlands, from 82 per cent to 58 per cent in West Germany and from 80 to 60 per cent in the United States.[1] Since these rates have been calculated by counting job-seekers as part of the labour force, the decrease has been even sharper than we might imagine by looking at the figure. This remark holds, in particular, for Great Britain which, if we take into account only those who have jobs, joins the list of countries whose

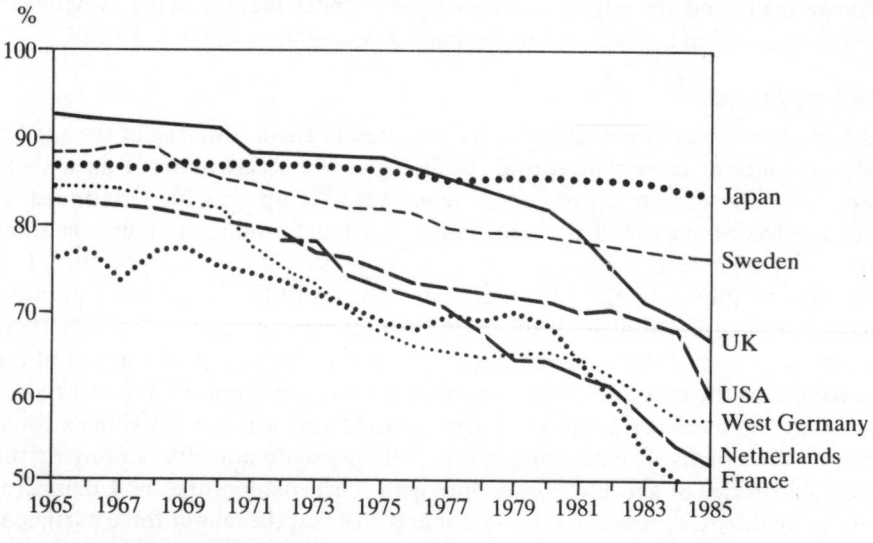

*Source:* OECD, *Labour Force Statistics*, Paris, 1984-86.

**Figure 9.1** *Labour force participation rates from 1965 to 1985 for men from 55 to 64 years old*

**Table 9.1** *Labour force participation rates and employment activity rates from 1965 to 1985 for men 55 to 64 years old in industrialised countries*

| | 1970 | 1971 | 1972 | 1973 | 1974 | 1975 | 1976 | 1977 | 1978 | 1979 | 1980 | 1981 | 1982 | 1983 | 1984 | 1985 |
|---|---|---|---|---|---|---|---|---|---|---|---|---|---|---|---|---|
| **Labour force participation rates: age 55–64/male** | | | | | | | | | | | | | | | | |
| USA | 80.7 | 80.0 | 79.1 | 76.9 | 76.2 | 74.6 | 73.3 | 72.8 | 72.3 | 71.8 | 71.2 | 69.9 | 70.2 | 68.8 | 67.9 | 59.7 |
| Japan | 86.6 | 87.1 | 86.6 | 86.8 | 86.3 | 86.0 | 85.9 | 84.8 | 85.0 | 85.2 | 85.4 | 85.0 | 84.9 | 84.7 | 83.8 | 83.0 |
| France | 75.4 | 74.6 | 74.6 | 72.1 | 70.8 | 67.9 | 67.9 | 69.4 | 68.8 | 69.9 | 68.5 | 64.3 | *59.8 | 53.6 | 50.3 | 50.1 |
| West Germany | 82.2 | 77.8 | 75.2 | 73.4 | 70.5 | 68.1 | 66.5 | 65.7 | 65.1 | 65.4 | 65.5 | 64.5 | 62.6 | 60.2 | 57.6 | 57.5 |
| Netherlands | – | 80.8 | 78.7 | 74.6 | 73.0 | 72.5 | 71.3 | 68.3 | 65.7 | 63.6 | 60.8 | 59.1 | 57.8 | 55.9 | 53.8 | – |
| Sweden | 85.4 | 84.7 | 83.5 | 82.7 | 82.0 | 81.3 | 81.3 | 79.7 | 79.1 | 79.2 | 78.7 | 78.1 | 77.7 | 77.1 | 76.2 | 76.0 |
| UK | 91.3 | *88.4 | 88.2 | 88.0 | 87.9 | 86.8 | 86.8 | 85.7 | 84.4 | 83.3 | 81.8 | 79.1 | 75.1 | 71.0 | 69.2 | 66.4 |
| **Unemployment rates: age 55–64/male** | | | | | | | | | | | | | | | | |
| USA | 2.8 | 3.3 | 3.2 | 2.4 | 2.6 | 4.3 | 4.2 | 3.5 | 2.8 | 2.7 | 3.4 | 3.6 | 5.5 | 6.1 | 5.0 | 4.3 |
| Japan | 2.1 | 2.1 | 2.1 | 1.8 | 2.1 | 3.2 | 3.8 | 3.8 | 4.3 | 4.4 | 3.7 | 4.3 | 4.3 | 5.0 | 5.0 | 5.0 |
| France | 1.9 | 2.2 | 2.6 | 1.9 | 2.1 | 2.6 | 3.1 | 3.6 | 4.3 | 4.0 | 4.7 | 4.8 | *5.3 | 6.0 | 6.2 | 6.7 |
| West Germany | 0.9 | 1.2 | 2.0 | 1.6 | 2.3 | 3.9 | 3.9 | 3.7 | 4.0 | 4.3 | 4.3 | 5.4 | 7.0 | 8.5 | 10.0 | 10.2 |
| Netherlands | – | – | – | – | 2.4 | 3.1 | 3.6 | 3.5 | 3.3 | 3.2 | 3.3 | 3.9 | 5.2 | 13.7 | 13.7 | 11.9 |
| Sweden | 1.5 | 2.3 | 2.3 | 2.1 | 2.4 | 1.6 | 1.4 | 1.1 | 1.8 | 1.8 | 1.6 | 2.2 | 3.1 | 4.0 | 4.2 | 3.5 |
| UK | 5.0 | *5.9 | 6.6 | 5.7 | 5.4 | 6.3 | 7.6 | 7.8 | 8.2 | 8.1 | 9.5 | 15.2 | *17.6 | 13.9 | 13.3 | 13.4 |
| **Employment activity rates: age 55–64/male** | | | | | | | | | | | | | | | | |
| USA | 78.4 | 77.4 | 76.6 | 75.1 | 74.2 | 71.4 | 70.2 | 70.3 | 70.3 | 69.9 | 68.8 | 67.4 | 66.3 | 64.6 | 64.5 | 57.1 |
| Japan | 84.8 | 85.3 | 84.8 | 85.2 | 83.2 | 82.6 | 82.6 | 81.6 | 81.3 | 81.5 | 82.2 | 81.3 | 81.2 | 80.5 | 79.6 | 78.9 |
| France | 74.0 | 73.0 | 71.5 | 70.7 | 69.3 | 67.1 | 65.8 | 66.9 | 65.8 | 67.1 | 65.3 | 61.2 | *56.6 | 50.4 | 47.2 | 46.7 |
| West Germany | 81.5 | 76.9 | 73.7 | 72.2 | 65.4 | 63.9 | 63.9 | 63.3 | 62.5 | 62.6 | 62.7 | 61.0 | 58.2 | 55.1 | 51.8 | 51.6 |
| Netherlands | – | – | 75.3 | 72.8 | 70.7 | 69.9 | 68.8 | 66.0 | 63.6 | 61.5 | 60.8 | 58.4 | 56.0 | 53.8 | 51.8 | 50.9 |
| Sweden | 84.1 | 82.8 | 81.6 | 81.0 | 80.4 | 80.7 | 80.2 | 78.8 | 77.7 | 77.8 | 77.4 | 76.4 | 75.3 | 74.0 | 73.0 | 73.3 |
| UK | 86.7 | *83.2 | 82.4 | 83.0 | 83.2 | 82.3 | 80.2 | 79.0 | 77.5 | 76.6 | 74.0 | 67.1 | *61.9 | 61.1 | 60.0 | 57.5 |

*Break in time series

*Source:* OECD, *Labour Force Statistics*, Paris, 1984, and our calculations.

labour force participation rates have plummeted (see Table 9.1, 'Employment activity rates'). By comparison, Sweden (as well as Japan) has not been swept up in this trend. On the question of women, a cross-sectional analysis is not very revealing since large numbers of women have entered the labour market during this period; an identical trend towards early labour force withdrawal can be clearly seen through a cohort analysis (Jacobs *et al.,* 1988). Given that data about men are more interpretable, the following remarks will be based primarily on them. Likewise, five countries were selected where the early withdrawal trend is the most noticeable; and Sweden was added to the sample as evidence of the contrary. In effect, the boundaries between work and retirement in Sweden have shifted but only slightly in comparison with the other five.

After a slow evolution over nearly half a century that gradually set the retirement age at 65 (the most common age of entitlement to a full old-age pension), the chronological thresholds used both to determine personal identities throughout the life course and to organise the transition to old age have been torn up during the last fifteen years. The age when persons stop working has been lowered significantly. This change affected, at first, the 60–64-year-old age group (see Figure 9.2); its labour force participation rate has fallen by about 50 per cent over the past twenty years. By 1979–80 in most countries, excepting Sweden (and Japan), this change concerned 55–59-year-olds (see Figure 9.3); their economic activity rate fell by an average of 20 per cent.

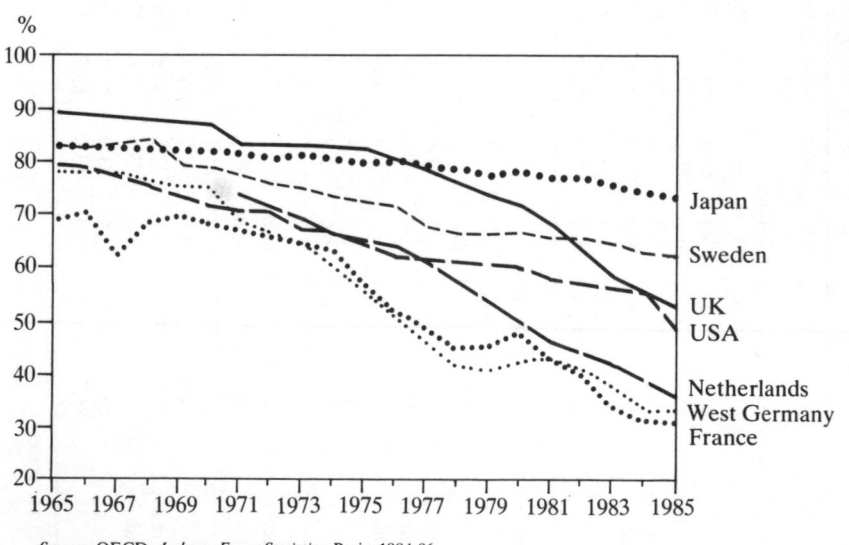

Source: OECD, *Labour Force Statistics,* Paris, 1984-86.

**Figure 9.2 *Labour force participation rates from 1965 to 1985 for men from 60 to 64 years old***

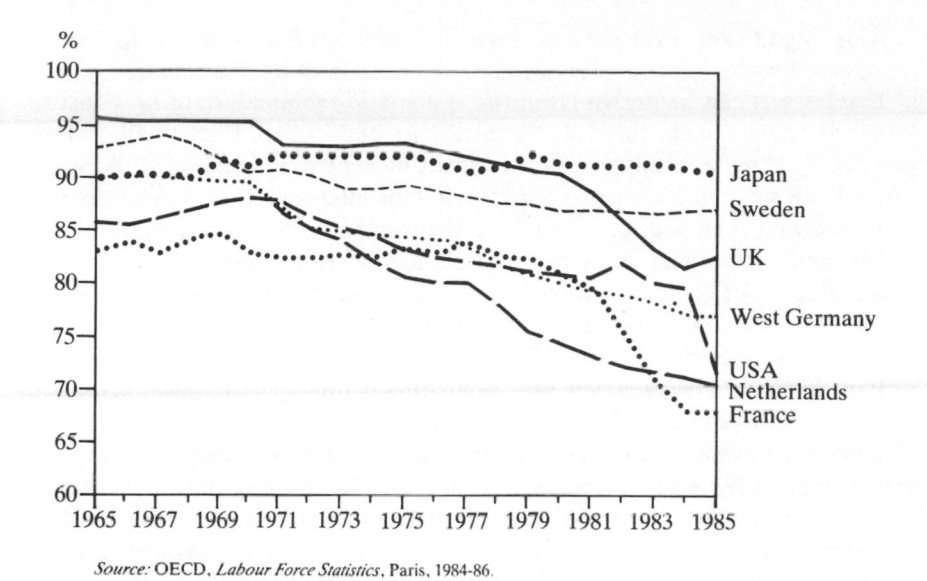

*Source:* OECD, *Labour Force Statistics*, Paris, 1984-86.

**Figure 9.3** *Labour force participation rates from 1965 to 1985 for men from 55 to 59 years old*

## Comparative analysis of the institutional arrangements ensuring early withdrawal

Given this lowering of the threshold for definitive withdrawal from the labour force, it is necessary to examine the institutional arrangements that have author-ised this shift in the boundary between inactivity and activity if we want to understand the meaning of this trend and to propose an interpretation. The nature and characteristics of these arrangements can be studied as being the means used to socially construct the relationship between the life course and work. The rules governing these institutions and the eligibility requirements under these arrangements reveal how the transition towards retirement is being socially redefined. Analysing these institutional arrangements can shed light on the principles that govern how work and non-work are distributed in the later years of life. This analysis also helps explain how the elderly are socially categorised as a group, and how old age is socially constructed.

The institutional arrangements to be taken into account cannot be defined a priori; they must be discovered and examined country by country. At the start, this meant studying each country to observe the principal pathways by which persons withdraw early from the labour force and the complicated institutional arrangements that have opened these pathways. The following analysis brings together the principal results of this empirical investigation of the six countries under review here. The aim is, above all, to see the similarities in the operation of such institutional arrangements. These cross-national points of convergence provide significant evidence of how national welfare systems are being reorganised with, as a consequence, a reorganisation of the life course.

Two lessons can be drawn from the systematic examination of how institutional arrangements in these six countries are converging. First of all, old-age pension systems are declining as the means of regulating exits from the workforce. In all six countries, people are leaving the labour market long before they start receiving such pensions: exit from the workforce, in most cases, no longer corresponds to a direct entry into the old-age pension system. In fact, only a small minority of persons now receive old-age pensions upon retirement immediately after they stop working: in these countries, excepting Sweden, only about 20 per cent of men still fit into this pattern. Second, and as a consequence, the new institutional arrangements now regulating definitive withdrawal bring into play other subsystems of the welfare system than old-age insurance. These new arrangements connect, in original ways, various of these subsystems so as to create unprecedented and unstable possibilities for moving out of the labour market and reaching the moment of entitlement to an old-age pension. These arrangements, their rules and requirements, both govern passage towards inactivity and set the threshold of old age as a period of life after work.

### The decline of the retirement system as a means of regulating withdrawal

A crucial change is that retirement systems are no longer as important for managing definitive exit from work. The generalisation of old-age pensions has been, during the development of industrial society, a major factor in the institutionalisation of the life course following a model of three ordered phases: education-work-retirement. Retirement has served as a compensation for the alienation of work, a time when people rest at the end of their lives; after contributing to production, they are entitled to rest. Work has thus been placed at the centre of the individual's life to the point that we talk about his 'working life'. It conditions the right to this time of rest. Analysing retirement as an 'element of the moral economy' in industrial societies, Martin Kohli (1987) considers it to be a pivotal means of social control. He sees the institutionalisation of the three-phase life-course model as a major means of socialisation in industrial society. Retirement has significantly contributed to the 'chronologisation' and 'standardisation' of the life course: as old-age pension coverage was generalised, the lifespan has been chronologically marked with reference to it (the age of entitlement to a full pension, the number of years of contributions necessary for entitlement, etc.).

Given the way retirement has helped construct a life course model, what are the implications of its decline? Does it not imply that this model is also waning? The fact that retirement systems are losing control over early withdrawal runs counter to the interpretation that the latter amounts to a change of calendar, a sign of the acceleration of an age-old trend towards lowering the retirement age. On the contrary, this decline is evidence in favour of another interpretation, namely that the threefold organisation of the life course is coming apart. This hypothesis will be used to examine the new institutional arrangements that are taking over, from the retirement system, the management of definitive withdrawal from the labour force.

## The new institutional arrangements and their implications

As old-age insurance and the pension system no longer fully manage the transition out of the labour force, other welfare subsystems have become significantly involved in redefining the boundary between working life and life after work. The principal subsystems are unemployment compensation and disability insurance. In France, the Netherlands and West Germany, definitive withdrawal has been managed through new measures within the framework of unemployment compensation and/or disability insurance. The same holds for Sweden and England, but not to the exclusion of all other arrangements. In the United States, public welfare programmes have had little effect on labour force departures; but many companies have adopted early withdrawal policies, notably the Early Retirement Incentive Program (ERIP), which has spread widely since the early 1980s (Meier, 1986). All this has taken place despite the 1986 amendment to the Age Discrimination in Employment Act, which forbids age discrimination with regard to dismissals as well as to retirement. Let us look at the two principal means of handling early withdrawal and examine their implications.

### *The disability insurance pathway*

Disability insurance provides one of the major pathways out of the labour force in the Netherlands, West Germany, Sweden and Great Britain. It has, in some cases, been used along with other arrangements, particularly under unemployment compensation, so as to complete the bridge from the workforce across early withdrawal till the normal retirement age. The building of this bridge has usually involved, as we shall see, broadening eligibility requirements under disability insurance.

In the Netherlands, the most common pathway for early withdrawal led until the late 1970s through disability insurance, and this is still a well-used route. The number of beneficiaries increased 130 per cent from 1973 to 1979; in 1979 nearly 60 per cent of persons receiving disability benefits were over 50 years old. Under these arrangements, health insurance covers the first stretch of fifty-two weeks; and then, if total disability is recognised, disability insurance takes up the remainder. The impact of these arrangements increased after 1973, when eligibility requirements under disability insurance were broadened. Accordingly, partial, even minimal, disability can be reclassified as total if the applicant is unable to find, in the local labour market, a job adapted to both his qualifications and handicap. According to a Dutch study (Van den Bosch and Petersen, 1983), one-third of persons receiving disability benefits in 1978 could be described as having a purely 'economic disability' that had nothing to do with any medical criterion. After 1980, two other sorts of arrangements began competing with disability insurance. First, early retirement provisions (VUT) have been placed in collective agreements; this arrangement was, at the start, financially encouraged by the Dutch government, which saw it as a means of transferring the costs of early withdrawal from public funds (disability insurance) towards the private sector. However, these VUT provisions have limited scope and concern but a fraction of potential beneficiaries from 60 to 64 years old. A second sort of arrangement, involving unemployment compensation, has been developed since 1975 and has covered as a result a significant proportion of 55–59-year-olds. Its success signals the failure of the government's effort to transfer the cost of early withdrawal towards firms.

In the Federal Republic of Germany, the prevailing pathway for early with-drawal has operated through disability insurance since the early 1970s. In 1984, 47.7 per cent of new admissions at the normal age into the retirement system had passed through disability insurance (Jacobs *et al.*, 1987). As in the Netherlands, the success of this arrangement has come from broadening eligibility require-ments beyond strictly medical criteria, so as to take into account variables related to the labour market. Since 1976 a partially disabled person may receive full disability benefits if there is no part-time job adapted to his situation. Conse-quently, this arrangement has been widely used by 55–59-year-olds, an age group that cannot enter the retirement system and whose situation in the labour market is, owing to age, precarious. Although the tightening of eligibility requirements since 1985 has somewhat narrowed this pathway, it is still important, despite the passage of a May 1984 Act in favour of 'pre-retirement' contracts that seeks to involve private companies in the cost of early withdrawal. In 1987 about 30 per cent of new beneficiaries of old-age pensions had still taken the pathway via disability insurance.

In Sweden and Great Britain, disability insurance has not been expanded as far as in the Netherlands and West Germany. Nonetheless, it has been used to cover more and more early withdrawal cases.

In Sweden, eligibility requirements under disability insurance were slackened in favour of ageing jobless persons; a criterion of 'employability' was added on to strictly medical ones. Since 1976, a jobless person at least 60 years old may, if he does not find a job corresponding to his qualifications, claim disability benefits till the normal retirement age of 65. Companies have not missed the chance to incorporate this early withdrawal arrangement into their personnel strategies. The opportunity thus presented should not be underestimated since the target population is, on one hand, very often the least productive age group in the workforce, and, on the other, the group that both has the best legal protection against dismissal and benefits from an active public policy for keeping ageing workers in the labour force (Casey and Bruche, 1983). This country, though characterised by such an active public policy, has opened a breach in this system of protection, since it has broadened the definition of disability. This new pathway for early withdrawal has, since 1980, come into competition with a 'partial' retirement programme. This programme, which has been very successful since it was set up in 1976, makes it possible to adjust the time an ageing person spends working by combining a part-time job with part-time retirement. However, expanding disability insurance has opened a pathway for getting around this active policy in favour of job flexibility for ageing workers: it authorises total early definitive withdrawal from the labour force and could thus threaten the retirement system by limiting its essential function of regulating definitive withdrawal. For the time being, however, what characterises Sweden is both the relative stability of labour force participation rates for persons over 55 years old and the maintenance of the retirement system's power over definitive withdrawal. The linkage in Sweden between the lifespan and the welfare system has not changed much during the period under study, unlike in the five other countries where new welfare subsystems have been set up to regulate exits from the labour force.

In Great Britain, a growing number of ageing workers have also withdrawn early from their jobs under disability insurance, which, however, has not been purposefully restructured, nor its eligibility requirements broadened as in the other countries. A British study (Piachaud, 1986) has revealed a strong correlation between the number of persons receiving disability benefits and the jobless rate. In effect, physicians are responsible for judging whether persons are unfit for work, and they apparently take into account conditions in the labour market. Nonetheless, only a small proportion of ageing wage-earners – mainly manual workers over 60 years old – have been capable of negotiating this sort of arrangement.

As the above cases show, disability insurance has become a predominant means of early withdrawal in countries where eligibility requirements have included, besides purely medical criteria, the criterion of the 'employability' of ageing workers given the situation in the labour market. Disability has been redefined in terms that are more economic than medical. What is often the result of age discrimination by employers is now euphemistically called worker's disability.

In several countries, a large percentage of definitive withdrawal cases are now regularly handled by arrangements under disability insurance instead of provisions under the retirement system. This means that the criteria for definitive withdrawal have been redefined; they are no longer a function of the age of entitlement to a pension but of the inability to work. Functional criteria, not age itself, are the basis for admission; disability benefits are acquired following procedures that have nothing to do with chronological age: the condition for receiving them is to be unfit for work. This change in definitive withdrawal can be interpreted as a new way of marking the end of the lifespan with functional labels rather than chronological milestones. It may reflect a 'dechronologisation' of the life course, a process that inevitably involves 'destandardising' it. Since a person's ability to keep working as he grows older depends upon the social group to which he belongs, these functional criteria lead to major differences among individuals in the timing of transitions between phases of the life course. Another consequence is the emergence of a new social construction of age and of its relationship to work. The ageing worker is no longer primarily someone said to be close to the age of entitlement to retirement; instead, he is defined as being unable to work. When, as in West Germany or the Netherlands, nearly half of those who reach retirement age have previously been managed by disability insurance programmes, economic inactivity no longer means having the right to rest; it means being unfit for work.

### The unemployment compensation pathway

Unemployment compensation is another welfare subsystem that has decisively redefined the boundary between working life and life after work. Towards the mid-1970s special procedures were adopted, almost everywhere in Europe, for compensating older unemployed persons for lost jobs. Of the six countries under study, this holds for France, the Netherlands, West Germany and Sweden.

In France, arrangements under unemployment compensation were a principal and massive means of managing early withdrawal: a guaranteed income scheme was set up in 1972 for persons over 60 years old dismissed from their jobs and was extended in 1977 to those who resigned. Other measures introduced in 1982 provided similar treatment for wage-earners over 55. Under agreements between the government and firms, wage-earners at the age of 56 years and 2 months (and sometimes at 55) can be dismissed but will be covered by a special allocation from the National Employment Fund until the normal retirement age (fixed in 1982 at 60 for persons who have contributed to the Old Age Fund for thirty-seven and a half years).

The Netherlands adopted a new rule in 1975 stipulating that anyone between 60 and 64 years old who receives unemployment benefits (WWV) should continue receiving them till the legal retirement age of 65. Under these new rules, persons can leave the labour force at the age of 57 years 6 months. Unemployment insurance and unemployment welfare assistance together successively provide benefits to such jobless persons till the age of 65, the normal age for receiving an old-age pension.

West Germany has gradually loosened the conditions for providing unemployment benefits to jobless persons over 54. In 1987, given the maximal length of coverage, a person at the age of 57 years and 4 months who is dismissed from his job can receive unemployment benefits until he is 60, the age that entitles him to a normal retirement pension, as a long-term unemployment case. Hence, the so-called '59er rule', which has worked as a means of early withdrawal for a long time and ever more intensively since 1975, has become, *de facto*, a '57er rule' (Kühlewind, 1988). In 1986, 11 per cent of new retirees had withdrawn from their jobs under arrangements with unemployment compensation.

In Sweden, a combination of arrangements under the unemployment and disability insurance funds opens the way to definitive withdrawal as early as the age of 58 with unemployment benefits till 60 and then disability benefits till 65, the normal age for receiving an old-age pension. In comparison with the five other countries, however, this pathway is still not often taken.

In Great Britain, no special protection has been offered to the ageing jobless; and no particular pathway opened for early withdrawal under unemployment compensation. However, unemployment assistance compensation for cases of long-term unemployment are very often provided so as to supplement the incomes of aged 'discouraged' workers (Laczko, 1987) who have stopped working early either owing to partial disability or thanks to occupational old-age pensions that are paid early. Occupational pension funds are one of the major means of early withdrawal in Britain.

In all six countries under study, facts are linked in the same way. Making it easier for older workers to receive unemployment compensation also makes it easier for companies to dismiss, first of all, those who benefit from better coverage. Firms can thus get rid of such workers at the least economic and social cost. Adopting measures that compensate older workers for lost jobs is a factor that reinforces age discrimination in the economy, all the more so as the economic situation worsens.

The growing importance of unemployment compensation and/or disability insurance as a means of regulating definitive withdrawal from the labour force has considerable significance and meaning. Three implications will be pointed out. First of all, the new boundary between economic activity and inactivity is more directly modified as a function of the labour market and of the definition of age groups thus produced. Early withdrawal under unemployment compensation depends on the employer and his power to dismiss, not on the employee and his claim to a right to rest. Even though it is optional in some cases (for example, the French guaranteed income scheme), this recourse to unemployment compensation mainly depends on companies' employment policies. Second, the right to receive social transfer payments (disability and/or unemployment benefits) entails surrendering the right to a job. In contrast, the principle of the retirement system is to separate the right to a job from the right to a pension; in general, a person does not have to give up his job in order to receive a pension. Using unemployment compensation, or disability insurance, to manage labour force withdrawal has considerably weakened the older worker's right to a job. Third, with respect to the life course, replacing the retirement system with these other two sorts of arrangement has opened a gap between the individual's working life and his life after work. He loses control over the transition to the later years of his life. There is greater age specialisation. After a working life comes the time when one is denied the right to work and forced to stop working (Guillemard, 1985a). To continue working at an advanced age becomes morally questionable by public opinion in a context of high unemployment (Guillemard, 1986a). Meanwhile, the transition towards the last phase of the life course is less foreseeable. The chronological reference marks of retirement have been swept away and, with them, any principle providing for an orderly transition out of the labour force. There is more flexibility in organising the end of the lifespan, which is increasingly governed by the labour market and companies' employment policies. The subsystems of unemployment compensation and disability insurance are handy; they are, in each country, constantly being reworked in relation to the labour market.

### The decline of the 'pre-retirement' pathway

The description of the institutional mechanisms used to manage early withdrawal would not be complete without mention of 'pre-retirement' arrangements. These have been the third principal pathway out of the labour force in most of the countries under study: solidarity pre-retirement contracts in France, the Pre-retirement Act in West Germany, the Job Release Scheme in Great Britain, and the VUT in the Netherlands. The main characteristic of pre-retirement arrangements is that they are intended to improve the situation in the labour market by proposing voluntary early withdrawal to ageing wage-earners and, in many cases, by stipulating that such departures must be replaced by new hirings of jobless young people. Despite their diversity (whether they derive from public policy or come out of collective agreements, how they are financed, etc.), such measures tend to manage labour force exits similarly to the retirement system: age remains an essential eligibility requirement, and the choice of whether to go on pre-retirement is left up to the ageing worker himself. Although eligibility requirements have changed frequently as a function of the labour market, they nonetheless provide for a regulated transition out of the workforce without placing beneficiaries in successive, precarious positions, as arrangements under unemployment and disability insurances do.

Significantly, pre-retirement schemes have, in most cases, either been abandoned (in France in 1986 and West Germany in 1988) or been restrictive (such as the British Job Release Scheme). Only the Dutch VUT programme is still in effect, and even that has apparently been called into question.

This decline of pre-retirement schemes corroborates the interpretation advanced herein of changes in definitive labour force withdrawal. These changes should not be taken to be simply the result of lowering the age of withdrawal. The tendency to let pre-retirement schemes expire furthers the decline of the retirement system since the former, like the latter, uses chronological criteria to manage a regular transition out of the labour force. This too is a sign of the dechronologisation of the life course.

## The deinstitutionalisation of the life course and cross-generational transfers

This attempt to interpret international data reveals the scope of the changes under way. Although we might, at first, think that these are simply a means of setting the calendar of retirement ahead, they turn out, after analysis, to be a deep trend that upsets the way the life course is organised along with the welfare system.

The retirement system has lost its central function of regulating labour force withdrawal. The other subsystems (principally unemployment compensation and disability insurance) that now do this introduce their own logic for regulating the transition from work to non-work. As a result of this replacement of retirement, the chronological milestones that used to mark the life course are no longer visible; and functional criteria have assumed importance in organising the later years of life. This change is especially noticcablc when disability insurance has thus replaced retirement. Other observations than those presented here reinforce this interpretation. For instance, the US law against age discrimination in employment can be interpreted as indicating a different way of organising the lifespan, one that places less importance on the age criterion but greater emphasis on functional criteria based on the individual worker's capabilities and effectiveness: only these criteria can now be legally used by employers to dismiss or retire employees.

This dechronologisation entails destandardising the life course, undoing the threefold model with which we are familiar. The transition to the last stage of life is being rearranged more flexibly, but this new flexibility does not mcan that individuals have more freedom of choice. In fact, the large majority of early withdrawals are not voluntary (Guillemard, 1986b, p. 288; Casey and Laczko, 1988, p. 13). This early withdrawal trend is a reflection of the employmcnt situation and of companies' strategies in relation to it. As pointed out, the new boundaries being drawn between economic activity and inactivity are directly modulated by conditions in the labour market and the definition of age groups thus produced. Given the broader eligibility requirements under disability insurances or unemployment compensation, early withdrawal mainly depends on a judgement about the 'unemployability' of older wage-earners, a judgement that comes out of negotiations about jobs. Thc timc for definitive withdrawal from the labour force is, for the individual, no longer fixed ahead of time; it is not predictable. Since the chronological milestones of retirement are being torn up, the threefold model, which placed the individual in a foreseeable life course of continuous, consecutive sequences of functions and statuses, is coming apart. As a consequence, an individual's working life now ends in confusion.

Jobless ageing persons' conceptions of their situation provide evidence of this fundamental change. A minority of this new 'inactive' population between 55 and 65 years old identify themselves as 'retirees'. There is clear evidence of this for France (Guillemard, 1986), but also for Great Britain. According to Casey and Laczko (1988) (using the results of the *Labour Force Survey*), one-quarter of the ageing jobless British population between 60 and 64, and only 12 per cent of those between 55 and 59, classify themselves as retirees; the rest define themselves mainly a being unemployed or 'discouraged' workers no longer looking for a job. These data measure the impact that the previously described institutional arrangements for early withdrawal have had on the organisation of the life course. Retirement is no longer the unifying principle, which gives a homogeneous meaning to a third phase of life that opens with departure from the labour force. The elderly no longer have a clearly defined social status. Definitive withdrawal, old age and retirement no longer concur with each other:

occupational old age begins with definitive withdrawal, well before retirement and physical old age. The life course as an institution is coming undone. Retirement is no longer a central means of socialisation that determines the identities and symbolic universes of individuals. There is less and less of a definite order to the last phases of life. The life course is being deinstitutionalised. It would, by the way, be interesting to compare the results of the numerous studies about how people enter the labour force with those of the scarcer studies about how they leave it so as to see if the interpretation advanced herein would be confirmed.

Deinstitutionalising the life course undermines not only the possibility of forming a continuous, foreseeable idea of one's life but also the system of reciprocity across generations. Doubt is being cast not only on retirement but also on the underlying contract of the commitments binding generations together. What are the prospects of this long-term contract involving several *successive* generations? The reciprocity of commitments across generations is no longer so reliable in a society where time is accelerating, where the lifespan is no longer part of a long run with fixed, standard chronological milestones, where, on the contrary, flexible diversified models are taking shape that provide for unpredictable life courses. People still working are starting to doubt whether coming generations will pay for their pensions as willingly as they are now paying for those of current retirees. In effect, the temporal strategy underlying this transfer implies that compensation for the alienation of work be delayed in exchange for the right to rest at the end of life. But the motivations behind this strategy are weakening since the life course no longer makes individuals part of a foreseeable continuity.

The passage from a society of 'managed time' (Roussel and Girard, 1982) to an ephemeral society, from a society that tries to control the future to one that is running beyond time and has no future, tends to give rise to a new conception of solidarity among generations. Short-term solidarity with immediate reciprocity *between* generations is now preferred to long-term solidarity *across* generations. As a consequence, the equity of such exchanges tends to be evaluated only over the short run, here and now. An alarming example of this is the pressure group Americans for Generational Equity (AGE), which criticises the redistribution of social transfer payments in favour of the elderly (Jones, 1988; Preston, 1984). In current debates about the equity of *inter*generational exchanges, the transfer of public funds among various age groups is measured instantaneously in order to denounce imbalances; no thought is given to the long-term *cross*-generational reciprocity of which these transfers provide but a partial image.

The institutional arrangements used to ensure early definitive withdrawal from the labour force provide evidence that the contract binding generations is being focused on the present. This early withdrawal trend has often been justified by the argument that the transfer of work between old and young balances the transfer of money (in the form of pensions) from young to old (Commissariat Général du Plan, 1986). This intergenerational solidarity involves an immediate reciprocity that has been given form through these new institutional arrangements. Rather than work being shared, it has, in most countries, been transferred from one generation to another, as older persons have seen their right to a job restricted. As a consequence public expenditures on the ageing, economically inactive part of the population have exploded. In France, for instance, half of what was spent on unemployment compensation in 1985 went to beneficiaries at least 55 years old (Ragot, 1985). In all the countries under study, public authorities have been attempting to shift the costs, but without much success, towards the private sector (Casey, 1987).

Yet another consequence has been how society now constructs the reality of ageing. Younger generations now see the aged as a relatively privileged, excessively costly group who accumulate the right to both social benefits and free time, an image that is all the stronger insofar as the other part of this exchange – transferring jobs from old to young – has not been up to expectation (Franck *et al.*, 1982). Older generations thus appear to be well-off and to have free time whereas the prospects of younger generations are not so bright, given the ageing of the population. This new conception of an immediate balance of intergenerational exchanges can be taken to be the result of remodelling the organisation of the life course, in particular from the labour force towards retirement. As a consequence, the cultural base underlying retirement and legitimating the contract binding generations is cracking. We are thus forced to recognise the long-term instability of the organisation of cross-generational transfers. Changes in retirement should not be considered, as they too often are, to be the mechanical effect of demographic ageing, nor should the future of old-age pension systems be predicted merely in terms of the cost analysis of a growing proportion of old people in the population. In effect, the processes of legitimation and the quest for meaning are just as decisive as budgetary considerations for shedding light on the prospects of the retirement system and for understanding how the welfare state is being restructured in relation to the life course.

*(Translated from the French by Noal Mellott, Centre National de la Recherche Scientifique, Paris)*

## Note

1  These graphs and tables were drawn by an international research group (Anne-Marie Guillemard, Martin Kohli, Martin Rein and Herman Van Gunsteren) that has worked on six countries (the United States, the Netherlands, France, West Germany, Sweden and Great Britain) in collaboration with F. Laczko and C. Phillipson (for Great Britain), Harold Sheppard (for the United States) and E. Wadensjö (for Sweden). The information thus gathered is the basis of a personal interpretation of the changes under way, one that reflects my own point of view.

# References

Casey, B. (1987), 'Early retirement: the problems of instrument substitution and cost shifting and their implications for restructuring the process of retirement', *International Social Security Review*, IV.

Casey, B. and Bruche, G. (1983), *Work or Retirement*, London, Gower.

Casey, B. and Laczko, F. (1988), 'Recent trends in labour force participation of older men in Great Britain and their implications for the future', paper given at the *Futuribles* conference on 'The Ageing of Population in Europe: Trends, Challenges and Policies', Paris, 4–5 October.

Commissariat Général du Plan (1986), *Vieillir solidaires*, Paris, Documentation Française.

Franck, D., Hara, R., Magnier, G. and Villey, D. (1982), 'Entreprises et contrats de solidarité de préretraite-démission', *Travail et Emploi*, XIII (July-September).

Guillemard, A. -M. (1985a), 'Preretraite et mutations du cycle de vie', *Futuribles*, LXXXVIII, pp. 31–8 (May).

Guillemard, A. -M. (1985b), 'The social dynamics of early withdrawal from the labour force in France', *Ageing and Society*, V, 4, pp. 381–412 (December).

Guillemard, A. -M. (1986a), 'State, society and old age policy in France from 1945 to the current crisis', *Social Science and Medicine*, XXIII, 12, pp. 1319–26.

Guillemard, A. -M. (1986b), *Le déclin du Social: formation et crise des politiques de la vieillesse*, Coll. Sociologies, Paris, Presses Universitaires de France.

Jacobs, K., Kohli, M. and Rein, M. (1987), 'Early exit from the labor force in Germany: country report', paper presented at the international conference on 'Early Exit from the Labor Force', Tampa, Florida, November.

Jacobs, K., Kohli, M. and Rein, M. (1989), 'The evolution of early exit: a comparative analysis of the labor force participations of the elderly', in M. Kohli, M. Rein, A. -M. Guillemard and H. Van Gunsteren (eds), *Time for Retirement* (in press).

Jones, J. R. (1988), 'Conflit entre générations aux Etats-Unis', *Futuribles* (October).

Kohli, M. (1987), 'Retirement and the moral economy: an historical interpretation of the German case', *Journal of Aging Studies*, I, 2, pp. 125–44.

Kühlewind, G. (1988), 'Age and procedures of retirement in Germany: present situation, past evolution and forecast', paper presented at the *Futuribles* conference on 'The Ageing of Population in Europe: Trends, Challenges and Policies, Paris', 4–5 October.

Laczko, F. (1987), 'Older workers, unemployment and the discouraged worker effect', in S. di Gregorio (ed.), *Social Gerontology: New Directions*', London, Croom Helm, 1987, pp. 239–51.

Meier, E. (1986), *Early Retirement Incentive Programs: Trends and Implications*, Washington DC, AARP Public Policy Institute.

Piachaud, D. (1986), 'Disability, retirement and unemployment of older men', *Journal of Social Policy*, 2, pp. 145–62.

Preston, S. H. (1984), 'Children and the elderly in the US', *Scientific American*, CCLI, 6, pp. 36–41 (December).

Ragot, Maurice (1985), *La cessation anticipée d'activité salariée*, rapport présenté au nom de la section du travail, Conseil Economique et Social, Paris (June).

Roussel, L. and Girard, A. (1982), 'Régimes démographiques et ages de la vie' in *Les Ages de la Vie*, Proceedings of the 7th Conference on Demography, vol. 1, Paris, Presses Universitaires de France, pp. 15–23.

Van den Bosch and Petersen (1983), 'An explanation of the growth of social security disability transfers', *De Economist*, CXXXI, 1, pp. 65–79, quoted in B. de Vroom and M. Blomsma, *The Netherlands: An Extreme Case*, Working Paper, Leyden Institute for Law and Public Policy.

# 10

# Changes in Life Course and Retirement in Recent Years: The example of Two Cohorts of Parisians

## Françoise Cribier

French public opinion has been struck by two changes over the last fifteen years. The first concerns the lowering of the retirement age, the transformation of entry into retirement and the improvement in resources prior to retirement for those no longer in work. The second involves the improvement in pension payments. For the first time, per capita income for households headed by a retired person is not below the average per capita income of all households.[1] The average standard of living of the male recently retired, which a few years ago was the same as that of the average active person, now equals that of a lower executive in mid-career, largely because in France there is a great increase in salary through the life cycle, seniority advantages being particularly important.

The data given here are the result of research into two cohorts of Parisians retired under the general pension scheme, formerly workers in the private sector. As 30 per cent were also, at some time during their working lives, either salaried workers in the public sector or self-employed, our samples represent 85 per cent of these generations of Parisians.

The two populations of Greater Paris which we surveyed first drew their pensions in 1972 and 1984, that is, with an interval of twelve years (the average age difference will be seen to be 13.6 years). The differences between these two cohorts were marked, whether we consider age at the end of working life, circumstances surrounding the end of employment activity, living standards or attitudes towards work and retirement. It will be seen that there were several other differences between these two cohorts, that those born prior to the First World War (1906–1912) and those born after the war (1919–1924) differed throughout their lives and continued to do so upon retirement. These differences, viewed by the public as period effects, attributable to changes in the labour market and in retirement legislation in the 1970s and 1980s, are also cohort effects, created by rapid and continuous social change.

The aim of this article is to show the extent of the disparity between two generations who were nevertheless very close to each other in years. Many differences do not represent true inequalities, but by considering the totality of these differences we can appreciate the disparity in treatment given to two successive generations of retired people by the welfare state.

The first survey, of Parisians who had retired in 1972, was begun in 1974. It was planned as a longitudinal survey examining the life course process, both retrospectively, from childhood to retirement, and prospectively, following a generation of retired people up to the end of their lives.[2] We aimed to learn about the lives of people in the various classes of a class society, the disparities between the lives of men and women and between those born in Paris and the greater number of Parisians born in the provinces or abroad. We wished to discover what people had made of their lives and what their lives had made of them. Life experience is cohort-specific. Therefore we studied occupational history, from childhood to retirement, family history, residential history of households and social strategies. Part of this material only is discussed here.[3]

The 'older cohort' refers to those who first drew their pensions in 1972. We were able to analyse 1,300 retirement files and to interview half those remaining in Greater Paris in 1975. Over the subsequent years we followed up the whole of the cohort (two out of three remained in the Paris area, with one in three having settled in the provinces; Cribier, 1982). Since 1974 we have been following a representative sample of 1,374 people. For the last survey in 1986, we obtained responses from 92 per cent of the survivors. Copies of birth, marriage and death certificates were gathered, in-depth interviews conducted, and biographies and life histories collected. The purpose of our study necessitated both quantitative and qualitative data, for social scientists need both to measure and to understand what they are measuring.

Our observations on the older cohort concerned the 96 per cent born between 1906 and 1912 (the 4 per cent born prior to 1906 had stopped working long before) and their median date of birth was 1908. The younger cohort was that first drawing a pension in 1984. Here too only 96 per cent of the newly retired were concerned, those born between 1918 and 1924, and their median date of birth was 1921–22. There was an 86 per cent response rate when we interviewed them in 1987 but we did not have access to the retirement files (the law concerning access changed in 1978). In order that these two populations can be compared at the same stage in their life cycle, they will each be described at R+3 (three years after retirement), the older cohort in 1975 and the younger cohort in 1987.

Since the average age at the commencement of pension payments fell from 63.7 years for the older cohort in 1972 to 62.1 years for the younger cohort in 1984, the age difference at the time of the first payment (as at R+3) was 1.6 years.

# The two cohorts

Some of the disparities between these two cohorts can be explained by different social and geographical origins, as will be shown later. Above all they both lived through a period of such intense social change that, at the same age, each generation lived in a highly different socio-economic environment (Chesnais, 1985). The older cohort left school around 1920, while the younger benefited from the inter-war advances in schooling. The older cohort was aged 25 years during the economic crisis in 1932 and the younger cohort reached this age in 1947, at the beginning of twenty-five years of sustained economic growth. The former brought up their children in the 1930s and during the Second World War, without family allowance or social housing, the latter's families grew up after the war, when social policy favoured the family. Many of the former were only able to go on holiday after 1950, when they were aged around 40, the others were able to do so in their youth. Many more examples could be provided. Differences between the cohorts in work patterns and family and residential history were marked.

## Geographical origins

The proportion of natives of Greater Paris was higher in the younger cohort (47 as against 39 per cent), that of natives of the provinces was smaller, and the proportion of people born outside Metropolitan France was constant across the two cohorts, at around 16 per cent. The proportion of Parisians born and brought up in the countryside fell from roughly 40 to 20 per cent, since natives of the rural provinces in the younger cohort, less numerous, came to Paris at an earlier age. For the first time in a century, over half a generation of Parisian 60-year-olds were brought up in Paris, in an age when school amenities and occupational training were far better in Paris than in the rest of the country.

## Education and work career

There were large differences in the level of education and the occupation of the two cohorts. First, there was a great increase in schooling during the inter-war years. Among those who remained in Greater Paris after retirement, the proportion of retired persons without any qualifications decreased from 40 to 20 per cent among men and from 48 to 27 per cent among women. The proportion of women with higher qualifications increased particularly from 3 to 8 per cent.

The low-skilled workers and low-qualified employees categories constituted half the newly retired population in 1972 and a third of that in 1984. The proportion decreased from 31 to 13 per cent for men and from 69 to 42 per cent for women. This is linked to progress in education and to the fact that low-skilled male jobs in the 1945–55 period were taken up by foreigners (many of whom had only worked a few years in France) and by French provincial migrants (more of whom than Paris-born Parisians left Paris upon retirement, Cribier, 1988b), whilst the men educated in Paris most often had skilled jobs.

Technicians, middle and senior executives increased from 27 to 40 per cent for men and from 8 to 15 per cent for women. The higher category remained essentially male. In both cohorts, women had a lower level of education and training than men. When compared with men at the same level of training, women were frequently lower placed in the job hierarchy. Many 'unskilled' women were as competent as male 'skilled' workers, and many female middle executives could have been senior executives if only they had been men. Moreover, with equally recognised skills, they were lower-paid (see Table 10.1) and they did not benefit from the 'best' supplementary funds as did their male

**Table 10.1** *Average salary and pension income (in constant French francs) for seven occupational groups, by sex, for the newly retired Parisians (a) of 1972 (National Pension Fund) (b)*

|  | Salaries 1970–72 (value on 1 January 1975) | | Individual pensions (value on 1 January 1975) | | % loss in purchasing power | | Proportion of supplementary pension in total pension | |
|---|---|---|---|---|---|---|---|---|
|  | Men | Women | Men | Women | Men | Women | Men | Women |
| 1 Service workers (c) | – | 1,088 | – | 598 | – | 45 | – | 24 |
| 2 Unskilled workers | 1,715 | 1,511 | 1,097 | 984 | 36 | 35 | 40 | 29 |
| 3 Skilled workers and foremen | 2,462 | 1,723 | 1,608 | 1,109 | 35 | 35 | 46 | 36 |
| 4 Unskilled employees (in shops, offices, factories) | 1,948 | 1,586 | 1,325 | 1,123 | 32 | 30 | 45 | 33 |
| 5 Skilled employees | 2,788 | 2,415 | 1,571 | 1,525 | 44 | 37 | 50 | 49 |
| 6 Technicians, lower and middle executives | 3,663 | 3,707 | 2,168 | 2,196 | 41 | 42 | 56 | 49 |
| 7 Engineers, senior executives | 9,021 | – | 4,330 | – | 48 | – | 77 | – |
| Total Sample | 3,269 (difference 44%) | 1,838 | 1,886 (difference 39%) | 1,143 | 40 | 36 | 51 | 35 |
| Manual (d) | 2,388 | 1,642 | 1,506 | 920 | 37 | 44 | 43 | 29 |
| Non-manual | 4,659 | 2,145 | 2,465 | 1,472 | 47 | 41 | 62 | 49 |

*Notes:*    This is a representative sample of 432 newly retired persons, interviewed in depth. All of them had remained in Paris, but the average salary and pension of those who had moved to the provinces was the same: retirement migration is not a middle-class pattern.

(b) For some categories we had a small number of cases (category 3, women, category 5, men) or a very small number (category 1, men, category 7, women).

(c) Charladies, cleaning staff, porters. Some of them were working part-time.

(d) Includes category 1, 2, 3, and half of 4.

counterparts. The inequality between men and women in the labour market basically stems from gender ideology (Kergoat, 1982).

Information on salaries and pensions according to sex and occupational category is given for the older cohort in Table 10.1. It should be stressed here that inequalities among the social classes and between men and women were far more important within each generation than between the two generations.[4] The social class to which the household, here the couple, belonged was most important regarding standard and style of living. From 1972 to 1984 the change in social category of the couple was considerable. The number of households in which at least one spouse had been a technician, middle or senior executive rose from 19 to 36 per cent.

If we construct just four large household social groups, based on occupation, among the salaried workers, from top to bottom of the social scale, almost half the married women – in both cohorts – belonged to a lower individual group than their husbands; as a couple they were placed in the husband's group, since it was higher. That is to say, the social positions of these married women were poorly described by their individual occupational group, as they would be defined in most studies (Cribier, 1980). The result is that there are three 'genders' in the retired population: men, married women – half of whom are placed higher up on the social scale than they would be were they not married, the other half having the advantage of living in a double-salary and then double-pension household – and, finally, single women, existing either on a small widow's pension or having to live solely on their own pension (Cribier *et al.*, 1979).

### Civil status at the time of retirement

The average age of the younger cohort at R+3 was 1.6 years lower than that of the older (65.1 as against 66.7 years). This partly explains why there were fewer widows in the younger cohort. Yet the differences in marriage status at R+3 were less the effects of age than of cohort, insofar as there had been a number of changes in family history over the years under discussion. These were:

(a) a slight decline in female celibacy, observed in the Census data for Greater Paris as well as for the country as a whole;

(b) a rise in the proportion of married persons: 85 to 87 per cent for men and, notably, 39 to 47 per cent for women. This was partly due to the fact that married women with less than fifteen years' work experience could receive a pension in 1984 but not in 1972; but the proportion of married women versus widows hardly increased in the later years in this age group, thanks to an increase in male longevity;

(c) a small rise in the proportion of non-remarried divorced women in all social groups and a small rise among men in higher social groups (because cohabitation is more acceptable among these groups;

(d) a marked decline in widowhood amongst women, particularly over the last decade for 50- to 70-year-old women, due both to the age difference (1.6

years) and to the increase in life expectancy for men. In Greater Paris, the proportion of widows in the 60–69 age group decreased from 29.5 to 25.1 per cent between the 1975 and 1982 Censuses; the proportion of widows among married women aged 60–64 was 40 per cent in 1975 and 33 per cent in 1982.

Looking at marriage history as a whole, there was no striking increase in the number of divorces and second marriages because these were already numerous among the older cohort (15 per cent of married men and women had married at least twice, and 25 per cent of women were divorced or had been abandoned). In the younger cohort, one in every eleven couples had a child from a previous marriage.

### Children and parents of the newly retired

It is said frequently that the family is changing. Public opinion, in France as elsewhere, tends to believe that this is for the worse, whilst the social sciences have firmly established that the family is a solid and adaptable institution. However, before looking at the real transformations in family roles, it is necessary to show to what extent the family situations of the newly retired have changed over the twelve years of this study, beginning with the number and place of residence of their children and the proportion still having an aged parent.

On average, the younger cohort members married younger and have had more children. Among men with children,[5] the average number of offspring increased from 2.3 to 2.7, and the proportion of men without children decreased from 19 to 16 per cent. There were more large families in the younger cohort: 30 per cent of men in the older cohort with children had three or more, while for the younger cohort the figure was 42 per cent. One reason is that the older cohort married principally between the years 1925 and 1937 (median year 1931) in a period of low birth rates, and the younger cohort married in the 1940s and early 1950s (median year 1947) during a period of high fecundity. However, the birth schedule changed between the two cohorts. Thus the age at birth of the last child (median age is 31) is the same for both cohorts, the age dispersion in the younger cohort being smaller.

Three further points must be made concerning children. First, one of the results of the higher fecundity of the younger cohort is that the proportion of retired persons with at least one daughter upon retirement increased from 57 per cent of the total male population of the older cohort to 63 per cent of the younger cohort. As daughters play a major role in the support of aged persons, this could make a great difference in the later life of the younger cohort.

Second, the median age of the parents in both cohorts on the departure of the last child was the same, 56. The children of the younger cohort continued their education for longer and their departure was sometimes delayed by unemployment in the 1970s and 1980s. On the other hand the older cohort often had children belatedly, after the Liberation, and also still had to accommodate their older children, born between 1925 and 1935, even after marriage, between 1945 and 1955, due to the housing crisis.

Third, the younger cohort of Parisians lived closer to their children than did the older, contrary to what might be popularly assumed. This is both because the former had more children on average and because their geographical distribution in Greater Paris was much less central than that of the latter. In the younger cohort, 25 per cent lived in central Paris on retirement as opposed to 36 per cent of the older, and 40 per cent as opposed to 28 per cent lived in the outer suburbs. The younger cohort's generation was the first to have settled in large numbers in the suburbs, in the 1950s and 1960s, and its geographical distribution was therefore closer to that of its children. In 1987, 68 per cent of the newly retired with a child living apart from them, but still in Greater Paris, lived less than half an hour away from the nearest child. In 1975, this was the case for only 62 per cent of newly retired persons.

Next, two questions relating to the parents of the retired cohorts will be addressed. How many of the interviewees in the two cohorts had a retired father? How many newly retired households still had a parent at R+3?

It has been shown elsewhere (Cribier, 1981b) that almost three out of four retired persons in the older cohort were the first retired persons in their family line. The proportion of those who had not known their father or who had lost him in their youth, notably during the First World War, was very high (20 per cent). Many fathers had died before retirement and many had died aged but still at work, especially farmers, small businessmen and artisans, or low-paid salaried workers who 'worked up to the last'. Only 27 per cent of the cohort had had a retired father, whilst for the younger cohort, generally less rural in origin and born just after the Great War, the proportion was about 50 per cent.

The proportion of those who had at least one parent or parent-in-law increased from 11 per cent for the older cohort in 1975 to 26 per cent for the younger in 1987. The latter were not only younger but were also more often married and, above all, their parents lived longer. However, the likelihood of living with a parent has not increased in the same way. In 1987 2.7 per cent of the newly retired in 1984 lived with a parent; in 1975 2 per cent of those retiring in 1972 did so. But although the increase in the proportion of the households still having a parent at R+3 has been so high, in 1975, 18 per cent of the newly retired who still had a parent lived with them (even though many of these parents lived in the provinces), while in 1987 the proportion was only 10 per cent. This difference is due to the improvement of the living standards of the aged parents of the newly retired, and to living-at-home policies (rent allowance, home help, home care).

Family roles have changed in less than one generation. There is strong evidence of a contrast between the two cohorts in intergenerational relationships. First, the amount of help given by each cohort to their parents differed. The older cohort had to support their aged parents financially. The majority had to give them money, while some had to take in an old parent, but were often forced to turn to the hospices in the later years. A greater proportion of the parents of this cohort – among those who lived to old age – entered institutions than of the parents of the younger cohort. In the younger cohort, a lower proportion of retirees provided financial assistance to their parents, who themselves received better pensions, but this was still the usual pattern in the working class. Although fewer of these very old parents, of all classes, entered residential homes, the interviews revealed more anxiety, perhaps even guilt that they were failing to 'do enough' and to show sufficient care for their parents; the future of these older parents was a constant source of concern for the newly retired.

A second contrast related to the exchanges made between each cohort and its children at the time of retirement. In the older cohort, many accepted financial help from their children and many more gifts in kind (from a colour TV set to 'a beautiful piece of meat for Sunday lunch'). This was because they recognised the economic progress made by their children, and because nearly all those who were helped by their children had helped their own parents twenty or thirty years earlier. However, for all of them the great worry was that they could be a 'burden' on their children later on. In the younger cohort, the majority of the parents were still better off than their children and they were happy to continue to help them when they needed it, whether they were out of work, needed to raise a deposit to buy a home, or were experiencing a personal crisis (divorce, illness, accident). The younger cohort was more successful in preserving their independence from their children.

## Household composition at R+3

The proportion of persons living with their spouse and only the spouse rose from 62 to 68 per cent for men and from 35 to 40 per cent for women. This was due to the decline in female widowhood and in all types of co-residence. This household type has become the social norm at the beginning of retirement. In fact, it is rather a male norm, for women living in a couple were already fewer at R+3 than women living alone.

The proportion of newly retired living alone did not change over the twelve-

Table 10.2 *Timetable of the residence and co-residence of the cohort of Parisians newly retired in 1972; proportion of parents living with at least one child (%)*

|      | Age |      | Total | At own place | At a child's place |
|------|-----|------|-------|--------------|---------------------|
| 1967 | 59  | R–5  | 49    | 49           | 0                   |
| 1972 | 64  | R    | 27    | 25           | 2                   |
| 1975 | 67  | R+3  | 22(a) | 17           | 5                   |
| 1986 | 78  | R+14 | 13    | 5            | 8                   |

*Note:* (a) 25 for men, 19 for women.

year period. For men, the proportion was 11 per cent and for women, 45 per cent. In 1987, 2.7 per cent of the interviewees (2 per cent in 1975) lived with a parent, but the proportion of those with a living parent and co-residing diminished greatly, as has been shown. There was a small decline in the number of newly retired living with a child (22 as opposed to 25 per cent among men and 16 as against 19 per cent among women). The reasons for this were that they were younger by 1.6 years, and that income and living conditions among the newly retired unmarried women had improved. In 1975, 8 per cent of the recently retired women were already living at a child's home but only 3 per cent in 1987.

The schedule of co-residence with children, for the older cohort, is shown in Table 10.2, from R-5 to R+14. Those who settled in the household of one of their children have been distinguished from those 'still' having a child living with them. In fact, some of these latter children had left the household and returned at a later date when they needed their parents (because of divorce, sickness, unemployment or depression). Among those 75-80-year-olds who still had a child living with them at R+14 in 1986, in one out of four cases the child was likely to be handicapped and in one out of five the child would have returned to the household. The co-residence of 75-80-year-olds and their children often functions as form of aid to the children, contrary to what is usually assumed! (Wenger, 1984).

In the younger cohort, half the children had already left at R-6, and 19 per cent of parents still had a child living with them at R+3 (less than 2 per cent were at their child's home).

### Salaries, pensions and living standards

The differences in salary on the eve of retirement between the two cohorts were 15 to 20 per cent in constant money rate, and in individual pensions at least 20 per cent (supplementary pensions seemed to be more often underdeclared by the younger cohort.[6]

Until the mid-1970s, a favourable economic climate led to a gradual rise of salaries from one generation to the next (Guillotin, 1988). During the 1980s, purchasing power increased as employees in general aged, but there was no improvement from one generation to the next. The wage earners who entered the labour market just after the Second World War (our younger cohort), like all generations entering the labour force between then and the mid-1960s, had an advantage over the previous (born before 1920) and following generations (born after 1945). The reasons for this privileged situation were the rapid economic growth of 1945-75, better training compared with their elders, and a scarcity of skilled workers in the face of strong demand, a scarcity which benefited men much more than women, at least in the 1920-24 birth cohort.

Over the twelve-year period 1972-84 there was an increase both in qualifications and in salaries for those reaching retirement, the maturing of pension schemes, and the extension of supplementary pensions, notably that of the 'Caisse des Cadres' (pension fund for 'executives' to which many technicians, supervisors and foremen also contributed). There were more working lives for which thirty-seven and a half years were declared (giving the right to the maximum pension) in 1984 than in 1972. For women, the declared working life in the younger cohort was very similar to the true one, whilst in the older cohort the working life was often underdeclared because of the frequency of poor declaration levels before 1945, especially among the lower-skilled.

The living standard of households increased even further with the increase in the number of couples with two pensions, and capital income (our survey did not include this question, impossible to investigate in France in this type of survey) was most certainly higher for the younger cohort. Taxation data show that in 1979 9 per cent of the income of retired households came from capital (Canceill *et al.*, 1987).

The proportion of second home owners among those remaining in Paris upon retirement increased from 10 per cent in the older cohort to 29 per cent in the younger. This proportion was over 50 per cent for both cohorts among those having retired to the provinces. The proportion of owners of their main residence, among those remaining in Greater Paris, rose from 42 per cent in the older cohort to 54 per cent in the younger, and the proportion of those still paying a monthly mortgage at the beginning of their retirement was greatly reduced. The older cohort became owners of their homes in the Paris area at the average age of 46 and the younger at the average age of 39 (Cribier *et al.*, 1987). Through the increase in home ownership and housing in council flats ('*HLMs*')[7] and through the decline in poor accommodation in low-rent, ageing housing in the private rental sector and in gratuitous accommodation (usually provided by a child, and which fell from 8 to 3.5 per cent of total housing), it is evident that 'better-quality' housing tenure had become more widespread.

There was a remarkable improvement in housing from the older to the younger cohort. City housing was much improved in France after 1950 (until then there had been little improvement since 1914) and the younger cohort benefited from the changes far more than the older. We shall give a few measures of the changes from the older to the younger cohort: from 14 to 6 per cent of retired persons living in one room, 49 to 70 per cent living in more than two orooms,[8] 21 to 4 per cent in dwellings without an inside toilet, and 35 to 62 per cent in dwellings with a bathroom.[9] The younger retired were better housed and had been so for a long time: the majority of the younger cohort were already adequately housed at the age of 45. This improvement from one cohort to the other was not simply the result of the increased proportion of more qualified people. Every social category experienced a marked improvement in housing, a very important aspect of social change in France after the Second World War (Prost, 1987).

Let us add that an objective improvement in health clearly occurred even though we only have subjective evidence of this. The fall in the death rate, which has been so rapid over the last twenty years for the population aged between 55 and 70, was largely the result of the improvement in health of this age group.

Moreover, the newly retired in 1987 considered it quite normal to be healthy at the beginning of retirement!

## Entry into retirement

What were the characteristics of the entry into retirement of the Parisian salaried workers in 1972 and in 1984? Two points deserve closer examination. First, there is the commencement of pension payments in the years 1972 and 1984. This means the moment at which one receives one's first retirement pension payment, whilst up until then one lived on a salary, a sickness or invalidity benefit, unemployment benefit, pre-retirement pay (in France, this is paid out by the unemployment funds) or, perhaps, one's husband's income, for the numerous women who stopped working long before retirement. The second point is the end of occupational activity. For half the men and just under half the women, this occurred in the same year as the commencement of pension payments, but it can occur beforehand or, especially in 1972, afterwards (French law authorises retired persons to work provided they are not 'invalid', 'disabled' or in pre-retirement).

Most of the mass, large-scale data available describe the commencement of pension payments without knowledge of the date upon which the individuals stopped work. Or, on the contrary, they give the activity status (from employment surveys), but then the date of commencement of pension payments is not known. Hence the relevance of surveys such as this one.

Retiring in 1972 was already quite different from retiring in the early 1960s, a period of full employment, even for ageing workers. In 1972, half the newly retired had stopped working before reaching the age of 65, without the public really being aware of the fact.

The survey conducted on the older cohort revealed that only half the interviewees still in active employment three years prior to the commencement of pension payments retired directly after being in work. A third had stopped working beforehand (12 per cent less than one year previously, 21 per cent between one and three years before) and 17 per cent had continued working after receiving their first pension payment. In the latter case, this was generally for one or two years. All those who had already ceased working three years previously, that is, 11 per cent of the men and 22 per cent of the women, had stopped long before. A third of these men were long-term unemployed and two-thirds were disabled or unfit; half of the women already inactive in 1969 had stopped working for reasons of health or redundancy and the other half for personal reasons (one out of every two before 55 and even one out of every four before 48). If we exclude now those 15 per cent of women for whom ceasing active employment did not mean true retirement, only 43 per cent of the newly retired had stopped working in the same year as the commencement of pension payments; 14 per cent ceased working afterwards and 43 per cent beforehand.

Frequently, the date and conditions of the end of working life were unforeseen. In 1972, four out of ten of the newly retired had not foreseen the date and conditions, whether they had been certified as unfit, made redundant or had fallen ill.

Scarcely a quarter of the newly retired in 1972 had ceased working at the age of 65. Half had stopped before the age of 65 (and half of these before 60 years of age), whilst one out of four men and one out of five women were still in work at the age of 66, when in fact 65 was the official retirement age for nearly all these salaried workers. The reasons for continuing work after the age of 65 were, for the most highly qualified workers, the desire to keep one's job (25 per cent managed to do so) and, for unmarried and low-qualified women in commerce and in the service sector, the need to earn a living (30 per cent worked after 65 because they 'had to').

In total, 30 per cent of the newly retired in 1972 were certified as disabled or unfit (in that year, this was the case for 33 per cent of all French newly retired). However, this certification of 'disability' was to some extent a way of managing exit from the labour market.[10] The proportion of workers certified as unfit or disabled increased from 20 per cent in the period of full employment in the 1960s to 31 per cent in 1972. The doctors on the committees responsible for unfitness and disability certification in fact had orders to facilitate the 'exit' of tired and worn-out workers and they certified as disabled the majority of those who wished to stop working, but also many unfortunate people who begged them not to withdraw them from work.

Two-thirds of the older cohort did not choose the date on which they ceased working and those who did choose did so through need in two cases out of three, continuing work in order to have a salary or 'three-month terms' of contributions. (Time worked is measured in three-month terms for the purposes of pension entitlement.)

The reasons for stopping work before the normal age, if we exclude the women who stopped before age 55 'to be at home', were disability for 60 per cent, sickness for 21 per cent, redundancy for 15 per cent and personal reasons, other than looking after their own children, for 4 per cent.

Many sick and disabled had been unemployed just prior to the sickness or disability and thus the unemployment level was underestimated. In fact nearly 20 per cent of this older cohort had been 'on the dole' at the end of their working life in the late 1960s and early 1970s.

Health problems (disability or sickness) were the cause in eight cases out of ten of involuntary ceasing of active employment. The social classes are affected by such problems in a very unequal manner: one out of five qualified employees, technicians and executives, one out of three low-qualified employees and half of all manual labourers and factory workers (Cribier, 1983). The follow-up of the over 1,400 subjects in this cohort showed that unfit persons die earlier than do others in all employment categories (Cribier, 1988a).

The involuntary nature of the end of active employment was highly marked. Whether or not it was welcomed is another matter: in fact 42 per cent of those obliged to stop working before the normal age did not wish to continue. Let us add that many of the unemployed and sick were unaware, on their last working day, that they would never again take up their jobs. Most experienced some uncertainty before retirement and for some this was a period of considerable anxiety.

It is interesting to compare now the way in which the two cohorts finished their active working life, in different socio-economic climates. In both 1972 and 1984 there was a population of 20 million actively employed in France, but in 1972 there were 500,000 unemployed persons and by 1984 these numbered 2,500,000. From 1972 onwards, new forms of early retirement were created. An indication of their importance will be given here by describing, with the help of a national survey (Heller, 1986), the formerly active population aged 55–65 years in 1985.[11]

In 1985 there were in France 1.6 million retired persons aged 55–65 years. Their mean age was 61.4 years. Many belonged to the public sector, in which retirement has always been taken at an earlier age; those in the private sector had taken their retirement for reasons of unfitness or disability and a small number had benefited from the 1983 Act (which reduced the normal retirement age from 65 to 60). In the same age group, there were 750,000 people in pre-retirement, virtually all former employees in the private sector. Their mean age was 60 years in 1985, but lower at the time they stopped working.

There have been four main pre-retirement schemes and many special schemes. There are two major types of unemployment compensation. First, there is the guaranteed income scheme for people made redundant, including the 'guaranteed income after redundancy' scheme and the programme under the National Employment Fund. This is mandatory. A second set of guaranteed income schemes, consisting of 'guaranteed income after resignation' and 'solidarity contracts', is optional.

The employment survey (Heller, 1986) enumerated 425,000 persons aged 55–65 years in pre-retirement in the whole of France, for whom retirement was mandatory. In addition, there were 234,000 persons who were given an option; yet it will be seen later that many did not really have a choice (the remaining 88,000 pre-retired persons under special schemes cannot be allotted to either of these two large groups). Thus 64 per cent of pre-retirements taken were mandatory and removed (permanently) from the labour market people who were on average seven to eight years below the normal age of retirement.

Table 10.3 gives the age at the commencement of pension payments, in 1972

Table 10.3 *Age on entry into retirement (first pension payment) (cohorts of 1972 and 1984) %*

|  | 60 | 61–64 | 65 | ⩾66 | Total |
|---|---|---|---|---|---|
| Cohort of 1972 | 14 | 21 | 47 | 18 | 100 |
| Cohort of 1984 | 35 | 29 | 27 | 9 | 100 |

**Table 10.4** *Age at end of work (cohorts of 1972 and 1984) (%) (a)*

|  | 1972 cohort Total | 1984 cohort Total | Men | Women |
|---|---|---|---|---|
| Before 55 ('unfit' only) | 5 | 5 | 4.9 | 5.0 |
| 55–59 | 10 | 27 | 29.5 | 24.3 |
| 60 | 13 | 28 | 30.2 | 25.7 |
| 61–64 | 23 | 29 | 25.0 | 33.5 |
| 65 and over | 48 | 11 | 10.4 | 11.5 |
| Total | 100 | 100 | 100 | 100 |
| Mean age | 63.4 | 60.0 |  |  |

*Note:* (a) Women who had ceased working before 55 for personal reasons (other than unfitness) are not included.

and 1984, for a sample of 10 per cent of the newly retired in the Paris area (that is, around 10,000 people). However, in order to interpret the differences correctly (commencement at 65 years and over has decreased by 41 per cent and that at the age of 60 has more than doubled), it is necessary to be aware of two facts.

First, in 1984, a new Act of 1983 allowed salaried workers to obtain their retirement at the full rate from the age of 60 if they had contributed 140 three-month terms. All such salaried workers aged 60–64 years in pre-retirement or unemployment had to take retirement and the others could take it if they wished – or if their employers pushed them into doing so. Hence, this was a year of transition.

Second, those women who had stopped work well before the age of 60 and who received their first pension payments in 1984 were greater in number than in 1972, for at this time at least sixty three-month terms were required (or fifteen worked years).

More interesting than the age at the first pension payment are the age at the end of work and the work status of the newly retired just before the first pension payment, particularly if the women already no longer active by the age of 55 (but not because of unfitness) are excluded (as in Tables 10.3 and 10.4).

One might think that the difference between the two cohorts was due to the new legislation of 1983. Actually pre-retirement schemes had been important ever since 1972, the decrease in age at the end of work was continuous from 1972 to 1984,[12] and the participation of the male population aged 55–65 in the work-force declined more rapidly in France than in other European nations (Scott and Johnson, 1988).

The mean age at the end of work was 3.4 years lower than in 1972 for the newly retired Parisians of 1984. The proportion of those who stopped at 60 or before was higher for men, because the proportion of men working in industry was higher than of women. The decline in industrial employment was

**Table 10.5** *Work status of the newly retired (cohorts of 1972 and 1984) (%)*

| | 1972 cohort | | 1984 cohort | |
| --- | --- | --- | --- | --- |
| | Men | Women | Men | Women |
| In active employment | 50 | 50 | 49 | 47 |
| Sick or disabled | 36 | 34 | 9 | 9 |
| Unemployed | 14 | 16 | 10 | 14 |
| In pre-retirement | — | — | 32 | 30 |
| Total | 100 | 100 | 100 | 100 |

continuous since the early 1970s, and the development of pre-retirement was particularly important for factory workers (Gaullier, 1986, 1988; Guillemard, 1985, 1986). This is why more men than women retired between the ages of 55 and 61, and more women than men between 61 and 64, the proportion of those having worked up to 65 being roughly the same, one in ten.

Clearly, the proportion of those who went into retirement directly after working changed very little between 1972 and 1984 – it was about half in both cases. However, for those who were without work before retiring, the situation in 1984 was much improved – and this was the opinion of those concerned. Three out of five persons benefited from pre-retirement pay, a more stable resource and one which provided a much higher replacement income of the previous salary than the unemployment or sickness benefit funds did for the older cohort. In 1972 those people retiring who were either sick or unemployed before retirement experienced a rise in income with their first pension. In 1984 many of those in pre-retirement experienced a slight drop in income when they received their first pension, even though the 1984 pension payments were some 20 per cent higher in purchasing power than those of 1972.[13]

## Attitudes to retirement

Attitudes to retirement and images of retirement also changed considerably. The lowering of retirement age had become, for a majority of people, a normal feature of life. It was already the social ideal of the majority of the population.

In 1977 a study was conducted by the Institut national d'études démographiques (INED) with a national sample of the non-agricultural population, active or retired, aged 50–70; 953 retired and 1,404 active persons were interviewed. Their answers clearly showed that retirement was a desirable goal for the majority, and early retirement particularly desirable (Monnier, 1979). The 65–70-year-old former salaried workers in the private sector stopped working, in the early 1970s, at an average age of 63.6, while the average desired age was 61.2. For salaried employees in the public sector, the figures were respectively 59.7 and 58.9, and for the self-employed 64.0 and 62.9. The younger workers were when they retired, the more satisfied they were with the age at which they retired.

Desire for early retirement was stronger among workers, employees and mid-level executives (at about 60), who formed the greatest part of the population, than among shopkeepers and higher-level salaried executives (at about 63). If the retired salaried workers of the private sector surveyed in 1977 could have benefited from their full retirement pensions at the age of their choice, 55 per cent would have stopped work at 60 or earlier (including 19 per cent at 55 years), only 31 per cent at 65, and 9 per cent later. Even among former shopkeepers and artisans, 37 per cent would have stopped at 60 or earlier, and only 13 per cent later than 65. A comparison between retirees aged 65 to 70 years old and non-retirees aged 50 to 59 shows that the desired retirement age was, in 1977, two years lower for the generation born in 1918–27 than for those born in 1907–12.

This change in attitudes was the result of the pressure of the labour market, of the rise in the standard of living and of an important increase in pensions, particularly supplementary pensions. Adequate income and financial security remained the best statistical 'predictors' of retirement satisfaction. Cultural changes also played an important role, especially the growth of leisure as a more central value throughout society and the positive image of active and independent retirement life – the 'third age' which is a genuine part of 'adult age', before 'real old age'.[14]

The younger cohort had a more positive view of retirement, either as a mixture of rest, family life and chosen activities (often useful ones), or as a new stage of life with more social, intellectual and leisure activity. Retiring 'early', that is, around 60, gradually became, between the mid-1970s and the mid-1980s, not only socially acceptable but the new social norm: all the surveys showed an increase both in the proportion of people content to retire and in those who would like to retire early. Retirement was seen as a positive stage of life by a majority of the mature active population,[15] but the newly retired often had ambivalent attitudes, and personal circumstances and characteristics varied a great deal within social groups themselves.

The most interesting differences in reactions to retirement will be outlined here. First, in 1975 many of those who had had to cease working before age 65 explained that they were not lazy, but could not find any work or were too worn-out to continue working. By 1987 it was those who worked up until the age of 64–65 years who justified themselves, explaining that they were not 'stealing jobs' but that they needed the salary, that they had to complete their insurance record or that their employers needed them. Only senior executives did not feel the need to justify themselves in this way.

Second, in 1975 40 per cent of the interviewees said that they would have liked to have stopped working earlier, 27 per cent at the age that they did and 33 per cent later (most of the last had been sick, unfit or unemployed). However in 1987, in the younger cohort, who had stopped working an average of three years younger, there were no more people who would have liked to have continued working for longer.

Third, in 1975 38 per cent of the newly retired wished to retire, 18 per cent accepted it as normal, 16 per cent both wished to retire and were afraid of retiring, 4 per cent were dreading it and 24 per cent would have wished to continue working. In 1987 the proportion of those showing apprehension towards retirement had diminished, basically because poor, sick, lonely and ill-housed about-to-retire persons were far fewer in numbers. Apparently, six out of ten newly retired persons in 1984 were very keen to retire in that year. However, we need to be cautious, because the image of retirement has become so positive (the active and independent senior citizen, living a life of leisure and enjoyment and at the same time fulfilling a social duty by vacating a job for the young) that it was now difficult for interviewees to say whether they would have preferred to continue work, that work was more interesting than retirement, that after work they felt themselves no longer 'needed' in society, or simply that they would have wished to see that part of their life last for longer.

Fourth, was there any difference in attitudes towards retirement between the younger and older cohorts and what was the experience of pre-retirement of the younger one? Not all those taking pre-retirement through redundancy wished to continue working. The employment survey of 1985 (Heller, 1986) revealed that at least 40 per cent were fairly happy or relieved to be retired. Not all those who had 'chosen' solidarity contracts and resignation – that is, who had retired, supposedly optionally, in order to leave a job free for a younger person – had wanted to stop working: at least 20 per cent would have liked to stay in their job. This survey showed that those who chose the optional scheme were prompted sometimes by health reasons, but above all by financial reasons (there were considerable advantages in comparison with the old system, and real security). Multivariate analysis of the responses to this survey revealed that the pre-retired enjoyed their retirement in the same way as retired persons and that dissatisfaction in retirement was in both groups linked more to situations of ill-health, loneliness and low income than to the way in which retirement was taken.

Our survey, conducted upon a smaller, Parisian population (603 subjects in 1987 who had remained in Paris and so were comparable to the subjects of the 1975 survey) showed that in the younger cohort, 82 per cent of men and 75 per cent of women were satisfied or 'fairly satisfied' with their life in retirement. There was the same proportion of satisfied persons amongst those who stopped work at the age of 65, at 61–64 or at 60. But there were far fewer among those who stopped earlier than 60: many of them had stopped working for health reasons, had been unemployed or had had to accept a pre-retirement scheme, compulsory or 'optional'.

In total, 36 per cent of the interviewees, both men and women, would have liked to continue working and 35 per cent said that they had been forced to take retirement through lack of work, but here the difference between men and women was noticeable (39 per cent of men, 32 per cent of women), because men more often worked in the industrial sector. The proportion of those who were forced to retire, through lack of work, and would have wished to continue, was

23 per cent (25 per cent of men, 20 per cent of women). This proportion was not much greater than in the older cohort! The proportion was higher for men among skilled workers and senior executives (some of the latter see retirement before 65 as an unfair punishment) and for women among skilled employees, technicians and executives, those with the most interesting jobs – and the best health. It was a little higher for non-married women than married women, although the difference was small (22 and 17 per cent respectively).

Those who found the retirement life 'a little difficult' or even 'hard to bear' (21 per cent of men, 30 per cent of women) were more often than the others, at the time of the interview, in poor health, poorly housed, anxious for a spouse, recently widowed, and with a low income. They were also more often unemployed or on sick leave before receiving their first pension, and had more often to accept (or even to ask for) a pre-retirement contract, which was the only possible solution to their difficulty.

Both surveys yielded results along the same line. The majority of the younger cohort adapted well to early retirement, under conditions scarcely expected a few years before.

Fifth, many of the newly retired of 1972 were pessimistic in 1975 when speaking of the life of retirement before them ('it will be all right as long as we are not handicapped, or thrown out of our homes, as long as I can walk, as long as I still have my husband. . .') and they feared, wrongly as the subsequent survey showed, a lowering of their standard of living in the years to come.[16] This pessimism was much stronger at the individual than the collective level and corresponded to the working and lower middle classes' traditional pessimism concerning old age. The purchasing power of retired people, in fact, has risen by more than 10 per cent in the eight years following retirement, and special forms of assistance (such as housing benefit and home help services) have multiplied.

The newly retired of 1984 were, in 1987, much more optimistic about *their* retirement and most of them expected a long period of 'good life' in retirement. Yet what they said about the collective future revealed true concern. It is argued here that this concern was based not only upon the economic calculations usually advanced. It came from a confused feeling that the new 'affluence' of half the newly retired could not be maintained if the situation of the young actively employed or young unemployed stayed at a low level, this imbalance no longer being acceptable to society.

## Conclusion

This, then, may be the most important new feature in attitudes towards retirement, but speaking here of the attitudes of the non-retired, especially the active population under the age of 45. For them, a whole fringe group of the newly retired appears today as a privileged population in what is seen as the 'Golden Age of pensions' (Babeau, 1985), and this situation runs the risk of strengthening the latent conflicts between age groups which, at present, the French generally refuse to recognise (these problems have been discussed openly for many years in the USA; Neugarten, 1982). But most people understand that even if a strong minority, especially of single women, still lives in difficult circumstances the younger generation of retired people is, as a whole, no more the victim of an unequal distribution of resources between the generations than were their parents in the 1950s and early 1960s. But we have to include the class dimension to fully understand the changing position of the elderly.

In our younger cohort, born in 1920–24, the middle class corresponds very neatly to what David Thomson so appropriately calls the welfare generation, the generation who benefited from changes in the labour market, economic growth, social policies, and also inflation, and which has been a 'net beneficiary of the welfare state' (Thomson, this volume). The working and lower middle classes, however, have had to pay for these advantages by long working hours, often in poor conditions. Low salaries forced many to make sacrifices where buying a house was concerned. Many also had to assist their ageing parents, and to keep their children in school up to the age of 16 or 18. They consider themselves better-off than their parents, but certainly not on the winning side in the sharing out of wealth.

*(Translated from the French by Stephanie Condon)*

## Notes

1   See Canceill *et al.* (1987). The data come from 1979 tax records. Actually the per capita income used was not very convincing. The income per 'consumption unit' would have been more relevant. The average income of different types of households headed by a retired person (single, couple with one or two pensions, with an active child, etc.) were unfortunately not observed in this survey. Furthermore, there are economically active persons in many retired households; 13 per cent of the total income of households whose head is a former salaried worker is composed of salaries, 78 per cent of retirement pensions, and 9 per cent of capital income, while of course many retired persons, often the most modest, live with and in the household of active persons.

2   This follow-up was conducted regularly each year with the help of the Caisse Nationale d'assurance – vieillesse (National Pension Fund), with the result that there were no losses from the follow-up. This older cohort was interviewed recently at 'R + 14'. Half the men were still living and 69 per cent of the women.

3   This research study was conducted by a team in which Marie-Luce Duffau and Alexandre Kych played a very important role throughout.

4   This is also the view of Paul Johnson and Jane Falkingham for Britain, as shown recently (Johnson and Falkingham, 1988, p. 144).

5   The difference in fertility between the *women* in our two samples was greater still, but this was because the pension allowance rules have changed: more mothers of large families, often having worked for a shorter time, had the right to a pension in 1984. This is why our comparison was done on men.

6   The 1984 retired population were far more reticent in talking about their income. This was partly because these incomes were more often high and because in France this subject is much more 'taboo' than in the USA or Britain. Yet I suggest it was also because the younger cohort felt that they had a good retirement income compared to young people's

salaries and payment to the unemployed that this question was an uncomfortable one for them.

7  Of the older cohort, 12 per cent lived in council housing at R+3 (8 per cent had done so in their forties), and 22 per cent of the younger (33 per cent in their forties). The latter had begun to form families in the age of large-scale social housing construction (Cribier *et al.*, 1987).

8  The main rooms excluding the kitchen, bathroom, etc. were counted here.

9  However, in the fifteen years following retirement, the proportion of persons in the older cohort living in dwellings with a bathroom would increase from 34 to 49 per cent, thanks to settlement in modern suburban accommodation, to the fact that access to council flats ('*HLMs*') is good after retirement, to the fitting out of ageing dwellings and also to rent assistance (Cribier *et al.*, 1987).

10  The definition of disability (in French '*inaptitude*') is being 'no longer capable of carrying out his work without seriously damaging his health', between 60 and 65. 'Invalidity' concerns people under 60 – some of them may be quite young.

11  For this special nationwide survey, conducted with the annual employment survey, a sample of 3,106 persons, either retired or pre-retired (aged 55–65), were interviewed (1 in 900).

12  From 1972 to 1984 the activity rate, for men aged 60–64, dropped in France from 63 per cent to 31 per cent, for men aged 55–59 from 84 per cent to 69 per cent. On the French '*pré-retraites*', see Gaullier (1986, 1988, chapters 1 to 4), and Guillemard (1985, 1986, chapter 3).

13  During the 1960s and 1970s there was a marked and regular increase in the purchasing power of the active population and, even more rapidly, of the retired. In the 1980s the retired are the *only* group in French society whose purchasing power has notably increased. However, the fact that the rate of increase in pension expenditures in France was maintained almost at the same level in 1974–80 as in 1960–73 should be interpreted with care (Babeau, 1985, p. 37). The rise in spending for the period 1974–80 stemmed largely from the fact that, since 1972, pensions have been calculated according to income during the best ten years and no longer that during the last ten years. There was a consensus in France that a rise in pensions should be a priority.

14  The success of the expression the 'third age', much used in France, stems from the background presence of the 'fourth age'. The notion of the 'third age' places the first stage of retirement still in maturity, isolating 'true' old age. Hence the very old are distanced from the rest of society more than ever (Cribier, 1981a).

15  This aspiration for early retirement was widely held by the *petit* and *moyenne bourgeoisie* in nineteenth-century France: it is Balzac's story of the shopkeeper who lived on 'beans at 3 pence a litre' in order to be able to retire at 50, having accumulated enough capital.

16  Between 1970 and 1979, the average national income of households headed by persons born in 1906–10 increased in France by 15 per cent, using constant franc values. The rise in purchasing power during this period was such that income did not decrease, even for this generation which had gone into retirement, according to Lollivier (1986). In my opinion this was partly because in 1970 many of those born in 1906–10 were already no longer employed: some were retired, others were on sick leave, many were receiving unemployment benefit, and many women were already widowed. In this generation many people received more money with their first pension payment than between the end of work and this first pension.

# References

Babeau, A. (1985), *La fin des retraites*, Paris, Hachette.

Canceill, G., Laferrère, A. and Mercier, P. (1987), 'Les revenus des ménages en 1979',

*Collections de l'INSEE*, M 127, Paris.

Chesnais, J.-C. (1985), 'Les inégalités démo-économiques entre générations', Paris, *Economica*, pp. 147–56.

Cribier, F. (1980), 'Constitution et structure des groupes socio-professionnels du salariat: une génération de retraités parisiens du secteur privé', *Consommation, Revue de socio-économie*, III, pp. 47–90.

Cribier, F. (1981a), 'Le temps de la retraite', *Temps libre*, IV, pp. 73–83.

Cribier, F. (1981b), 'Changing retirement patterns: the experience of a cohort of Parisian salaried workers', *Ageing and Society*, I, 1, pp. 51–73.

Cribier, F. (1982), 'Aspects of retirement migration from Paris: an essay in social geography', in A. Warnes (ed.), *Geographical Perspectives on the Elderly*, London, Wiley, pp. 111–37.

Cribier, F. (1983), 'Itinéraires professionnels et usure au travail: une génération de salariés parisiens', *Le mouvement social*, XXIV, pp. 11–44.

Cribier, F. (1988a), 'La mortalité des travailleurs après la retraite', *Gérontologie et Société*, XLV, pp. 80–99.

Cribier, F. (1988b), 'Le logement à l'heure de la retraite', in *Transformations de la famille et habitat*, Travaux et documents de l'INED, CXX, Paris, Presses Universitaires de France, pp. 107–27.

Cribier, F., Duffau, M. L. and Rhein, C. (1979), 'La vie professionnelle d'une cohorte de retraitées parisiennes', *Gérontologie et Société*, VI, pp. 137–65.

Cribier, F., Duffau, M. L. and Kych, A. (1987), *Les conditions de logement de deux générations de Parisiens*, Paris, CNRS.

Gaullier, X. (1986), 'The management of older workers in a flexible career cycle: the case of France', *Ageing International*, XIII, 4, pp. 34–40.

Gaullier, X. (1988), *La deuxième carrière*, Paris, Seuil.

Guillemard, A. M. (1985), 'The social dynamics of early withdrawal from the labour force in France', *Ageing and Society*, V, 4, pp. 381–412.

Guillemard, A. M. (1986), *Le déclin du social*, Paris, Presses Universitaires de France.

Guillotin, Y. (1988), 'Les carrières salariales en France de 1967 à 1982', *Economie et Statistique*, CCX, pp. 13–20.

Heller, J. L. (1986), 'La retraite anticipée: choix ou contrainte?', *Economie et Statistique*, CXCIII-IV, pp. 97–109.

Johnson, P. and Falkingham, J. (1988), 'Intergenerational transfers and public expenditure on the elderly in modern Britain', *Ageing and Society*, VIII, pp. 129–46.

Kergoat, D. (1982), *Les ouvrières*, Paris, Le Sycomore.

Lollivier, S. (1986), 'L'évolution temporelle du revenu des ménages', *Economie et Statistique*, CXCII, pp. 75–81.

Monnier, A. (1979), 'Les limites de la vie active et de la retraite: l'âge du départ en retraite', *Population*, IV-V, pp. 804–24.

Neugarten, B. (ed.) (1982), *Age or Need? Public Policies for Older People*, Beverly Hills, California, Sage.

Prost, A. (1987), *Histoire de la vie privée*, V, Paris, Seuil.

Scott, P. and Johnson, P. (1988), 'The economic consequences of population ageing in advanced societies', Discussion Paper no. 263, London, Centre for Economic Policy Research.

Thomson, D. (1989), *Selfish Generations: The Ageing of the Welfare State*, Wellington, Allen & Unwin.

Wenger, G. C. (1984), *The Supportive Network: Coping with Old Age*, London, Allen & Unwin.

# Index